The Romantic Will

The Romantic Will

Michael G. Cooke

New Haven and London, Yale University Press 1976

Library of Congress catalog card number: 75-43313
International standard book number: 0-300-01961-0

Designed by Sally Sullivan
and set in Baskerville type.
Printed in the United States of America by
Vail-Ballou Press, Inc., Binghamton, N.Y.

Published in Great Britain, Europe, Africa, and Asia (except Japan) by
Yale University Press, Ltd., London.
Distributed in Latin America by Kaiman & Polon,
Inc., New York City; in Australia and New Zealand by Book & Film
Services, Artarmon, N.S.W., Australia;
in Japan by John Weatherhill, Inc., Tokyo.

In the beginning was darkness concealed in darkness; all this was an indistinguishable flood of water. That which, possessing life force, was enclosed by the vacuum, the One, was born through the power of heat from its austerity.
Upon it rose up, in the beginning, desire, which was man's first seed.

Rigveda 10.129

What properly belongs to us besides energy, strength, and will?
Goethe

CONTENTS

PREFACE

When it was fashionable to treat romanticism as a sort of bouquet of mental tendencies and literary turns,* there would often be included in the gathering a quality of apprehending the world of physical phenomena in fresh and singular ways. Wordsworth with his stationary blasts of waterfalls, his violet by a mossy stone, his forty cattle feeding as one, afforded amplest illustration of the case, but the opening stanza of Shelley's "Hymn to Intellectual Beauty" gave surprising evidence of its validity; so in fact did all the major poets and many a minor one, including Clare, Hood, Samuel Palmer, and Thomas Wade. And Dorothy Wordsworth's *Journals* stood to prove that singularity of perception was not a hothouse growth of poetry alone; it assumed the condition of something representative and pervasive in romanticism.

A special interest attaches to the idea of singularity of perception, if one may briefly hark back to the bouquet criticism of the period. That idea appears as an anticipation, on however modest a scale, of our present preoccupation with romanticism and consciousness. It is at least a variant of the consciousness theme. And it helps, by its very modesty perhaps, to raise questions as to how far consciousness is radical and axiomatic for romanticism. What might the romantics' singular way of perceiving convey? What might it stem from, how should we construe its function? What place might it

---

*Love of nature, desire for solitude, a taste for the medieval and the oriental, soft-focus description, balladizing and generally experimenting with form, individualism and revolutionary fervor, blatant melancholy, idyllicism, etc.

hold in the romantic complex? It is not enough to say that it evinces a passion for novelty, or (in a tautological vein) a passion for perception. The romantics may have found themselves in an environment of novelty or revolution, but they did not solicit or idolize novelty: they opposed values that were merely hereditary and traditional, but only to the extent that these might prove a filigree of social accident, and always with an eye to the basic fabric of humanity, an eye to what is *immemorial*. In Aphorism 1 of his *Aids to Reflection* Coleridge is explicit on this point:

> In philosophy equally as in poetry, it is the highest and most useful prerogative of genius to produce the strongest impressions of novelty, while it rescues admitted truths from the neglect caused by the very circumstance of their universal admission.

The conjunction of novelty and truth may sound like nothing so much as a Popean prescription, but it is otherwise in fact. The universal truth of Coleridge's philosophy (equally with his poetry) is connected with and arises from his experience as a sublimating ground; while deploring the way his age suffered from a "general contagion of mechanic philosophy," he tended still to be an idealizing empiricist. The perception of novelty becomes part of a faithful search for lost, and not merely neglected, truth. The habit of redefinition—of genres and feelings, concepts and states—in the romantic complex expresses the same search. There is an open situation, in which perception does the work of establishing fact and context for the self and establishing the self in fact and context.

In the entire system of relationships that we find highlighted by a trait of singular perceiving in romanticism, a metaphysical dimension is fundamentally present. And it is a metaphysics of surprise. Perceiving is not end and triumph, but signpost and uncertain promise. In Wordsworth's "Nutting" intense perception metamorphoses into empathy, immediate sensual attraction into a stable spiritual affection. A sharp outer world of acquisitive passion and sensationalism spins unwittingly into a fine inner world of compassion and generosity. The upshot is a new universe of spiritual values, a sort of revelation that converts the singular lust for perception in which it originates. The metamorphosis of perception in *Christabel* is even more complex—and sinister. It will not do to make perception merely phenomenal, in the manner of the bouquet critics; but it is not enough to isolate consciousness, however rich and resonant this term. The dynamics, even perhaps the pragmatism and personality, of consciousness in romanticism have been noted; Walter Jackson Bate calls attention to "the remorseless deepening of self-consciousness" in romantic poets, and Geoffrey Hartman, from another vantage point, focuses on the poets' attempt to cultivate "anti–self-consciousness." These two positions are not in accord, but need not be incompatible; without coming between such mighty opposites, one may observe that consciousness in either case enters problematically into a situation larger than itself. It is useful here to recall Coleridge's remark in *Aids to Reflection*, that it is "a duty of conscience to form the mind to a habit of distinct consciousness." This sounds like a claim for the paramountcy of consciousness, but Coleridge introduces a clear purpose beyond consciousness, namely, to avoid "snares and pitfalls" as one goes in mortal "twilight" (Aphorism 19).

Coleridge, of course, speaking in a religious vein, puts a moral construction on the case. In the romantic context, a metaphysical construction of the factors of consciousness would seem more generally appropriate. But if we recognize a morality of being, rather than of specific conduct, Coleridge affords us clear and valuable instruction. His evaluation of consciousness is in keeping with a remoralization of philosophy (common to Kant, Schopenhauer, Schiller, and Schelling) that revises the privileged position of induction and inference in Hume's universe of skeptical naturalism. It also exorcises the demon of consciousness-for-its-own-sake, or at least reduces it to less than monstrous proportions, for the moral-metaphysical role of consciousness does not require that knowledge be infallibly founded or absolutely ascertained. Even Kant at his sternest does not require that we do what is right (perfect knowledge) but only what we could posit for others in our case (perfect commitment).

It must be stressed that calling consciousness metaphysical is not to make it more abstract, but more engaged, more basic to the enterprise of being. This is the enterprise, at once self-reliant and self-learning, arrogant and poignant, that informs *Endymion* as well as *Alastor, Jerusalem* no less than *The Prelude, Childe Harold* and also *The Rime of the Ancient Mariner*. One may see it as the central enterprise of romantic literature, reaching out to encompass Goethe's *Faust* and Schiller's *Letters on the Aesthetic Education of Man*, Coleridge's *Biographia Literaria* and De Quincey's *Confessions of an English Opium Eater*.

What emerges in romanticism is the metaphysics of action, a constant engagement—at once practical and symbolic—upon a radical problem of being. This study seeks to enunciate its terms in relation to English romantic poetry in particular. It centers on the question of will as the concept which *for the romantics* consummately expresses the metaphysics of engagement; Coleridge in his *Table Talk* calls the will "the law of our nature," and Schopenhauer, again displacing consciousness into act of being, declares that "the self-consciousness is intensely, really even exclusively, occupied with willing." Ultimately knowing, willing, and being fuse in the romantic vision, as witnesses Coleridge's remark in *The Statesman's Manual* that in his free will a man "intuitively knows the sublimity, and the infinite hopes, fears, and capabilities of his own nature." Jakob Boehme, whose writing exercised so pervasive an influence on German romantic philosophy and its consideration of the will, provides a sharp statement of the principle of symbiosis relating will to understanding and being: "Every life is essential and is based on will. . . . Will is the motive power of the essences. . . . Will is dumb without life, wherein is no feeling, understanding or substantiality. . . .

Life is the essence's son and will is the essence's father, for no essence can arise without will."*

It is clear that we are confronting a will differing in important respects from both the Platonic-Christian and the skeptical-materialist conceptions. At the same time the romantic position on the will seems not so much original as independently eclectic. It combines the elements of (1) predestinarianism with teleology, (2) egotism with consent in what may be termed the will of life, and (3) dejection or defiance with faith. And it is, I think, symptomatic that Godwin's optimism and Schopenhauer's pessimism alike repudiate the specifically purposive will. As Boehme put it in his *Mysterium Magnum*, "Unquietness is the life of self-will. . . . The pain of the damned consists in this, that they will the particular [*Eigenheit*] . . . . "

The depth to which the question of will enters into romantic literature can be gauged from Wordsworth's depiction of his voyage over the Alps in *The Prelude*, book 6. Wordsworth is, he says himself, in quest of "trophies," and is thrown into consternation to find that he *"had crossed the Alps"* unawares, without enjoying a "summit experience." But the loss of his personal, specific aim (or will) becomes somehow the occasion of a greater and deeper experience, one that is not aesthetic, selfish, and transitory, but universal and permanent: an imaginative epiphany befalls him. The episode, in fact, stands as part of a major pattern in *The Prelude*, for Wordsworth, whether stealing a ride in a rowboat or climbing a mountain to "see the sun/Rise," cannot seem to achieve what he sets out to achieve (or wills), though his "failures" somehow produce incalculable gains. Again, while a type of consciousness is central to these episodes, our view of them remains partial if we ignore the dramatic context and the contribution of "willing" to the development of "Imagination."

Six Theosophic Points 1: 1-6.

For many students of the period mention of the will in English romanticism may well conjure up Byron and the spirit of romantic self-assertion variously categorized as lawless, headlong, idiosyncratic, defiant. This sort of self-assertion is a striking feature of the case, but it may not be finally a central one. It is rather a matter of wilfulness than the substance of the romantic will. In an earlier study, *The Blind Man Traces the Circle: On the Patterns and Philosophy of Byron's Poetry*, I have sought to show that such wilfulness, however engrossing in itself, constitutes only a special incident or episode in an extensive, complex phenomenon of thought and behavior. Whether it is evinced by the poet in *Alastor* or in *Sleep and Poetry*, by Byron's Prometheus or, before his regeneration, by Shelley's, it involves a Pyrrhic ecstasy, something that at best sinks back crushingly on itself, and at worst sets its face against life. In this study I have endeavored to look through the dazzle of the will-unto-itself in romanticism and have sought ways of investigating a more radical and widely distributed activity of will in, for example, the romantic theory of imagination, in Wordsworth's "The Solitary Reaper" and Keats's ode "To Autumn," in Byron's *Childe Harold* and Blake's *Jerusalem*. In sum I am dealing with the will and art of being in English romanticism.

It has seemed well, even so, to be on guard against the danger of finding the will (like Sir Thomas Browne's quincunxes) everywhere. But the further this study has gone, the more it has seemed that the will offers itself as a pervasive issue in romanticism—and as a substantial issue in itself. In a sense the study is organized to follow the shape of the will. Instead of dealing with, say, Coleridge, or Byron, and the will, I have taken up salient features, conditions, and relationships of the will and drawn on various authors and works in substantiation of those features and conditions and relationships. This is not to subordinate the poets to the topic; a topic is always a means of asking questions of writers and their work, and I hope that my topic and my questions have elicited fresh and fruitful responses concerning romantic poetry and the romantic period as a whole.

For context and comparison I have had recourse to philosophy, especially in the first chapter, where the presence and the force of the will in romanticism require establishing; and to literary history, especially in the second chapter, where it is necessary to establish what is peculiar in the functioning of will in romanticism. At all points, however, it has been my object to convey the special qualities of important documents of romantic writing in light of the given topic of will, and to chart the singular play (or evolution) of the will in individual poets. The latter purpose has led to a pattern of a few long chapters, the former to the inclusion of frequent subheadings which may allow the reader to browse without entirely losing sight of the extension and interrelation of the analysis.

There is a prudential as well as a professional reason for insisting that mine is a literary study. The existence of the will has been disputed in philosophy from the beginning (Coleridge calls this dispute basic to philosophy as such); but it is the twentieth century that has most massively tended to deny its existence. For a layman to enter into the field, and presumably on the affirmative side, is for a bantam to utter song for foxes. No more is intended or implied here than that the romantic poet considered the will a viable issue and spoke and acted in his poetry as if it existed. Whether the will comes out equal to phlogiston or to ultraviolet the judicious reader alone will be in a position to say.

Our hopes bear a certain, or an uncertain, ratio to our debts. At any rate, my debts to others in the course of this study have given me hope to sustain it. Many debts are imperfectly recorded in the body of my discussion and in notes. A few should be singled out. For specific and timely support of the undertaking, and for valuable suggestions concerning it, my special thanks go to four friends and colleagues, A. Dwight Culler, Geoffrey H. Hartman, Paul deMan, and Harold

Bloom. J. Hillis Miller and W. Max Byrd generously read portions of the manuscript; they thereby helped to keep me going, and on a better footing. My colleagues in the Columbia Seminar on Romanticism and the Nineteenth Century gave a hearing to my ideas and stimulated as well as taxed them in a lively discussion. Thomas F. Weiskel, my former colleague (much lamented), did much to promote my labors with his fine tact in listening and in probing dialogue. So did Leslie Brisman, whose interests richly complement mine, and with whom my conversation is both personal and literary. The spontaneous interest and encouragement of my friends at Brown, Michael S. Harper and James D. Boulger, proved a real benefit, and Professor Boulger added appreciably to my thinking on Coleridge. At a crucial juncture came the generous support of a John Simon Guggenheim Memorial Foundation Fellowship, without which the faults of my study would have been much greater, and the study itself much slower to appear.

Kathy John typed the versions, conversions, and reversions of the manuscript with unmatched cheerfulness and skill. And I was fortunate enough to have Ellen Graham and Lynn Walterick of the Yale University Press shaping and guiding the text in its progress from recorded thought to published book. I hope the book can somehow sustain the care, and grace, and judgment they brought to it.

NOTE ON EDITIONS

The following editions have been cited throughout this study. Specific form of citation is noted for the reader's convenience.

Blake, William. *The Poetry and Prose*. Edited by David V. Erdman. Commentary by Harold Bloom. Garden City: Doubleday, 1965.
Quotations from *Jerusalem* are given according to Blake's headings, that is, by chapter, plate, and line numbers, but chapter numbers are suppressed after the first reference where many occur in a brief compass.
Quotations from *The Four Zoas* are given according to Blake's headings, by Night, page, and line numbers. Again, "Night" numbers are suppressed after the first reference where many occur in a brief compass.

Byron, George Gordon Noel, Lord. *The Complete Poetical Works*. Cambridge ed. Boston: Houghton Mifflin, 1933.

Coleridge, Samuel Taylor. *Biographia Literaria*. Edited with his Aesthetical essays by J. Shawcross. 2 vols. Oxford: Clarendon Press, 1907. Cited by volume and page numbers.
———. *The Complete Poetical Works*. Edited with textual and bibliographical notes by Ernest Hartley Coleridge. 2 vols. Oxford: Clarendon Press, 1957.

Keats, John. *Complete Poems and Selected Letters*. Edited by Clarence DeWitt Thorpe. New York: Odyssey Press, 1935.
———. *The Letters. . . , 1814–1821*. 2 vols. Edited by Hyder Edward Rollins. Cambridge: Harvard University Press, 1958. Cited by volume and page numbers.

Pope, Alexander. *The Poems. A One-Volume Edition of the Twickenham Text.* Edited by John Butt. New Haven: Yale University Press, 1963.

Schiller, J. C. F. von. *On the Aesthetic Education of Man.* Edited and translated by Elizabeth M. Wilkinson and L. A. Willoughby. Oxford: Clarendon Press, 1967.

Schopenhauer, Arthur. *The World as Will and Representation.* 2 vols. Translated by E. F. J. Payne. New York: Dover Publications, 1966. Cited by volume and page numbers.

Shelley, Percy Bysshe. *The Complete Poetical Works.* Edited by Thomas Hutchinson. London: Oxford University Press, 1943.

Wordsworth, William. *Poetical Works.* Edited by Thomas Hutchinson. A new ed., rev. by Ernest De Selincourt. New York: Oxford University Press, 1956.
Quotations from *The Prelude* are given by book and line numbers.

1

THE WILL IN ENGLISH
ROMANTICISM

INTRODUCTION: CONSCIOUSNESS AND CONDUCT

The harm in Freud is not that he vigorously flung open the
Pandora's chest of the unconscious once and for all, but that
he remained the while so decisively devoted to the operations
of the consciousness. He makes of the unconscious not a
mysterious field of power, but as it were a territory to be
annexed. He proves analytical, clinical, pragmatic, in his biases,
and there is no better measure of his penchant for neat self-
subsistent systems and the expulsion of the unexpected or
the antiformal phenomenon than the fact that, while he was
unveiling the unconscious, he tended to resist what Jung and
Ferenczi proposed, the claims of the occult. When he turns
his attention to the occult, as in the essays published under
the title *Studies in Parapsychology*, he drives toward what
Philip Rieff calls an "*explanation* of the whole range of the
uncanny," a "laying *bare*" of "hidden forces" (italics added).
Freud observes that people "vary . . . greatly in their sensitivity to [the] quality of feeling [the "uncanny"]," and himself "plead[s] guilty to a special obtuseness in the matter,
where extreme delicacy of feeling would be more in place."[1]

Unlike Descartes, or even Hegel, Freud is less than explicit
about his bias to formal clarity, and it must seem paradoxical
that he, the archexplorer of the unconscious, has proven the
fountainhead of our twentieth-century affair with conscious-

ness. Where a moralist once said, to know all is to forgive all, we seem to say, to know all is all. With a premium on the act of bringing to consciousness, the inward gesture of acknowledging and, ideally, of accepting what may lie hidden becomes an acme of metaphysical accomplishment; and it almost seems a laudable proof of virtue to be in a position to admit subtle forms of vice. Indeed, one may often wonder whether the point of analysis is not to display a daring ingenuity, a capacity for plastic integration by the analyst of the patient's tumbled life, leading to a triumphant unveiling on the one side, and on the other all too often a frayed admiration and thwarted apprehension. Certainly Freud's epochal analysis of Dora exhibits such a pattern. Even so, in this dispensation, to appear well is superficiality, to mean well is hypocrisy, but to think well, in the form of presenting the unconscious to consciousness, is triumph.

But it continues true, that if the unexamined life is not worth living, the examining of life is not living. Thus there arises the danger that concentrating on the synecdoche of consciousness, within the system of being, may make this subject ever larger and more fascinating until it reaches a point of exclusivity where the part becomes the whole, in a sort of allegorical absorption and distortion of the being in its consciousness.

It is well to be mindful of the fact that faith in pure thought, as in pure science, is a phenomenon and a superstition of our century, and one that need not win universal praise. Perhaps it is prudential in origin. Darwin's life was not actually threatened, but the effect of his ideas proved for him personally as ominous as did Galileo's. Darwin speaks of his discomfort in his *Autobiography*, and it seems generally agreed that Alfred Russel Wallace, had he not shied away from the subversive implications of his observations, might have beaten Darwin to the theory of evolution. This from a social standpoint. From within the psyche the disavowal of responsibility for the Manhattan Project on the part of a few theoretical physicists must afford them some consolation. Here it is tempting to quote the poet: "After such knowledge, what forgiveness?" But it is hardly decisive to do so. For in the end it is not knowledge as new information but knowledge as altered organization or *new consciousness* that challenges forgiveness. Surely it is according to the latter sense of knowledge that Plato regarded the idea of the purest idea as practical in implication.

The real situations in which consciousness occurs demand something more than a plea of *sapientia causa sapientiae*. Indeed, within man as within society, as the Adamic myth suggests, the cause of consciousness institutes something more. In the first place, *consciousness of* has a double value, one forthright and the other tacit but very significant: consciousness of an object, and consciousness of the subject whose response enters critically into the occasion of consciousness. As Kant relentlessly shows, we know things in relation to ourselves, and cannot know the *Ding an sich*.

This subjective dimension of consciousness is easy for us now to take for granted, but it came very much to the fore in the romantic period and proved so much trouble to cope with that a self-protective reaction toward "anti–self-consciousness" began to take shape.[2] We may well ask, what made it troublesome? And the answer would seem to lie in the fact that consciousness, even though it suggests mental or intellectual events and contents, is really largely the bringing to light of passional, emotional, spiritual, perhaps even psychological data that may be kept private even from the self. Consciousness in this light becomes the statement of a problem, a problem of dimension and of organization, in the inner economy of life. This is, I think, the way the romantics saw it. Certainly Rousseau in undertaking a "history of [his] feelings" implies an embarking on unprowed seas, in which the authority of feeling or unanalyzed being would usurp the place of reason (apparently, but not truly, germane to consciousness). Similarly, Wordsworth, in striving to combine more than usual passion with more than usual order, sought to bring a sense of coherence to bear on the extravagances of available experience. What we are dealing with is no abandonment to feeling or wallowing in it—the sort of blind indulgence F. L. Lucas charged romanticism with.[3] Rather it is an exploration of the possible authority of feeling[4] and an experiment in placing licentious personality and mystical states under the discipline of language and discovered common values.

The presence of the subject, furthermore, suggests another dimension of consciousness, namely, *consciousness for.* It will be clear what this means if we extend the distinction between knowledge and consciousness. Knowledge may be pure and inert and neutral, and has something of the cumulative character of a reservoir to be drawn on to suit particular occasions. But consciousness remains practical and suited to particular occasions, and is always in some measure personal. Perhaps this is a question of whether one focuses on what one knows (knowledge) or on oneself as knowing (consciousness), but the difference is more than paltry. For if one may apply knowledge to an external circumstance, one experiences oneself in consciousness, one invests and reveals oneself in consciousness, and one may elide and refuse consciousness in a way that one does not elide or refuse knowledge as such. Knowledge becomes something one has, consciousness implies something one is. As Merleau-Ponty pregnantly remarks, there are "many ways for consciousness to be conscious."[5] In this regard *consciousness for* conveys the personal engagement and extension of the self into the object encountered and the shaping or becoming of the self that this entails. Thus, even if we see neoclassicism as teleological, and so biased toward conduct, and romanticism as aetiological, or biased toward consciousness, the full implications of the latter really subsume some of the terms of the former position, to the extent that consciousness as here defined implies a conduct of being. In the context of our present understanding of romanticism, the theme of consciousness is clearly paramount, while this definition of it raises problems and possibilities not so far sufficiently explored.

THE QUESTION OF THE WILL

Who can view the ripened rose, nor seek
To wear it?

Byron

Is there a flower, to which [the infant Babe] points with hand
Too weak to gather it, already love
Drawn from love's purest earthly fount for him
Hath beautified that flower. . . .

Wordsworth

In the past decade, roundly speaking, a critical focus on the world of the mind rather than the world of action has brought forth major gains in our view of romantic poets and of the romantic scheme—so much so, in fact, that romanticism has come to be virtually identified with a primary introspective concern with the mind and self, or, in a word, consciousness.[6] So far is this true that critical debate centers on consciousness in its varieties and modes, with scarcely a question of alternative orientation; Charles Altieri, taking exception to Hartman's reading of Wordsworth with its "progressive mounting of the mind towards self-consciousness," writes:

Wordsworth not only accepts (the dynamic part of the self which continually posits and escapes . . . definitions) . . . but he reconciles himself to the problematic aspects of identity by recognizing that while each act of self-consciousness is incomplete and in a sense self-denying, each act also creates new dimensions of consciousness which enrich the dynamic potential of consciousness to experience itself more deeply and more capaciously in subsequent acts. Like nature, consciousness destroys or frustrates itself only to build and grow in unexpected ways.[7]

Little room is left for anything but consciousness where the whole complex of living, moving situations in *The Prelude*—on the one hand stealing a ride in a rowboat or going to college or taking a sojourn in London or France or climbing

Mount Snowdon, and on the other involved hopes and ambitions and passions and fears and crises and satisfactions—becomes homogenized as a serial "act of self-consciousness." But consciousness is only one aspect *of experience* for the poet who saw his life as "*action* from without and from within" (italics added).

There have been certain notable exceptions to the prevailing mode, in studies of the incorporation of contemporary politics into romantic literature and art.[8] But introspection and apocalypse have seemed to stand not only in their own right, but also as fountains and termini of practical politics in the romantic scheme. Perhaps Rousseau can be used in illustration: as his *Confessions* makes manifest, his passion for the public good and for liberty springs from private emotional experience, while he tells us himself in the *Reveries* that the thwarting of this passion sends him back to his truest pleasure in "solitary meditations."[9] What is outward is contingent, to be engaged or suspended according to impulse; the inward alone is authentic and substantially permanent.

In apparent accord with such a bias, the lyricization of the epic and of dramatic and narrative poetry in the romantic scheme needs no documenting: *The Prelude, Childe Harold's Pilgrimage, Manfred,* and *Prometheus Unbound* gather ostensibly objective materials into a common field of gravitation inward. More important, perhaps, various romantic writers take up the inner being, the mind and the self as regarded from within, as explicit and central issues. Schiller in *Naive and Sentimental Poetry* and *Letters on the Aesthetic Education of Man*, Wordsworth in *The Recluse*, Coleridge in *Biographia Literaria*, Blake in *Jerusalem* with his call for "intellect" over the "piety" of outward forms, Shelley in *A Defence of Poetry*—all are occupied with consciousness, and that somehow at the expense of conduct. Rousseau once again furnishes a telling summary of the case, as he interiorizes and singularizes the instruments and the very idiom of objective science: "I shall apply the barometer to my soul."

But without questioning how much the concern with consciousness has amplified our response to romanticism, it may be observed that all is not as simple or as positive as it seems. The full import of Rousseau's position develops only in conjunction with another statement he makes:

> Those hours of solitude and meditation are the only ones . . . in which I am fully myself, and for myself, without diversion, without obstacle, and where I can truly say I am that which nature has designed.[10]

For if, with the "barometer" image, Rousseau pursues knowledge of himself, in the statement on solitude he *assumes* knowledge of himself. In one case the self is learnt in time, in the other given for all time. The statement on solitude, in fact, reveals that Rousseau wishes more than to know himself; rather than an end, knowing himself may serve as but the instrument of his deeper purpose: to *be* himself, with an unlocalized metaphysical will. Certainly he suspends a programmatic attitude toward action or society, but action is not repudiated finally, nor society ignored. Rather Rousseau is placing demands of extraordinary idealism on action in society, as well as on the actions of society. He is instituting the principle that society must make for the prosperity—material, psychic, and moral—of each of its members or be written off as subversive of human nature. This is a paradoxical hypostasis of society which Western civilization has yet to resolve, caught as it remains between Coleridge's notion that man can only become himself through the cooperation of other men, and Mill's notion that man can only be himself if others do not gratuitously interfere.[11] The implied conclusion is: let me, let every man be "that which nature has designed" and sociopolitical programs become eccentric, or superfluous.

Even this position proves less simple than it seems. "The self-sufficing power of Solitude," as Rousseau's collision with a "great Danish Dog" in the *Reveries* quickly taught him, is a sometime thing, and the career of self-knowledge liable to many mishaps. Society and opinion violate Rousseau's sense of self by setting into action a susceptibility that otherwise lies dormant in him. They do not invade him so much as un-cover him, and what shows may be rather unpalatable than untrue. Put another way, to identify "that which nature has designed" can in any case lead into veritable thickets of inter-pretation. A Rousseau may slash his way through these, but that act is a phenomenon in the self, a synecdoche of personal rhetoric. The self is in it, and exceeds it as clearly as power exceeds any single gesture that expresses it. By the same token an interfusion of consciousness and conduct appears as axiomatic in *Wilhelm Meisters Wanderjahre,* where Goethe sums up life and wisdom as a matter of *denken und tun, tun und denken*, "thinking and doing, doing and thinking." And the pragmatism of consciousness is professed by no less a mind-first philosopher than Fichte. Early in his career Fichte had written, "I want not only to think, I want to act. . . . I have only one desire . . . to act on my surroundings." A do-mestic confirmation of this purpose comes from Fichte's son, who declares that the *Wissenschaftslehre* was aimed "at directing the spirit of the age"; and a philosophic confirma-tion is explicit in the "primacy of practical reason" in Fichte's eyes. The point is not knowledge, but *realization*, not philos-ophy but life: "Fichte's philosophy was indeed designed to breed a passion for perfection, a superimposing of logic on life."[12] Two questions rise promptly from this. The first is, how much a matter of personal election, of personal imposi-tion even, is the self announced as known by Fichte, or again Rousseau? And the second: given the influence of the adventi-tious in the world of self-knowledge, given the fact that the self must negotiate the outer, other world on the way to self-knowledge, how much a matter of implicit choice and ante-cedent purpose is the shape self-knowledge takes?

It is striking that romantic philosophy—and it should suffice at this point merely to cite Schopenhauer's *The World as Will and Representation* and Hegel's *The Phenomenology of Mind* —all but rests its distinctive investigation of self-conscious-ness on the fundamental presence of the will. Coleridge, that archexplorer of consciousness, calls the will our only "absolute Self," and he is seconded by Schopenhauer: "The self-consciousness is intensely, really even exclusively, occupied with willing." Goethe in his *Maximen und Reflexionen* declares that "whoever understands also wills," and Schelling sums up the "understanding," in his essay *Of Human Freedom*, as "actually the will in willing." Indeed, as Coleridge illustrates in the beginning of chapter 5 of *Biographia Literaria*, romantic philosophy could see the will as the perennial issue for philosophy: "There have been men in all ages, who have been impelled . . . to propose their own nature as a problem, and who devote their attempts to its solution. The first step was to construct a table of distinctions, which they seem to have formed on the principle of absence or presence of the *Will*."[13] And this is no remote philosophical divagation. Goethe flatly calls the will, because it is "advantageous to the *individual* . . . the god of the modern world,"[14] and Schiller writes that "there is in Man no other power than the Will."[15]

Poetry and autobiography, the two forms in which creative writers most deeply engaged and expressed themselves in the period, do not give the lie to such opinions, but as it were act out what philosophy and criticism spell out. And this holds good in contexts as divergent as Byron self-consciously contemplating the immedicable disease of life in *Childe Harold*, canto 4, and Wordsworth pragmatically walking up Mount Snowdon in *The Prelude*, book 14. Byron exhorts "us"—mankind in and through himself—to "ponder boldly," and Wordsworth proceeds through "the dripping fog" "with eager pace and no less eager thoughts." If we take account of the adverbial qualifiers in either case ("boldly," "with eager pace . . ."), we can hardly fail to note that they are highly charged phrases of spiritual mode. We are dealing with more than a manner of climbing or of pondering: we are dealing with a manner of man climbing or pondering, a manner of being. Volition and, to the extent that any outcome must be influenced by the style of the agent, even a kind of direction enter into the scene. And we are moved to consider that what a man finds, climbing or pondering, may be conditioned by what he brings intrinsically to the situation (as Coleridge observes, "we receive but what we give"). What we seek responds at once to how we seek it and to what we are in doing so.

Perhaps, then, it is not enough to adopt the truism that for the romantic poet self-concern and self-consciousness are paramount, even with the corollary that these lead to a conception of human character and identity. For this truism may obscure what the problematical status of self-knowledge should convey: the way the question of self-knowledge is bound up in the way poet and man realize themselves in time, whether that time be personal-biographical (Wordsworth, Byron), social-historical (Byron, Coleridge), or transcendent-mythical (Blake, Shelley, Keats).

Say this were granted, though, it must still appear somewhat strange to put the will where, if an agent of realization had to be found, the peculiarly romantic imagination is ready to hand (and doubtless first in mind). But the will proves basic to the imagination, and focus on it should help to set imagination in an improved light. Prima facie it is the imagination which, in the universe composed of Nature and the Soul,[16] at once fuses and supersedes the triple elements of the classicoplatonic constitution of the soul. Coleridge is explicit on this point:

> The poet . . . brings the whole soul of man into activity.
> . . . He diffuses a tone and spirit of unity, that blends,
> and (as it were) *fuses*, each into each, by that synthetic
> and magical power, to which we have exclusively appro-
> priated the name of imagination.[17]

This statement about the poet goes not only in an aesthetic direction, toward poetry, but also in an ontological and practical direction, toward romantic man. Hence one of its bearings is that romantic man achieves self-orientation and definition through imagination.

On the face of it a new word for a new organization, this imagination, if it affords any overt link with the old semantic structure, would seem to do so in terms of reason, and not will. Even while being rejected in its standard, prescriptive-analytical sense, reason is deftly reordered and redeemed for a romanticism that is anti- rather than ir-rationalist. Wordsworth calls imagination "reason in her most exalted moods," and thus orthodox classical reason is not only endowed with obviously alien moods but is paradoxically carried by these moods into areas of exaltation.[18] Byron all but dissolves reason in uncertainty. He acknowledges "waking Reason," but in a context so far removed from moral objectives and institutional understanding that bewilderment is the order of the day, and pondering boldly is the best and "last refuge" of man. Whether reason is itself coming to wakefulness, or bringing others to it, "waking" is as far as it gets; the advancement and arrest of reason merge in a crepuscular permanence. Even Blake, for all his dispraise of Newton and Locke, enjoins us to an exercise of "intellect," of lucid and spirited seeing, as a way into the truth of vision.

But it is in this very reconstitution of reason that evidence of something pertaining to will emerges. Reason ceases to be an abstract operation and becomes a virtual expression of character in the man who will not despair though that appears the logical thing to do, or the man who will believe and dare though that appears imprudent. Reason, in romanticism, is radically affected by "moods," with a sense of Anglo-Saxon *mod*: expression of integrity or state of being, activity or affection of the innermost self, volition and intention.

It is well to be on guard against the presumption that the imagination, because it is usually defined in relation to the poet or in the context of poetry, is confined to the poet or to poetry.[19] Imagination constitutes a gift of the poet as consummate man. It goes beyond the status of a mode of consciousness, whether aesthetic or otherwise. It is a mode of being in relation to the complex of things available to consciousness. In terms of the history of philosophy, psychology, and moral culture, the romantic imagination is the focus of an experiment in dissolving the solid partitions of the soul into faculties or constituent parts, so that the whole being is brought to bear all together, without separation or even sequence, if sequence implies any discontinuity; this can obtain because mood (again, Anglo-Saxon *mod* reminds us that the basic meaning is "soul") informs the entire action. Judgment is accordingly addressed toward quality of being, rather than any precision of operation or orthodoxy of relationship of several "faculties."

And even so judgment arises as spontaneous recognition: there are no models, no hereditary rules, such as in the old dispensation made for uniform standards of conduct and evaluation. Indeed, there cannot be. It is not just that little time has been given for these standards to develop. In the nature of the imagination time is forbidden this result. The imagination evolves in the very situation in which it is applied, and involves its exponent in a vicious circle of negation: it must exist in order to be applied, and must be applied in order to exist. We may extend the idea that the imagination is more a mode of being than of consciousness and say that it does not so much know, and enact itself, as act, and, in the context of its own action, discover itself. It subsists, to adopt Coleridge's poetic phrase, as "cloud at once and shower." It is the equivalent of what Herder calls in his *Essay on the Origin of Language* an "entire disposition of man's forces . . . the total arrangement of all human forces, the total economy of his sensuous and cognitive and volitional nature."[20]

But if the vision that is imagination works according to an empirical and indeed experimental process, how does it come to work? Not mechanically, that is certain; the imagination is generated as an antidote to mechanistic philosophy. And not by obedience to established forms, or formulas; the imagination generates itself in an eventualist universe. The purest answer is a tautology, that the imagination works by working. Fortunately, this need not be the final answer. The imagination, otherwise, works by virtue of the vital activity of its possessor, by virtue of the self-expression which since Schopenhauer and Hegel[21] has been taken as inseparable from the possession of life. The factor of "mood," already defined, enters from the outset into the concept of imagination. Thus the absence of "joy," of positive knowledge and *experience* of integrity and goodness as the ground of things, impairs the function of the imagination in "Dejection: An Ode." As Coleridge remarks, joy is a "beautiful and beauty-making power"; this needs to be construed not in an aesthetic but in a vital sense, as a statement of the beauty of being.

But it is clear that more than mood is involved. Coleridge himself has the imagination "co-existing with the conscious will." The connection seems neither steady nor perspicuous, and yet Coleridge, relentless coiner and remolder of words though he is, neither analyzes nor amplifies on the concept of will. It is perhaps characteristic that the will comes up in a central position, and seems so obvious from an internal perspective that its possible obscurity from an external perspective stays altogether out of mind. We are left to pose ourselves the question, what must be the definition of will in this case?

It is possible, on the strength of "Dejection: An Ode," to set a limit on the meaning and power of will. The closing couplet of the third stanza and all of the fourth and fifth stanzas of "Dejection" indicate that the specific will, as a personal drive to have or be anything definite, is not a reliable, perhaps not even an available, power. The declaration "we receive but what we give" provides no more than illusory support to the idea of an arbitrary and decisive ego. It informs us that nature—the whole world without—has no affective value and remains but "objects . . . essentially fixed and dead," *unless* on his part man relates positively to it; looked at with an empty, unresponding gaze, as the Abbé Sièyes observed, the world seems to offer little of note or substance. Coleridge does not imply that man may specifically or as it were tendentiously choose either *to relate* or *how* to relate to the world without.[22] This whole notion is dramatically exploded in the poem. Coleridge, as the one who "would . . . behold" more than "that inanimate cold world," confesses and lives his impotence to bring about a particular state in himself. He only recognizes that without being in a particular state, certain conceivable relations to the outer world are aborted. The specifically tendentious will, some isolated formal faculty of maintaining engagement and choice, must then be given over. Joy is something the poet "cannot command at will," and in general his concrete, purposive will is powerless before his "moods."[23]

On the other hand, an unanalyzed or unisolated will does emerge in the lines as an effective power for realizing ourselves and for consummating our relationship with the world. "I may not hope," Coleridge writes,

> from outward forms to win
> The passion and the life, whose fountains are within.

> O Lady! we receive but what we give,
> And in our life alone does Nature live:
> Ours is her wedding garment, ours her shroud!
> And would we aught behold, of higher worth,
> Than that inanimate cold world allowed
> To the poor loveless, ever-anxious crowd,
> Ah! from the soul itself must issue forth
> A light, a glory, a fair luminous cloud
> Enveloping the Earth—
> And from the soul itself must there be sent
> A sweet and potent voice, of its own birth,
> Of all sweet sounds the life and element!

> O pure of heart! thou need'st not ask of me
> What this strong music in the soul may be!
> What, and wherein it doth exist,
> This light, this glory, this fair luminous mist,
> This beautiful and beauty-making power.
> . . . .
> Joy, virtuous Lady! Joy that ne'er was given
> Save to the pure, and in their purest hour,
> Life, and Life's effluence, cloud at once and shower,
> Joy, Lady! is the spirit and the power,
> Which wedding Nature to us gives in dower
> A new Earth and new Heaven,
> Undreamt of by the sensual and the proud—

> Joy is the sweet voice, Joy the luminous cloud—
> We in ourselves rejoice!
>   ["Dejection: An Ode," 45–72]

In saying that we rejoice in ourselves or otherwise we can rejoice in nothing, and in showing that this joy cannot be willed, except in vain, Coleridge is not repudiating all terms of will. He is indicating that will cannot anticipate itself. To will joy would be tantamount to willing what is in effect the will, and so regressing from actuality into interminable anticipation. The poem is based on the ironically helpless consciousness that joy, the spirit and power of life, is the will of the very condition of being. In "Dejection: An Ode" Coleridge is concentrating on its yield, but even so his awareness of the radical ontological will is there to be discerned. The idea of irreducible originality (fountain, birth, issue, cloud-shower) is plain enough, and the element of will emerges from this, in the difference between a light "issuing" from the soul, and a voice "being sent" from the soul. For if "issue" is a descriptive term, and "light" a given feature, the "voice" is more than given, it is an individually marshalled and enacted energy, and the "giving" of it stands as a definite communicative act involving a definite engagement of energy. That is to say, the difference between "issue" and "be given," in this context, implies a recognition of an effect of the soul (recognizable light) being carried to another dimension of activity and expression in the soul (uttered voice).

Another dichotomy in the passage should help to clarify and reinforce this point. Perception is "allowed" to the "crowd," but joy is "given" to the "pure," the joyful. The first verb, "allowed," suggests something circumstantial, and perhaps transient; the second, "given," indicates something intrinsically taken over, and permanent. The joy, then, is in one's possession and power, and no doubt this explains why the joyful soul, which has been given its state, also is a giver in this state; for we receive but what we give in relation to nature, but what we give is *given* in relation to authentic life.

Hence the implied and crucial tautology: joy is given to the joyful. Hence, also, the obvious paradox that nature "gave" Coleridge at his birth his "shaping"—independent, formative, even in relation to nature—spirit of imagination. This is not far from Wordsworth's protestation, in his own situation of crisis, that "thou must give,/Else never canst receive" (*Prelude*, book 12, 276-77).

The idea of will at once total and indistinguishable in a healthy state of being is manifest here and is corroborated by the way Coleridge described disease of being ("that which suits a part infects the whole"). His thinking is separated from his feeling ("not to think of what I needs must feel"); his will is separated from his basic thinking and feeling: "abstruse research" constitutes his "sole resource," his "only plan." In effect Coleridge undergoes a lapse, or relapse, from an integrated being informed with will to a divided being, possessed of will. He reverts from a romantic to a classical scheme of utilizing the will, and infection results. The upshot is that the soul, naturally radiant and communicative (light and voice), is thrust away from its proper place and state by abstruseness (*abstrudere*), and shut up in itself, for the phrase "habit of my soul" conveys not only unnatural ways of behavior but also unnatural clothing or shrouding.[24]

The limits of the will, then, have to do with its conceivable operation as "a completely undetermined power to will either one of two contradictory opposites without determining reason, simply because it is desired.[25] This isolated faculty engaged in an isolated moment belongs to an invidious tradition and represents an *infectious* orthodoxy. We must accordingly go about elucidating Coleridge's cryptic use of "will" in the definition of imagination without the prejudice of this sense. But we may note a positive direction implicit in what Coleridge rejects, a direction toward a fully integrated and creative will, which serves as a condition and source of being. In the context of his remarks on imagination, what does this amount to?

The IMAGINATION, then [Coleridge writes], I consider either as primary, or secondary. The primary IMAGINATION I hold to be the living Power and prime Agent of all human Perception, and as a repetition in the finite mind of the eternal act of creation in the infinite I AM. The secondary Imagination I consider as an echo of the former, **co-existing with the conscious will,** yet still as identical with the primary in the *kind* of its agency, and differing only in *degree*, and in the *mode* of its operation. It dissolves, diffuses, dissipates, **in order to** re-create; or where this process is rendered impossible, yet still at all events it **struggles to idealize and to unify.** It is essentially *vital*, even as all objects (*as* objects) are essentially fixed and dead. [*Biographia Literaria*, 1:202; boldface added]

Two features of this statement may be noted at once: the presence of the will itself, of course, and of numerous germane terms; and the fact that these terms, embedded as it were in the portrayal of the primary imagination, become explicit and definitive in relation to the secondary imagination. Coleridge appears to be *reconciling* Schelling's insistence on the imagination and Fichte's on the will as the radical creative power in man.

The thing to keep in mind in going through the statement on imagination is that it directs itself toward the enterprise of being alive and human and of negotiating at once the conditions and contingencies of being. It involves a metaphysical position and an experimental disposition, and it works in terms of responding to what man may make of himself, or grow into, given the ground of being. Taken in this light, the imagination is suffused with a quality of choice, and bears principal responsibility for the shape life (as well as art) takes. Its end is not exclusive as to objects, but specific as to being; the moment and the emerging totality of being are referred to it for recognition and ratification. The following analysis of Coleridge's statement concentrates on its character as metaphysical activity. The method of analysis is more solicitous of the text than of novelty, but its literalness may seem unusual enough in taking up the difficult pragmatics of our unprogrammed metaphysical state.

It is tempting to overestimate the primary imagination,[26] to think of it as universalizing, as intrinsically participating in a mode of perfection. And certainly the excited, if not exultant, spirit in which Coleridge speaks of it moves us in that direction. Wordsworth, too, as Earl Wasserman reminds us, exhibits this excitement; he begins to come into his own as a poet when he infuses into his poetry "a primitive, child-like wonderment that he experiences the outer world *at all*." And Wasserman suggestively dubs Wordsworth "an ur-romantic" on this basis, seeing him as one capable of "celebrating unphilosophically the forgotten basic miracle that the self may possess the outer world in some telling way, and making fresh the wonder of the act."[27]

We may note, too, that Coleridge both sings the glory of man's mimic "creation" and reminds man of his creatureliness in *Religious Musings*, where identification with God demands abandonment of identity:

> There is one Mind, one omnipresent Mind,
> Omnific. His most holy name is Love.
> Truth of subliming import! with the which
> Who feeds and saturates his constant soul,
> He from his small particular orbit flies
> With blest outstarting! From himself he flies,
> Stands in the sun, and with no partial gaze
> Views all creation; and he loves it all,
> And blesses it, and calls it very good!

But if one may say so without irremediably underestimating the primary imagination, it is *only* the excitement of a man's finding himself alive in the world (though it will also be necessary to pursue the idea that his "only" becomes the inception of "all"). To explain the excitement, it is important to bring out Coleridge's vision of how a man finds himself in the world, its absoluteness and at the same time commonness and dependency, its magnificence and at the same time pettiness and pathos. For if Coleridge seems to be recalling Schelling's position that "man's being is essentially his own deed,"[28] he is typically modifying and enlarging and particularizing this position, saying not only more than Schelling says, but also more than we could divine Schelling means.

With the primary imagination Coleridge is at bottom dealing with the fact that the world comes into being for each of us individually when and as it is perceived; hence his use of the word *primary*, and hence his drawing an analogy with the Creation—if we do not perceive it, individually, it does not come into being for us. Individual being, then, and individual perception interpenetrate and become identical in effect. It is of use to recognize in what Merleau-Ponty terms "perception" the lineament of the "primary imagination"; his compelling summary of the oddly reminiscent idea, "the primacy of perception," almost serves as a gloss on Coleridge's thought:

> By these words, the "primacy of perception," we mean that the experience of perception is our presence at the moment when things, truths, values are constituted for us; that perception is a nascent *logos*; that it teaches us, outside all dogmatism, the true condition of objectivity itself; that it summons us to the tasks of knowledge and action. It is not a question of reducing human knowledge to sensation, but of assisting at the birth of this knowledge, to make it as sensible as the sensible, to recover the consciousness of rationality.[29]

But both being and perception express or embody a "living Power" and signify more than just an occurrence or a datum that could say, this being is, wittingly, in and in relation to the world. Being and perception are an "act," analogous to the original act of God making the world, and so imply a self-manifestation as well as a self-discovery. If the secondary imagination is "vital" as over against objects which are "dead," the primary imagination has, in perceiving, a vitality or "Agency" that is opposed to any mind-world relationship of a "mechanical" or "materialistic" system.

Of course the character of this vitality remains institutive only, and not constitutive, of human being. With all the celebration due to the fact, rather than the *act*, of life, it is necessary to observe that the primary imagination places us in the world at the fundamental level of perception, and no more; and what we perceive is indeed the world of "objects, *as* objects, essentially fixed and dead." In short, if through the primary imagination the world becomes to us individually as new as to God when first it was made, we do not become as God. The world for God is whole, instantaneous, corresponds to his creative word, and expresses him as ordained; to man the world is partitive, sequential, susceptible of understanding, and is experienced as found. Hence Coleridge's phrase, "a repetition in the finite mind." As Hölderlin so lucidly says, "At the very point at which the beautiful world came into being for us, when we achieved consciousness, did we become finite."[30] It is for us to know what to make of what God as Maker knows, and so the secondary or second stage of imagination comes into play. Its specific charge is to accommodate the primary plurality and incoherence of the objects of perception, to arrive at a grammar and philosophy for what Paul deMan has called "the infinitely fragmented and amorphous language of pure denomination."[31]

The primary imagination moves toward perception or self-conscious existence, the secondary imagination moves toward conception[32] or meaning and value. Both move from the same center of active being, though, and in a sense imply each other. But it is important to remark that meaning and value do not arise on a putatively favorable, or even a neutral, base of perception. Rather, the isolate features of perception can fail to cohere, can repel one another, thus making the work of the secondary imagination a "struggle," as Coleridge says, or sometimes an "impossibility." Where conception does occur, it results not from any happy aggregation of the features of perception, but from a grasp of the "connection of the parts and their logical dependencies" (*Biographia Literaria,*

1:173). And as Coleridge declares, when it does occur it is properly an affirmative ontological act; connections and logical dependencies yield "a whole [which] is groundless and hollow," unless sustained "by living contact" and accompanied with a "realizing intuition which exists by and in the act that affirms its existence, which is known, because it is, and is, because it is 'known'" (*Biographia Literaria*, 1:173).

The secondary imagination, as the *sole* agent of conception, is the power whereby the unity and value which the world has veridically in the eyes of God become possible for human knowledge and use. Coleridge insists on its being continuous with, though distinguishable from, the primary imagination, and we may take this as a recognition of the fact that the primary and secondary imagination, together, make for the human version of God's creative consciousness, as conception completes perception. That is to say, the "infinite I AM" is positive, instantaneous, final; the "finite repetition" is analogous, partial, processive. It commences with perception, and with the secondary imagination it comes into its own, as far as may be. Once again here the fact that we are working in the finite state, that the Self is absolute in God while self is only synecdoche in man, must be borne in mind. The process of interpretation at work in the secondary imagination addresses itself to consciousness and at the same time to an activity of being. And to catch the peculiar combination of consciousness and activity in being, the term that most plausibly offers itself is "realization," in an epistemological as well as an ontological sense.[33] One realizes oneself and the state of things together, as one; even so, in the contingency of human experience,[34] a *development toward* fullness of realization has to be assumed, or as it were undertaken. If realization itself does not come into question, the terms of realization have to be met and matured piecemeal, according to what may well be called a blind teleology.

The weight and value Coleridge is placing on this act of realization can be gauged if we compare this repetition of the infinite I AM with a similar statement he makes in *Aids to Reflection*. Speaking of the imagination in *Biographia Liter-*

aria, Coleridge raises the individual mind toward divine creativity, or at least toward analogy with that divine power. His
invocation of the "conscious will" if anything strengthens the
analogy, and amplifies the praise of man and his imaginative
power. But a much more cautious, grudging note breaks in by
the time he is composing the *Aids*. "A finite Will," Coleridge
observes, "*constitutes* a true Beginning; but . . . the *finite* Will
gives a beginning only by co-incidence with that *absolute* WILL,
which is at the same time *Infinite* POWER!"[35] Analogy, even
ectype, has dwindled into "coincidence," and the "absolute
Self" of an earlier vision of the will has disappeared into the
inaccessible absolute of conventional godhead. The association of man with divinity through the imagination is paramount in the *Biographia*, and deserves every emphasis.

There is a danger, at this point, of overestimating the secondary imagination. Certainly the primary act of perception
seems to throw a considerable burden on the secondary imagination, and certainly the work of the secondary imagination
in coming to terms with the self and the world, in the form
of a blind teleology, seems to outrank the moment of finding
that the world is there. Such advantages to the secondary
imagination are specious, though, and are based on an invidious division which far exceeds the limits of the given distinction. Coleridge is at pains to advise us that the primary and
secondary imagination involve the same *kind* of operation,[36]
which has more than one phase, or *degree*, and more than
one pattern, or *mode*, of response.

The mode of activity of the secondary imagination—perhaps
the most elusive of the three terms of relationship between
primary and secondary—may be substantially described in the
light of Coleridge's own idioms for the *perceived* world and
the activity in question. In either case, the world is there to
be made something of, but it is first met, with the primary
imagination, as material, "fixed" and discrete, and inert. It
does not change its nature when the secondary imagination
comes into play, but as it were its guise; what has appeared
solid and static proves susceptible of a power that "dissolves,
diffuses, dissipates"; what has been material and separate

proves susceptible of a power that tends naturally "to idealize and to unify." From the perspective of the secondary imagination the world of objects loses mere individual and opaque solidity and takes on a dimension of fluidity and solubility,[37] whereby connections and relations that are in effect abstractive and conceptual arise in the very conglomerate mass of primary "creation."

The primary imagination gives information in terms of which the secondary imagination gives indications of meaning and value. In this respect there is no more ground for dividing the two phases of the imagination than for dividing the world perceived from the world conceived. It is one world and one imagination; the perceived plurality embodies the principle of unity, and both exist simultaneously, though made available in a time pattern that is subject to analysis. The chronology of the imagination really implies a use of time for purposes of *manifestation* and does not at all contain the notion of a product of time in evolution. The imagination, primary and secondary, remains essentially continuous, not subject to division or arrest.

It is worth stressing this indivisible activity of imagination, because it reminds us that Coleridge uses the terms "primary" and "secondary" to point to a mere practical chronology, rather than value,[38] and also because it brings out the fundamental wholeness of man's meeting with the world. Still, the presupposition of indivisible activity does not mean that the secondary imagination just happens along. Self-expression, an individual act, has already been seen as intrinsic to the primary imagination. This self-expression is manifest in a higher degree and in a more articulate mode in the secondary imagination. It is on this account that we find a higher incidence and specificity of terms designating the will in Coleridge's depiction of secondary imagination. Perhaps the phrase with which he introduces the will seems somewhat offhand, but this is misleading. The "conscious will"—the very phrase sums up the double emphasis I am seeking to establish—is so much a part of the imagination, so much present wherever it is present ("co-existing with" it), that Coleridge responds as though it were enough to point to it and pass on. And it is enough, in his mind. We need more, though. We may only conclude here that his statement is not so much offhand as shorthand and look to the remainder of the passage for explication.

At no point, we may note to begin with, is the secondary imagination held before us without explicit reference to will, and will as conscious and deliberate. The basic datum of "conscious will" itself suggests a fusion of intellectual and volitional modes of response, and this fusion continues into the praxis of the secondary imagination. It "dissolves, diffuses, dissipates" the things that are perceived, and it does all this with an explicit purpose, "in order to re-create." Its effect is to "idealize and unify," and where such an effect does not readily occur it "struggles" toward it. The presence of the will is insistent and radical, in these terms, and we need only ask how it should be construed. A partial answer has arisen in the foregoing discussion of the relation of secondary to primary imagination, and this may be amplified here.

The attainment of comprehension, as distinct from the accumulation that is peculiar to the primary imagination, has already come out as the business of the secondary imagination; so has the fact that this attainment, in any degree, is purposed ("dissolves . . . *in order to* re-create" [italics added]). Such a recreating, too, has been shown as a more sophisticated or profound—in effect a more complex—version of the initial "creation" of perception, and it has been shown to be, at least potentially, problematical. Beyond this, a few points need bringing out. The sense of "re-create" is made clear by reference to the specifying terms "idealize and unify." The secondary imagination recreates, or elaborates and articulates, the world as perceived by recognizing its implicit principles ("idealize") and its implicit coherence ("unify"). It brings about a consciousness of "the unity which . . . necessarily but unconsciously exists" within nature, "as in a seed."[39]

It means to bring this about. It wills what it does; it does in that it wills. The world of perception, though, does not for a finite being (it is always to be stressed that Coleridge is dealing with a *finite* version of absolute creation)—does not for a finite being necessarily yield up its principles and its wholeness on demand. And this fact leads to a reiteration of the intrinsic will in the secondary imagination. In the face of practical difficulty, even impossibility, the imagination "struggles to idealize and to unify." In short, the purely intellectual recognition that it is "impossible" to "re-create" does not lead to a conclusion in the state of the secondary imagination.[40] Such a conclusion, meaning either deduction or end, would imply that the secondary imagination had ceased to exist, and one would experience the kind of "death" which Coleridge so poignantly depicts in "Dejection: An Ode." By the same token, to struggle, even with impossibility, makes "failure" a positive achievement, a realization rather than defection of self.[41]

In some respects, then, the secondary imagination should be considered apart from its effects, though it is through these effects that it becomes most readily available for discourse. It is self-active, self-choosing, a *willed* evidence to being, and if it results in a finer knowledge and consciousness, that is not its end, which remains unalterably fuller realization of being. It is, in sum, what should be meant when we speak of the self-made man.

The imagination taken, as Coleridge enjoins, to be *one* activity susceptible of analysis into two modes of operation embodies a myth of human potentiality: "The potential works *in* them," Coleridge says of people in whom imagination is well developed, "even as the *actual* works *on* them." Imagination means development, with the qualification that its intrinsic mark is to struggle toward a position of idealist unity for the world, not necessarily to achieve it. Imagination is purposive, with the qualification that it exhibits at most an indefinite teleology. It is also important to stress the fact that, while referring or belonging to all men, this myth of potentiality is erected upon an incorrigibly individualist basis and must be separated from the Hegelian myth of history and Schelling's myth of the evolutionary God, both of which entail a specific teleology in a collective or transindividualist context.

We need to take full account of the *autobiographical* origin of Coleridge's statement on the imagination. Say what we may of the influences upon it,[42] the statement boils down to Coleridge's cryptic summation of the way he finds and realizes himself. The very concept of imagination has individualizing value, as it puts Coleridge's own definition over against the habits of his language and society, and helps to remind us that we have not given sufficient attention to a *penchant* for redefinition in romanticism. To illustrate, epic, lyric, ballad are redefined as genres, and pleasure, dream, imagination as philosophical and evaluative terms, in what is clearly an expression of a freedom and right to define meanings and the very structures of thought and value. The statement on the imagination is Coleridge's personal identification of the instrument and end alike of his (and at once, then, of man's) encounter in the world. Here it seems to entail a profound act of ontological courage, going one's own way in the world. When this courage fails Coleridge he specifically recants, by privately striking out the avowal of the imagination as "a repetition in the finite mind of the eternal act of creation in the infinite I AM"; this is recorded by Sara Coleridge in the second edition of *Biographia Literaria*.

But the occasion of *Biographia Literaria* was just such as to engage Coleridge in this vein.[43] Coleridge is more than showing his need for assurance that the human spirit could stand without specific recourse to divine authority and faith.[44] He is making man do, create, for himself what God has done for him, defining himself by translating passive gift into active product. And the autobiographical or individualist emphasis stands out all the more against Coleridge's lifelong tendency, in society, to "sacrifice" himself to others, and, in thought, to absorb single men into universal or institutional bodies. Clearly even such a Boehmian abandonment of the individual will has a voluntaristic dimension and entails an art of self-definition. This paradox will be taken up in due course. For now the presence of the will must be concern enough; and the recognition that "self-construction," the term Coleridge used for the autobiography itself, may be used equally as well as "self-realization" to describe the imagination and its intrinsic acts of consciousness and of will.

Of the face of it the statement on the imagination may remain liable to the objections raised by T. M. Raysor in his introduction to Coleridge's *Shakespearean Criticism*, namely, that as it stands it seems "unfortunate" and "eccentric." Looked at in light of an autobiographical postulate, the statement rises free of such charges and takes on both poignance and cogency. The adventure in momentaneous self-reliance and the ultimate spiritual poise that we recognize in the theory of the imagination Coleridge certainly gave over. He turned to a special blend of Christian orthodoxy, in religion, and of transcendent reason, in philosophy, as his stay against incertitude. But it may be argued that, in the world that does not boast the "integral *spirit* of the regenerated man" or enjoy "a pure influence from the glory of the Almighty," Coleridge kept a corner of his heart sacred to the idea of the creative imagination; in that world, the only one we know, he still saw the *discursive* understanding as equal to "Clearness without Depth," and insisted (in *The Statesman's Manual*) that "the completing power which unites clearness with depth, the plenitude of the sense with the comprehensibility of the understanding, is the *imagination*, impregnated with which the understanding itself becomes intuitive, and a living power."

As an individualist myth of potentiality the statement on the imagination enunciates a peculiarly Coleridgean order with a moving center and an expanding circumference. From the perspective of the single human being it affirms what from the perspective of institutional judgment (history) might seem anarchic, to wit, the nonviability of ready-made axioms of behavior or thought. Yet it is not licentious. If it substitutes opportunism for obedience,[45] its opportunism is strictly self-controlled. Fancy is in Coleridge's terms more licentious, indeed *because* it is more calculating and purposive in its treatment of the "fixities and definites" of perception. It is, like the secondary imagination, chronologically subsequent to the action of primary imagination, but it is marked by arbitrary superficiality and proves in quality as like the secondary imagination as rearrangement is like recreation. The "will" associated with fancy is a mere "empirical phenomenon," whereas the will associated with the secondary imagination informs individual being. Coleridge's depreciation of fancy, then, reflects his sense of its failing (1) to penetrate the opacity of phenomena on the level of consciousness, and (2) to reach beyond the technical command of phenomena on the level of will or personal being to a "disciplined and strengthened . . . ulterior consciousness" (*Biographia Litera-ria*, 1:168).

The propriety of the statement on the imagination as an integral part of the entire *Biographia Literaria* cannot be too strongly stressed. It is the statement of the way a man creates himself, set forth in the book in which Coleridge "constructs" the raw material of his experience into his life. In this story of an individual which modulated into a story of being ("my philosophical opinions are blended with, or deduced from, my feelings," Coleridge writes, and again conceives "my metaphysical works as *my Life*, and in *my* Life"),[46] the presence of the will, though it has gone largely unnoticed, is radical and pervasive. Chapter 12 of *Biographia Literaria*, well described as a "preparative discipline indispensable" (1:163), makes it clear that Coleridge has the will very much in mind:

> It has been shown, that a spirit is that, which is its own object, yet not originally an object, but an absolute subject for which all, itself included may become an object. It must therefore be an ACT; for every object is, as an *object*, dead, fixed, incapable itself of any action, and necessarily finite. Again the spirit (originally the identity of object and subject) must in some sense dissolve this identity, in order to be conscious of it; fit alter et idem. But this implies an act, and it follows therefore that in-

> telligence or self-consciousness is impossible, except by
> and in a will. The self-conscious spirit therefore is a will.
> ... [1:184–85, thesis vii]

It is also clear that he is not thinking of an "empirical" or
locally purposive will, but of the will in being, the will of
being:[47] "This principium commune essendi et cognoscendi
... subsisting in a *will*, or primary *act* of self-duplication"
(1:185, thesis ix). If we take a signal from Coleridge's "re-
perusing ... the Timaeus of *Plato*" on the verge of writing on
the imagination (1:161), we may recognize Coleridge's all
but explicit concern with accounts and hypotheses of creation. This confirms one other feature of the will already
mentioned, namely, that it is inseparable from creation even
in the finite mode and that creation is, again in the finite
mode, a personal act.

In light of the foregoing discussion, the presence of the will
in imagination becomes as patent as the presence of the self.
And it is a necessary and obvious step to hold that its presence in the imagination gives it centrality in the romantic
scheme. One may propose at this stage that, in the open system of romanticism, the will is the subject and center of the
emergent situation. It is in everything in general, but what it
means to be so defies understanding except in particular instances. In practice varieties of density and texture emerge,
and these must be analyzed and, as far as possible, interpreted
in proof of the power of the will in romanticism.

THE WILL IN ROMANTIC POETRY

For the contexts of the will, then, it should be of advantage
to begin by sketching in a few examples of the will at work in
a variegated grouping of poems. Coleridge's *Rime of the Ancient Mariner* allows us to see the will in a charged dramatic
context, emerging from silence and obscurity, under chastisement, into a compulsive and impracticable mode of prophecy.
Wordsworth's "The Solitary Reaper" allows us to see the will
in a charged reflective context, with overtones of spontaneous

ritual. Byron's "Prometheus" treats the will from an external, general viewpoint, granting it only the negative power of safe-guarding the self from an ill-constituted universe. And in Wordsworth's "Tintern Abbey" the will as it were meets a problematical universe with impunity and surges forth on the very stream of (grammatical) time.

There are two ways of construing the initial decision point in *The Ancient Mariner*, embodied in the line, "The Mariner hath his will."[48] It tells us first that the Wedding Guest is done for, *his will* overmastered by the character and spirit of the Ancient Mariner. But it also implicitly tells us that the Mariner's will, exhibited in this moment, goes beyond any particular case; the Mariner is a man marked, characterized by will, a man who possesses this power of will in notable de-gree. With Coleridge proclaiming it, there is no need to prove that the question of will makes one of the pivots of the poem. The question of the will of the Wedding Guest does not re-move this issue, but focuses it sharply on the Mariner as he proceeds from compulsive action to obsessive memory, and the poem itself shifts from a position of observation to one of participation: the will is not to be catalogued and dis-missed, but is implicated in the recapitulatory action.

As for the main action, three more decision points present themselves. The first really constitutes the beginning of the action proper, insofar as this action revolves around the Mariner: "I shot the Albatross." What precedes is the mise-en-scène, the establishment of the order of the universe in which any action will occur. But this "order," as the Mariner perceives it, seems random enough: one finds oneself simply, unceremoniously out somewhere on an ocean which itself may be calm or stormy, and one is driven this way and that. It is a universe of superstition, because one is desperate for signs, for orientation[49] —hence the other sailors condemn or praise the Mariner's act as they find themselves becalmed in mist or breezing along in the clear. The situation anticipates the shipwreck episode in Byron's *Don Juan*, where abandoned and desperate voyagers insist on locating an elusive Providence

in a rainbow or the corpse of a turtle. Forcing symbolic meanings onto transient occasions ("as if it had been a Christian
soul"), Coleridge's sailors are being consistent in the framework of superstition which alone their protean world seems
to afford. This background of meaninglessness, or unintelligi-
bility, affords a useful perspective on the Mariner's act. He
perceives, insofar as he describes a universe under the domination of blind matter and random motion; things, like the
Sun and the STORM-BLAST, are personified and active, while
people are present only as sufferers and objects ("and chased
us") or as obedient agents of the moment ("the helmsman
steered us through!"), or as terrified victims of a hostile
world ("we fled"). The sailors are lost in phenomenal nature
or lost in the collective body or in the metonymy of their
function—the singular person of "the mariner's hollo" embraces them all, under their function, without discrimina-
tion.[50]

"I shot," then, inevitably reverberates with the personal
identity and force of that "I." The idiom is ballad-wise austere and virtually neutral on the surface, but the very agitation
of the Mariner as he says it must warn us not to take this for
granted. Though we may feel baffled as we attempt to penetrate the cause of the shooting we cannot but recognize the
shooting as *his* act. Ultimately, the cause is *himself*: "I shot."
It is to be stressed that he alone makes decisions in the poem.
To take his act as another mere occurrence confuses the result
with the origin. He is as essentially present in it as in the
"wicked whisper" which "came" to him—as to Claudius—when
he "tried to pray." He is moved by the same impulse that in
another context led to the killing of the crow that saluted
Caesar. On the face of it an incongruous importance is being
attached to the bird, but it is possible to see through this a
sort of rough and proud assertion of individual primacy, perhaps even of human dignity, over against the extraverted
focus on the bird.

The fact is that no one hitherto has had a place, a definitive
place, in the universe of the story. In some sense, despite the

level of social development implied in the maritime activity of
the opening lines, the characters resemble Herder's "infallible
machine [much like an animal] in the hands of nature," but
suddenly one man, sensitively perceiving the universe but ostensibly passive in it, announces his presence, and as Herder
says "himself becomes a purpose and an objective of his efforts."[51] If the poem "depicts the soul after its birth to the
sense of separate . . . being,"[52] the mode of being born (or
borne) is far from passive and practical merely. It is active,
selective, and spiritually purposive. The Mariner does something that matters to the universe of matter, in which he finds
himself, materially, less than a person.[53] He has undertaken
the adventure of individuality, reasserting and expanding the
authority and significance conferred by his position as Mariner
or "Old Navigator, as Coleridge . . . delighted to call him."[54]
He is in charge of their course, of *them*, and will not brook
a rival for reputation. Though his adventure of individuality[55]
will bring him back to a collective vision of people going
"together to the kirk," and "all together" praying, that vision
is *his* vision, chosen and not mechanically given, and itself includes others as individualities:

> While *each* to *his* great Father bends
> Old men, and babes, and loving friends
> And youths and maidens gay!
> > [italics added]

   This is the same adventure of individuality which the poet
in "Kubla Khan" contemplates and which Christabel undertakes when she steps beyond the chartered castleworks of Sir
Leoline. And no doubt the horror of consequences they sev-
erally display is analogous to the Ancient Mariner's shudder
as he recollects his act. But such an explanation glances by
the essential point that the consequences, for the Ancient
Mariner, admit of no distinction from the act. The horror of
consequences is simple and final for the other sailors—the
irrationality of their deaths holds a warning of sorts to be
careful what you enter into. But the consequences for the

Mariner are complex and continuous, and speak of what he is. His "I shot" distinguishes him in the universe. By it he enacts himself, only to discover the implacable isolation and exposure of identity; not even the natural bond of family sustains itself, or him, in this case:

> The body of my brother's son
> Stood by me, knee to knee:
> The body and I pulled at one rope,
> But he said nought to me.

Propinquity ("knee to knee") and collaboration ("pulled at one rope") have no value as consolation, no effect on his personal condition. Identity means excommunication. Thus the "plague" the Wedding Guest sees working in him is not so much the memory of consequences as the recognition of himself therein. Only because he is indissolubly in the act does it continue to live in memory for him, and with it its wake of consequences. Though certainly no Columbus of the moral seas, or even a "stout" Balboa, the Mariner certainly ranks as a spiritual adventurer in a peculiarly eruptive and unpredictable scheme. This is not to make a hero of him; as Humphry House observes, epithets like "great" and "courageous" do not apply.[56] But it is just and necessary to see him as a puzzled ontological adventurer, finding himself and his world moment by moment.

But because he is more than he does at any juncture, these consequences at the same time function as a new set of circumstances leading to the second decision point in the main story, this in the form of the Mariner's second act: "I blessed them unaware." Here the relation between the essential man and the external gesture is somewhat clearer, since "blessed" conveys more of what is inside the Mariner than does "shot"; besides, we are prepared to make sense of the benediction by the context and by the seeding of the Christian vocabulary earlier in the poem, whereas the shooting comes upon us with all the abruptness of ego. But both acts, as the key qualifier "unaware" makes clear, spring alike from unanalyzed, unapprehended levels of his being. The blessing has nothing to do with his sense of propriety or faith; the conscious empirical will has failed already, as it so often does in Coleridge:

> I looked to heaven, and tried to pray;
> But or ever a prayer had gusht
> A wicked whisper came. . . .

Rather the blessing expresses the basic will or state of his being, now manifesting in itself a capacity for aesthetic admiration, for love, and for a sacred respect for other things *in themselves* (for we may recall that the Albatross is absorbed into the scheme of the ship's life, as parasite or plaything or portent, and is nothing in itself):

> Beyond the shadow of the ship,
> I watched the water-snakes:
> They moved in tracks of shining white,
> And when they reared, the elfish light
> Fell off in hoary flakes.
>
> Within the shadow of the ship
> I watched their rich attire:
> Blue, glossy green, and velvet black,
> They coiled and swam; and every track
> Was a flash of golden fire.
>
> O happy living things! no tongue
> Their beauty might declare:
> A spring of love gushed from my heart,
> And I blessed them unaware:
> Sure my kind saint took pity on me,
> And I blessed them unaware.
>
> The self-same moment I could pray. . . .

In this light, prayer becomes less an adoption of an established, formal mode of response than a spontaneous development within a pattern of self-expression. The pattern of action within the episode almost allows itself to be read symbolically, as the Mariner looks on the surface of things for what they may do for him, then comes to look into things for themselves: "I looked upon the rotting sea"; "I looked to heaven"; "I *watched* the water-snakes"; "I *watched* their rich attire" (italics added). But *watching*, looking into and not just looking, reveals that a changed expression in the self precedes and generates the changed recognition of what is without. In a sense that conveys more than the geography of far and near, the Mariner has indeed changed from something "beyond" to something "within." If he is sharing in the nature of the water-snakes as "happy living things," and thus easing his own despair, this stands as a given result, without a prior purpose. The sharing is spun out of himself, out of his capacity to characterize them as happy—a different thing from the personification of the storm-blast—and out of his coming into being at this new level of perception. That a birth or special awakening is taking place we may conclude from the progression between "hoary flakes" and the "flash of golden fire." This is the progression from winter ("hoary flakes," with reinforcement from "shining white"), to spring ("golden fire," with reinforcement from the warm and expanded color scheme, "blue, glossy, green, and velvet black").

"I blest," we may see, is as far removed from "I shot" as "I watched" from "I looked." The advance is not moral, though; one act is not to be chosen over the other for being better. The change is ontological, putting the Mariner in a deeper, fuller, and truer relation to the universe *and to himself*. The change, I have tried to show, is chosen and brought about essentially in himself; it is in that respect a willed manifestation of his being, a positive will to find and accept what one is capable of (dissatisfaction, a negative will, is obvious all along). The necessity of seeing the case ontologically comes about sharply when we consider the aftermath of the Mariner's second decision, the blessing. If it were moral, it would constitute or at least initiate an atonement with the nature offended by the shooting. It does not do this, though. To the contrary, the original act remains, repeating itself indefinitely and providing the foundation of a relationship between Mariner and Wedding Guest that is itself founded on will, not on morality or understanding ("sadder and . . . wiser" reach out to understanding, but probably refer to and commence in the ontological will). Morally, we expiate our actions; ontologically, we contain them and recognize in them the idea of ourselves as expressed in those actions and, with reservations that are no more than analytical, as satisfied by them.

This idea of something ontologically ineradicable will be remembered as a feature of *Christabel*:

> But neither heat, nor frost, nor thunder,
> Shall wholly do away, I ween,
> The marks of that which once hath been.

The immediate reference is of course the scarred friendship of Sir Leoline and Lord Roland de Vaux, but the statement is general, gnomic, and reverberates in the Geraldine-Christabel relationship. What makes for ineradicability[57] will probably clarify itself if *Christabel* is set beside not only *The Ancient Mariner* but also Blake's *Visions of the Daughters of Albion*.

Blake insists, and we are convinced, that Oothoon, ravished by Bromion, retains her innocence and is not essentially touched. Bromion has possessed her body, perforce and perchance. Her nature remains inaccessible to him; he does not *know* her. But Christabel's case, though force is again involved ("forced unconscious sympathy"), differs in crucial respects from Oothoon's. Geraldine possesses Christabel's *person*, revealing at once something about her and about the constitution of the universe she occupies; both are anomalously susceptible to moments of possession ("Off! woman, off! this hour is mine!"). That an inner metaphysical experience has taken place, far beyond the "resignation" of her "features" to Geraldine's mood, is clear enough in Christabel's cry, "Sure I have sinned!" with its strange mixture of bafflement and lucidity. More than this, the narration gives ontological substance to what on the level of behavior might seem a hypnotic freak. Christabel spends the time with Geraldine "dreaming that alone, which *is*" (italics added). The dreamt moment realizes itself as it occurs, it *is*, for Christabel, who in this light stands to Geraldine as does the Wedding Guest to the Ancient Mariner. Through the vital experience of dominated will, both grow sadder and wiser. And it may be more than incidental that both suffer overwhelmingly while carrying out commitments of their own, that is to say, in situations already fraught with will. The two episodes tacitly suggest that the will exists beyond specific election or practical consciousness, in all that we become; and befalling and becoming are one, since what befalls us takes its definition from what we bring to it and become in the face of it.

The obvious remorse the ancient Mariner feels about shooting the Albatross is based, once again, on his recognition of himself in the act. He is capable of trying to displace his part in certain situations, as when he tells us "a wicked whisper *came*" (italics added), or, more surprisingly, when he seems to attribute the water-snake blessing to his "kind saint." His attempt to theologize the action of the poem is a genuine but also an elliptical impulse in the poem as a whole. He cannot stuff his experience into the quiet bed of orthodoxy. We may note that he never tries to pass the fact of the shooting onto any wicked demon, and this is the cardinal act. If it is a "sin," then his original sin is *being* and there is no theology in the poem to which that can be referred. In fact, he cannot, as being, begin to renounce that act, albeit that he cannot bring it into order in private or public spheres. His remorse is a way of maintaining that act in a perpetual present of imagination and of recommitting it indefinitely. The retelling serves on one level as the public equivalent of this private remorseful retention. And because it involves repetition without variation in vision or mood—fixation, in effect—no reformation can occur. Indeed, there is from the first telling to the Hermit, a confession without a shriving, a solipsistic rather than religious unburdening that is accomplished directly by the Ancient Mariner's utterance of his tale, without any intercession on the part of the "holy man." The same force of the self which expressed itself in action before now expresses itself in language.

It is crucial here to stress that the tale originates in response

to the question "What manner of man art thou?" The Ancient
Mariner is more than remembering, he is identifying himself,
the person who includes the water-snake blessing without ex-
cluding the shooting of the Albatross. The self-obsession of
his tale is not an effort to see his life as a significant action
with a recognizable human shape, but an effort, given the action, to identify himself in it as an acceptable being. Still no
one accepts and cares, but each listens with a forced hypnotic
obedience.

Both the blessing and shooting are alike in their spontaneity
and at the same time opposed in temper and effect. The character of the Mariner in sum appears energetic but incohesive,
needing at once salvation—the assurances of orthodoxy—and
adventure, or the opportunities of ego and freedom. This is
the character that finds expression in the third and last decision point in the action, the Ancient Mariner's invocation of
his ideal world:

> O sweeter than the marriage-feast,
> 'Tis sweeter far to me,
> To walk together to the kirk
> With a goodly company!
>
> To walk together to the kirk
> And all together pray,
> While each to his great Father bends,
> Old men, and babes, and loving friends
> And youths and maidens gay!

Here, of course, is a decision point with a difference; it is not
action, nor even actuality. It is the self looking wistfully beyond the self, according to a mode of mere consciousness; it
implies all the reality of bitterness already uttered by the Mariner, the bitterness of being "the manner of man" he has
shown. This wistfulness itself also expresses the Mariner's will,
but in a speculative vein. The form of the poem does not
make room for any effort on his part to apply himself to the
realization of his ideal, does not make room for reformation.

Perhaps, in the light of the incohesiveness of the character, reformation is impossible, and we are dealing with a case of mistaking "wishing for willing."[58] At any rate, the Ancient Mariner is satisfied to enunciate and retail this ideal, while invariably repeating his spontaneous self, while remaining the "manner of man" it embodies. And he takes responsibility for this self as willed, with the implication at last that we are not only responsible for our mortal finiteness, bu intrinsically also will it.[59]

Where the will curtails the theoretical possibilities of the world in *The Ancient Mariner*, it is the world that limits the alternatives of the will in Byron's "Prometheus." The "immortal eyes" of the Titan see the "reality" of human existence and in the superiority of his vision sanction the view of it as being "sad" and "unallied"; at the same time the Titan's immortal nature and condition constitute a "symbol" or model for man, whereby he can recognize the only way possible for coping, namely, by invincible defiance. The poem explicitly cries up the virtue of "a firm will," and implicitly limits "the will" to its relation to "the suffering" (that is, to the "wretchedness" and "funereal destiny") of man in the world. Life reduces itself to "the strife" between these two forces. If the will prevails or at least survives in the face of "the suffering," then man is "triumphant"; if "the suffering" gets the better of man . . .

But this possibility is not even entertained in the compass of the poem. At the same time, neither the possibility of an Aeschylean detente between Prometheus and Zeus nor of a Shelleyan evolution into a postpolitical, ideal order is suggested; the Thunderer trembles, but things stay the same. The poem initially has Prometheus looking at us in relation to the world, and finally has us looking at him in relation to the world, but these are really two ends of one view. Monotony for the world, monomania for man: these are its effective amplitudes.

Even so there is a latent dimension in the poem, according to which the will has created the world that bilks it of any expression save defiance. The first section of the poem, as already noted, is oriented toward man and seems to lump man in one category, "the proud." In repudiating any relationship but one of pride, the poem has preordained the relationship between man and world. And the pride in question has a decidedly negative and static character. It works by concealment, silence, *privacy*; the elimination of everything but hostility and danger in the world may justly be recognized as a factor of, and a service to, the principle of privacy. That is to say, if there is nothing out there to tempt disclosure or to promise an ease of suffering, concealment becomes at once easier and more urgent; until finally—and this is where "Prometheus" finds itself—need modulates into law, and alternatives to a "sad unallied existence" have vanished from sight and thought. In this view (one which the biographical situation amply supports), the Promethean world is a dependent, rather than an illuminating, symbol, and tells us less about the world at large than about the world one man needs and wills. The casting of the poem in the form of abstract observation only partly achieves its objective of concealing the personality of the will in the poem. It embodies and confesses the tendency of that personality to secure itself in abstractions which silence the suffering that

> speaks but in its loneliness,
> And then is jealous lest the sky
> Should have a listener, nor will sigh
> Until its voice is echoless.

To seek such silence is to be paranoid about being paranoid, and the abstraction of the will in the poem emerges as an ultimate form of self-justification, a statement of justified paranoia. This is perhaps best understood in relation to Paul Ricoeur's summary of "that which Plato calls our Titanic nature; [the Titan] attests that the lowest degree of freedom is close to the brute, angry, inordinate force of the unleashed elements; Prometheus is in harmony only with the shapeless scenery of the Caucasus, not with the temperate landscape of

Colonus, which bathes the aged, transfigured Oedipus in sweetness. This savage possibility in ourselves . . . is incarnated in a crime older than any human fault; and so the Titan represents the anteriority of evil in relation to actual human evil."[60]

"Prometheus" suppresses, or at least converts into opaque generalizations, the personal events and narrative strain of *The Ancient Mariner*. It vastly inflates the capacity for inference concerning the "ideal" world. The Mariner's "sweet" is equivalent to the "pride" of the nameless speaker of "Prometheus," as a matter of abstract principle. But the engagement of the will with, say, the sacred beauty of the watersnakes is perfect, if momentary, for the Ancient Mariner and inconceivable for the speaker in "Prometheus." In both cases, whether we move toward action or toward definition, the will is the motive force and a particular "manner of man" comes forth. The divergence between the will seen as implicit personality, in *The Ancient Mariner*, and as explicit philosophy, in "Prometheus," is a matter of manifestation, a product of context and character.

The will may be regarded as one of the crystallized features of poems like *The Ancient Mariner* and "Prometheus." Within the romantic complex its occurrence is often less plain, without becoming less crucial, as in "Tintern Abbey," for example, or in "The Solitary Reaper." The following analysis of these two poems is meant to bring out the presence and effectual power of the will where, existing as it were in solution, it might well pass unnoticed.

"The Solitary Reaper" has been astutely identified as a "lyric of surmise," affected "by a *penseroso* element that sinks toward melancholy"; and analysis of Wordsworth's "reaction" to the singular reaper has justly been seen to embody an "archetypical situation for the self-conscious mind."[61] No better description of the freight and flow of the poem comes to mind. But the source of the poem's power, its basic energy remains obscure unless we identify the character and situation of the self whose consciousness is

the overt business of the poem, and unless we find the coherence point of the scattered "surmises" which overtly
establish its mode. To this end, it is crucial to penetrate to
the latent drama of the poem taking place between speaker
and subject, and reflexively between speaker and audience.
For the surmises in the poem run close to a Keatsian "wild
surmise," a giving of verbal expression to an abrupt and
amazed recognition. The speaker is not just sharing his reaction with an amorphous audience—the social dimension Hartman points out—he is enforcing a reaction upon an audience
whose susceptibility he himself determines. Though he is
himself involved in a present situation, and not with a remembered one,[62] he is an oblique Ancient Mariner, making
the audience insensibly play the part of the Wedding Guest.
His instrument will appear in the three imperatives, acts of
summoning, around which the poem pivots.

The initial summoning of the poem, "Behold," can be
called coercive, but it coerces attention or perception only,
and because sight is the one sense under our power to with-
hold or engage,[63] this coercion may not last. Practically
speaking, "Stop here, or gently pass" acknowledges the freedom to look or not to look. But this statement, the second
summoning of the poem, exerts its own coercion on the audience, and it is a deep coercion. Where "Behold" summons
attention more or less neutrally, "Stop . . . pass" summons
and commits the attitude or conception of the putative
passerby. The manner of passing, "gently," expresses however briefly the demand in the scene for attention and humility. No matter what the passerby does, he is obliged to
show reverence, to *be* reverent. Not observation, but an active
recognition and a taking part of the moment, must be understood as the core of the poem.

Its contemplative manner, the surmises and penseroso tinge,
constitute the manifest layer of the poem and in fact arise as
a tentative analysis of an indubitable condition of spirit. I
would propose that that condition is celebrative as much as
it is melancholy, wonderfully experiencing a consummate
moment of life, albeit life that includes death, as the *solitary*

reaper—reminder of death, embodiment of life—includes both. The force of the surmises, like the tumbling metaphors in the first stanza of Shelley's "Hymn to Intellectual Beauty," creates uncertainty as to knowledge, but certainty as to meaning. All the personal associations and cultural energy of the scattered surmises concentrate around the reaper and are included in her. All space—"Arabian sands" and "the farthest Hebrides"—and all time—"far-off things," "long ago," "matter of to-day," "may be again"—are present with her. Even if the "Vale profound" is the vale of tears, and even though her reaping song entails a memento mori, there is an idea of immortality in it—"as if her song could have no ending." The focus of the poem enlarges around, but never departs from, the reaper. Nor does it need to. She contains and causes the symbolic evidence of death and of an intense, even explosive life-consciousness to which Hartman calls our attention.[64] And there is an immediate access of energy from it, which the speaker transmits in the imperatives "behold," "stop," and "listen."

This final summoning, "listen," is as much an appeal as an imperative and appears to restore to the audience the freedom breached by "Stop . . . pass." But it is only the freedom to confirm the involuntary commitment with a practical choice; one listens on purpose to get the abundance of what one is hearing: "O listen! *for* the Vale profound/Is overflowing with the sound" (italics added).

So far it may be thought that the poem operates in terms of consciousness as regards the speaker and the reaper, in terms of will as regards the speaker and the audience. But there is no mistaking the fact that the speaker is passing on to the audience the possession of will he himself experiences. His authority over us, the audience, is more than a matter of rhetoric or of mechanical sympathy.[65] It develops as a form of communication, of discovering unity through language where the overt action gives evidence of separation. It embodies proof of the primary force and authority of a seemingly casual human situation. Considering the celebrative resonances of the poem, the question becomes, what is being celebrated?

Not death, though death may be very much in mind. At worst the poem could be taken as an elegy for a death that has no illustration, no substance; no one is dead, and the omnipresence of death leaves it thinner than the concentrated presence of life.

The subject of the celebration, then, would seem to be the unexpected, unmistakable presence of spiritual life transfiguring reaper and reaping for anyone who recognizes it. It is finally less important that the response is communal than that it is irresistible; the audience—the communal body—is called in as much to certify as to share its power. A basic clue to this power may be recognized in the way the speaker insists on the singer's separateness. A cluster of words—"single," "solitary," "by herself," and "alone"—suggests in the form of physical solitude (which the speaker seems careful not to disrupt) a character of independence and uniqueness that Frederick Garber has justly emphasized.[66] And yet the two things the Highland Lass does, reaping and singing, have distinctly social overtones in this context of solitude. What is the interaction between society and its antithesis, uniqueness and independence? What troubled forces congregate and are resolved around the solitary reaper?

The context of solitude may well be elaborated on first, as the conditioning environment for the specific action. It anticipates the idea of being stranded, bereft, homeless on the very edges of viable space, which appears in the "surmises" of the second stanza: "weary bands ... Among Arabian sands," and "the Cuckoo-bird,/Breaking the silence of the seas/Among the farthest Hebrides." To this extent, the surmises, as they are meant to do, expatiate on the cryptic data we have concerning the Highland Lass. The hushed reverence and exclamatory tone of the opening stanza recreate for us and communicate to us a vital shock of relief and joy at the human presence in an improbable and desolate setting. The scene is "charged with accumulations of long-gathering energy,"[67] existing at once as random and as symbolic encounter and therefore making present and known a basic susceptibility to and a basic need for the shock of a primary, radically human engagement. As far as possible from a paradisal garden or *locus amoenus* Wordsworth invokes a pristine relationship, suggesting what is deepest and truest in our being, and the shock of that deep truth.

The quality of this shock comes out strongly if we compare Wordsworth's invocation of our grievous mortality, of "time's consuming rage" against mere personal life, with that of Keats in the "Ode to a Nightingale." For the Keatsian version, though it involves long time and wide space and takes in "emperor and clown," is static rather than dramatic and one-directional rather than reciprocal: neither emperor nor clown nor Ruth's sad heart should be presumed to have waxed poetic and uttered an ode at the bird's song, for Keats is not proposing a perennial response to, but only the perennial existence of, that song. One acknowledges this existence, one can be overwhelmed by it, but one is not shaken into a cry of life and a substantive revelation of the human condition; rather one grows elegiac: "for many many a time/I have been half in love with easeful death. . . ."

A further expatiation, on the subject of the solitary reaper's singing, is contained in the third stanza of "The Solitary Reaper," but even while the details are melancholy with immemorial sorrows, the effect of relief and joy is not suspended; something "welcome" and "thrilling" is transferred from the second to the third stanza by the pivot line "Will no one tell me what she sings?" The details of mortal time are tempered by a perennial, and so immortal, human presence, just as the deficiencies of space are made up by a human presence. Only "reaping" has no overt expatiation (significantly it is left as an intransitive verb, unattended and unexplained), but it is not straining to see the melancholy of the song as an implicit expatiation of the symbolism of reaping.

Reaping and singing, in this light, are one. But if we take the fact of singing, and not the content of the song, a real disparity confronts us. Reaping is a mechanical or at best an agricultural function. But singing is a personal, perhaps even a spiritual, act. What does it mean that the poem insists on their presence together, inseparably, in the Highland Lass and stresses the singing, the act, as against the reaping, the function? Basically, I think the act of singing preserves and expresses the personal identity of the reaper while reaping, and beyond this, it affirms an invincible human capacity within the context of reaping, for all its overtones of relentless duty and alarming solitude and implicit death.[68] The singing conveys a triumph over the very melancholy it reminds us of; and it is not going too far to take it as a tacit activity of will and self, as what the Highland Lass makes of what befalls her. Thus it both facilitates and denies subjection to circumstances. The mortal implications of reaping are transformed by the spirit of the singer, even while they are also expressed in the tone of the song. In a sense the Highland Lass becomes a cryptoheroine in a tragic performance, insofar as she transcends loss on the level of phenomena, by virtue of the assertion of her spirit on the level of ontological will.

The true magnitude of her spirit, of her testimony to life, perhaps emerges best if we compare her situation with that of Vala in "Night the Ninth" of Blake's *Four Zoas*. Vala also seems to celebrate life, and more conspicuously than the Solitary Reaper. "Her garments," Blake tells us, "rejoice in the vocal wind and her hair glistens with dew" (page 126: line 35). Her celebration is far more self-conscious and articulate as well:

Rise up O Sun most glorious minister & light of day
Flow on ye gentle airs & bear the voice of my rejoicing
Wave freshly clear waters flowing around the tender grass
And thou sweet smelling ground put forth thy life in
    fruits and flowers
Follow me O my flocks & hear me sing my rapturous Song
I will cause my voice to be heard on the clouds that
    glitter in the sun
I will call & who shall answer me. . . .

[page 128:4–10]

It is clear that Vala is celebrating the presence and the phenomena of life; she does so, furthermore, under a guarantee of immortality: "Yon Sun shall wax old & decay but thou shalt ever flourish/The fruit shall ripen & fall down & the flowers consume away/But thou shalt still survive. . . ." The Solitary Reaper, inconspicuously and even inarticulately, does more. She manifests life, in an ambience of deprivation and death. Her song is not purposive, like Vala's: "I will cause my voice to be heard." She is practically oblivious not only of what lies abroad, but of the metaphysical values of her act. But this is what gives her such power, that her devotion to life is diffused through her being and act, expressing itself without effort and maintaining itself without support.

The expressive act of singing in "The Solitary Reaper" focuses three lines of will: the reaper's, the speaker's, and the audience's. It focuses also the situation of man in space and time, and is unusual in Wordsworth's poetry in two respects: in the excerpting of the moment in the reaper's life, which has no substance beyond the immediate scene; and in the generalized conception of time, which has no shape in individual life. In "Tintern Abbey" these two extremes are adjusted toward each other, and we are presented with a vision, more typical in Wordsworth's poetry, of an unfolding life and biographical time. There is a crucial point of contact between "Tintern Abbey" and "The Solitary Reaper," though, where the former, in the concluding verse paragraph, spins to *impart* the power of the speaker's experience of life and time, catching up the audience (here Dorothy) in an irresistible swell of personal feeling, philosophical conviction, and biographical prophecy. In all this, the will may be seen to have a significant part, not only where William as it were ordains Dorothy's existence and she tacitly consents to it, but also as each of them confronts the sort of life and time that might "prevail against" them and pervert their will.

The melancholy situation that must be overcome is clear enough:

evil tongues,
Rash judgments . . . the sneers of selfish men,

> . . . greetings where no kindness is . . . all
> The dreary intercourse of daily life. . . .

If anything, this intensifies the elegiac strain of "The Solitary
Reaper," and it must be acknowledged at once that the mode
of "Tintern Abbey" is more discursive and contemplative,
less dramatic and actualizing, than that of "The Solitary
Reaper"; little scope seems left for the will. But as soon as we
note the way Wordsworth talks to Dorothy, the way he *presents himself*, this difficulty disappears: his speech is the
equivalent of the reaper's singing, with surmise raised to certainty as affective sound gets articulated into effective vision.
There is a primary impact that Wordsworth wishes to have on
Dorothy and which differs little from the impact of the reaper
on him:

> oh! then,
> If solitude, or fear, or pain, or grief,
> Should be thy portion, with what healing thoughts
> Of tender joy wilt thou remember me,
> And these my exhortations!

The distinction between "me" and "my exhortations" deserves to be noticed; it warns us not to limit the power of his
argument to the power of the speaker's being. It is true that
he, by radical presence, becomes to her what the solitary
reaper is to him. But the very word "exhortations" pro-
claims the fact that the relation entails an engagement of
understanding and will; "me" refers to personality or ethos,
"exhortations" to principles or logic, and the basic situation
suggests an integration, a *chosen* integration of one with the
other.

   The introduction of Dorothy into the concluding verse paragraphs of "Tintern Abbey" goes along with a change in
Wordsworth's treatment of himself. Heretofore his responses,
no matter how far they have moved toward passion and even
ecstasy, have been predominantly factual or descriptive. Not
even the gradual increase of logical terms ("so," "for," "therefore") in the penultimate verse paragraph disturbs the factual

emphasis; to the contrary, as in the phrase "Therefore am I still a lover," the logic arises to account for the fact.

But at once there is a shift. "Nor perchance," Wordsworth writes in the final section,

> If I were not thus taught, *should* I the more
> *Suffer* my genial spirits to decay. . . .
> [italics added]

The comparable construction "If this be but a vain belief" has earlier led him into memory, into substantial fact: again and again he turned to the "sylvan Wye" for succor, and it always proved efficacious. Here, though, he is led into supposition concerning what is fitting ("should") and into the play of power and choice ("suffer"). There is an element of preference and an ignorant act of choice perhaps in the line "How often has my spirit turned to thee!" But Wordsworth is not aware of it as such. Here at the end of the poem, however, we must see that what happens to Wordsworth's "genial spirits" is in a measure at least what he allows (suffers) to happen. An expression of spirit and of will breaks in on and alters the value of the fact. The subjunctive and the invocation which quickly follow in the poem ("May I behold," "and this prayer I make") are very much in keeping with this factor of will. Not that Wordsworth controls the definition of events for himself, or of himself in relation to events. But he orients himself spiritually, establishing his position whatever comes.

This exercise of self-identification in the will is cardinal to the relation of Wordsworth to Dorothy. He sets himself to illustrate it for her, and to inculcate it in her. Thus it is that, as the subjunctive recurs in the middle of the verse paragraph ("let the moon/Shine on thee," "let the misty mountain-winds be free/To blow against thee"), Dorothy fulfills his dream by reenacting his will for herself. Thus also the future tense ("wilt") that chimes through the closing lines of the poem takes on such astonishing resonances, at once serene and minatory. It is a strong future, with overtones of the imperative mood,[69] as though the guarantee of Wordsworth's own history might be idle if Dorothy were not careful, did not choose to follow its pattern. Grammatical and ontological "will" merge into one another, as Wordsworth both forecasts Dorothy's future inevitably and obliges her to do nothing that would spoil his prophecy (there is a biblical precedent for this: "That it might be fulfilled what was foretold of Him"). The complete permeation of the scene with the will is apparent when we realize that Wordsworth is not only exercising his will so that Dorothy may know and will his life, his way, but is *consciously* willing it now for the first time explicitly himself, having only lived and described it before.

To bring out the work of the will in "Tintern Abbey" helps finally to shed light on the relation of man to nature in Wordsworth's poetry. For while Wordsworth himself turns to nature for solace and joy and urges Dorothy to do the same, the power of nature is only an available power, made efficacious by combination with the spontaneous power of the will; and by the same token, the will is but an implicit or unrealized power before nature engages or elicits it. In this case, though, nature means more than simply the "moon" and the "mountain-winds." There emerges in it, along with these, an abstract factor of time and change, involved equally in the separation from and the restoration to the scene above Tintern Abbey.

This is a factor of alienness or apparent discontinuity not only between Wordsworth and the outside scene but between Wordsworth and the given condition of his being ("Though changed, no doubt, from what I was"). In this respect the will engages with nature in three ways: by participation and perception and appreciation (first half of fourth verse paragraph), in memory and consolation (second half of the same), and in renewal and restoration (first and fifth verse paragraphs). It functions vitally at every stage of Wordsworth's development, is present alike in the "blood," in the "heart," and in the "purer mind." The perfection of the understanding, as already shown in the final scene of the poem, is (through the activity of remembered participation, consolation, and restoration) a mode and a furthering of the will.

The foregoing discussion of "Tintern Abbey," "The Solitary Reaper," "Prometheus," and *The Ancient Mariner*, as well as my introductory comments on the romantic ambience, should leave little doubt that the will qualifies as a prime *topos* in the emergence of romanticism. But of course it is not to be taken on merely because it is there. Its informing and amplifying effect on given poems, its implications as an organizing factor in other questions (e.g., the questions of imagination and of time), its influence on our conception of the place of man and the articulation of his world, its radiation into the meaning of art in romanticism[70] —these are some of the attractive principles of the will. Schopenhauer sets the basic position:

> Whoever is capable of somehow discerning the essential element, even when it is disguised under various modifications of degree and kind, will not hesitate to include among the manifestations of will also all desiring, striving, wishing, demanding, longing, hoping, loving, rejoicing, jubilation, and the like, no less than not willing or resisting, all abhorring, fleeing, fearing, being angry, hating, mourning, suffering pains—in short, all emotions and passions. For these emotions and passions are weaker or stronger, violent and stormy or else quiet impulses of one's will, which is either restrained or unleashed, satisfied or unsatisfied.[71]

This eloquently alerts us to the presence of the will and its moments without, however, recognizing the multiplicity of patterns in which it may occur or the multiplicity of visions to which it may be susceptible. In the long run, it is the relation of moment to context and the relation of context to context (one poem to another within a poet's *oeuvre*, one poet to another within the period) that must give the dimensions and force of the will. In combination with the historico-philosophical situation, a study of manifestations of the will in romantic literature bids fair to making a contribution to our view of romanticism itself.

2

THE EXTREMES OF SELF
AND SYSTEM

These, if ever, are the brave, free days of destroyed landmarks, while the ingenious minds are busy inventing the forms of the new beacons which, it is consoling to think, will be sent up presently in the old places.

Conrad

There is only one quarrel in this world: which is more important, the whole or the individual part.

Hölderlin

If the matrix of an artist's work is reality, to start with, and not feeling, and not imagination, and not the things he dreams . . . if that's the matrix of his work, it's absolutely inexhaustible.

Paul Strand

Every opportunity is a disguised form of risk, and the ultimate opportunity for man, namely, the world in which he finds himself,[1] gives also the unshakable evidence of his precariousness in being. The self that creates the world, according to an idea of duplication that we have seen in the primary imagination, is in the very pride of that creation obliged to recognize itself as a mere point of reference and even as a phenomenon in the world. Absorbing the individual into a comprehensive scheme in his instructional *Aids to Reflection,* Coleridge echoes the neoclassical Leibniz:[2]

Will any reflecting man admit, that his own Will is the only and sufficient determinant of all he *is,* and all he does? Is nothing to be attributed to the harmony of the system to which he belongs, and to the pre-established

Fitness of the Objects and Agents, known and unknown, that surround him, as acting *on* the will, though doubtless, *with* it likewise? . . .

Again: in the world we see every where evidences of a Unity, which the component parts are so far from explaining, that they necessarily pre-suppose it as the cause and condition of their existing *as* those parts. [Aphorism 6]

Other romantics were less complaisant about surrendering themselves to a presupposed harmony. A note of ambiguity and tension enters into much romantic reflection on the case. As Schopenhauer puts it:

This world is the succession of the representations of this [individual] consciousness, the form of its knowing, and apart from this loses all meaning, and is nothing at all. Thus we see . . . the existence of the whole world necessarily dependent on the first knowing being, however imperfect it be; on the other hand, [we also see] this first knowing animal just as necessarily wholly dependent on a long chain of causes and effects which has preceded it, and in which it itself appears as a small link.

The being's autonomy, qua self, conflicts with its dependency, qua element, and slender pride is supported by the corollary that the autonomy of the world, as *given* in the Kantian sense,[3] is neutralized or at least conditioned by the necessity of being *perceived*. The self and the world emerge in either case as confronted autonomies, at once necessary and antithetical to one another.

In relation to the self, this is a crucial confrontation for the will in romanticism, and it was vitally felt and vitally suffered. One feels that the resolutions offered in philosophy, by Fichte, say, or Schopenhauer, are less products of observation, analysis, intuitive experience, and practical conviction than of spiritual need; that is to say, it appears that an emotional temper, perhaps even a species of volition, helps to shape the conclusion reached about the relation of self and world, whether that conclusion is positive or negative as regards the self. As George Armstrong Kelly puts it:

> Kant attempted to show in his ethics the profound universality of the moral principles, unsullied by convenience, situation, or interest, and he called it the only valid *a priori* concept of reason—that is, unmediated by the forms and categories of the understanding. Fichte, however, *was not content* with this formulation of man's freedom in the world; he *insisted* that the moral self, acting by way of transcendental liberty, *must be shown* to create that world *in order to overcome it* through ethical will. [Hence arises] the *need* to eliminate all presumptive independent grounding of the reality of nature or the physical world.[4] [italics added]

This factor of primary *need*, and with it accordingly the presence of open possibilities in the relation of self to world, is precisely what makes for the innovative quality of the romantic situation. Frye is, I think, unduly positive when he declares that "in the romantic construct there is a center where inward and outward manifestations of a common motion and spirit are unified, where the ego is identified as itself because it is also identified with something which is not itself."[5] This Fichtean terminology ("Ich" and "nicht-Ich") deals with a *proposed* identification,[6] a perpetual and perpetually unfinished process or approach, à la Zeno, toward identification. Partly this results from the fact, to be developed presently, that it is impossible to do justice at once to the self and to the place where it finds itself—each emphasis is jealous of the other. But partly also the uncertainty arises from a desolidification of the meaning of self and not-self (and not-self may be equally nature, society, or a free mental construct). This desolidification, or placing in solution of self and system, is cardinal in our approach to the question of will in the romantic period; and while a comprehension of the poetry in light of this issue remains paramount, it seems very much in order, before taking up the self/world confrontation more fully in the poetry, to ask what it means to call it a matter of will in romanticism, rather than of the will in general, and to sketch in some of the literary-cultural factors that help to establish an answer.

If one were to raise the will as an issue in literature before romanticism, surely *Tamburlaine* would promptly come to mind, as would Satan in *Paradise Lost*, and Restoration heroic drama, most especially *The Conquest of Granada*. And we may recall Yeats's comment in his *Essays and Introductions* that the Elizabethan dramatists "celebrated [the soul's] heroical, passionate will going its own path to immortal and invisible things." But that dispensation has not survived intact. Using Satan as the pivotal figure, Peter L. Thorslev has argued that a new and refurbished "satanism" is a salient feature of the romantic sensibility. Thorslev calls attention to "the will to be God—the will to arrogate to the individual and finite mind those attributes traditionally reserved for God alone: self-sufficiency, creativity, and ultimate freedom . . ."; and he points out that the new "satanism" is exculpated of "pettiness" and sinfulness in the light of romantic theories of the sublime and romantic legitimizing of rebellion.[7] That is to say, ultimate loftiness belongs to man and ultimate authority belongs to the history of superstition.

But the very need for, or at any rate the fact of, a "metamorphosis of Satan" in the romantic order[8] suggests a discontinuity which is not explicitly taken up in the scope of Thorslev's penetrating and suggestive article. This discontinuity becomes clear in the different values accorded the terms "mind" and "place" in Renaissance and romantic contexts. We shall see that Satan, the exorbitant Renaissance hero, is trying to reconstitute the terms, but that the romantic tendency is to try to nullify one—place—so that a different order and kind of man result.

Though Satan identifies them, the terms "mind" and "place" clearly stand opposed, in a manner analogous to "self" and "world," personal autonomy and the ordained terms of existence. Satan, as Milton portrays him, runs up squarely against the impossibility of merging these two autonomies; the mind which is supposed to be free to make a Heaven of Hell finds itself obliged to confess, "which way I turn is Hell." Heaven is not in its power when it is not in Heaven. In effect, the "place" of the mind is not by itself viable. And we may note in passing that neither Tamburlaine nor Almanzor (in *The Conquest of Granada*) escapes from this limitation. Almanzor, for all his appearance of towering individual will, proves a quasi-adolescent sowing political wild oats, and emerges as a positive counterpart to Antony, giving up singularity and taking on culture and domesticity, and all for love. Tamburlaine, for his part, pursues a path of triumph that is inverted self-destruction; it is his own "shepherd" softness that he destroys as the relentless warrior, his own seed that he destroys in his sons. Each image of his mortality that he eliminates is but an image; his mortality lies in wait for him and proves at last the hopelessness of his quest. Whether we look at Satan, at Almanzor, or at Tamburlaine, we are forced to acknowledge the irreducible and inescapable substance of the world and the active power of its terms to check and chastise mere will. This is typical of the Renaissance, and is summarized in Shakespeare's *Troilus and Cressida* where Ulysses makes his classic speech on degree:

> . . . everything includes itself in power,
> Power into will, will into appetite,
> And appetite, an universal wolf.
> So doubly seconded with will and power
> Must make perforce an universal prey
> And last eat up himself. . . .

But the chastising presence of the world is not its only quality. It will be of advantage to show forth its positive relation to the self in the Renaissance and neoclassical regimen as an important and, at bottom, mutable alternative for the open romantic situation.

THE SYMBIOSIS OF SELF AND SYSTEM
IN THE NEOCLASSICAL REGIMEN

The project of a vast, if not total, dissemination of culture originates in neoclassicism, as we see in the positive attempt of Addison and Steele to educate the multiplying reading public to the highest values, and, negatively, in the satires of Pope and Swift with their efforts to excoriate folly and vice, to keep the culture homogeneous and clean. The two pairs of authors oppose as well as support each other, and in so doing imply an inherent weakness in the classical structure and economy—if the pairs, temperamentally and philosophically taken, are not kept in balance, then the system runs toward indulgent sentimentality (*The Conscious Lovers*) or toward fierce exclusivity (*Moral Essay* III or *The Dunciad*). It may be said of any "period"—but perhaps particularly of the Augustan age—that it contains its own centrifuge as well as its own equilibrium and undoes itself as much by unwieldy self-development as by falling prey to enemies. Sheer reaction plays no less a part than generous invention in literary history. In effect, then, my discussion of the Augustan period and of the problem of self and system will concern itself with the ways in which texts as various as *An Essay on Criticism* and *Polyeucte* hold their equilibrium and keep from flying off in desiccation or ecstasy.

The basic instrument of this equilibrium, whether we look at Addison and Steele or at Pope and Swift, proves to be the reader's self-interest. That is to say, formal efforts on behalf of the system can bear fruit only through the self. Thus Addison asks in *Spectator* No. 10, "Is it not much better to be let into the knowledge of one's self than to hear what passes in Muscovy or Poland?" Here we might ask, what self is he promoting? Clearly not the lurid *sub rosa* self of the Oedipus complex and the primitive lust for power, and not even that all-resisting self which is in the name of integrity suspicious of virtually everything except the private act of suspicion.

Though Addison commends self-knowledge, his may not seem a familiar self.

But it *is* one which Addison thinks universally possible and desirable. He defines it indirectly as he continues, posing the question whether it is not much better "to amuse our selves with such Writings as tend to the wearing out of Ignorance, Passion, and Prejudice, than such as naturally conduce to inflame Hatreds, and make Enmities irreconcileable?" The hoped-for extinction of hatreds and enmities implies the idea of community as a cardinal point in the definition of the self; the wearing out of ignorance, passion, and prejudice has as its corollary the establishment of knowledge, reason, and truth, which again, though to be possessed by single persons, would be possessed in common by all. In short, because neoclassicism is never merely scientifically descriptive, but always described with an ideal objective for the nation or for the individual, the realization of the self depends upon the possibilities of the system, that of the system on the endeavors of the self. No man is an island; and it is therefore necessary to look at the self in the light of the system (in the romantic period, I might interject, the self is seen rather in search of a system).

In a certain sense the more overtly modern philosophy of a Hobbes or a Mandeville, which we can well understand and perhaps sympathize with, depersonalizes us more than the typical philosophy of neoclassicism. Hobbes believed that man's egotism should be held in check for the welfare of the state, and Mandeville urged that that very egotism be given free rein for the welfare of the state. But both subscribe to a position of pragmatic naturalism which either manipulates or exploits man in society. Pope, with his neoclassical world view, does not look for society merely to work conveniently; he envisions its working right. The individual is part of a cosmic system and may with attainable knowledge, reason, and truth come to love himself as part of the whole of creation. The *Essay on Man* thus carefully constructs the ascent of self-love to social love to divine love, and ultimately offers itself as "*something* whose Truth convinced at sight we find,/ That gives us back the Image of our Mind."

Here, as in the phrase "What oft was thought, but ne'er so well expressed," resides a slippery point for our grasp of neoclassicism. Neoclassicism habitually assumes that the individual knows what it is taking great pains to teach him; that is why it abounds in satires which teach by chastisement the knowledge which everybody supposedly has, but which most people apparently forget, or neglect. Neoclassical psychology, though we see in it the beginnings of modern psychology, was not investigative but ultimately dogmatic. Pope recognizes, in the first *Moral Essay*, that "there's some Peculiar in each leaf and grain," but he is recognizing, not idealizing, peculiarity; he is quick to play down the question of human singularity by reference to "THE RULING PASSION," the universal "spring of action."

Even science in the late seventeenth and early eighteenth centuries was as much dogmatic as experimental. Newton expected his work in mathematics and astronomy to confirm religious orthodoxies and believed his biblical and theological studies would have more lasting importance than his investigations in physics. It has been claimed that Descartes's emphasis on reason "fostered intellectualistic views" and "increased man's sense of his own dignity and importance," but we must remember that one person's "inner light" of conviction was, to the neoclassical world, a slug of irrational enthusiasm if it did not ring true on the counter of common sense and reason. We can see by the possibility of error in irrational enthusiasm that the harmonizing of the self and the system is not simple or automatic. The relation of self and system becomes vital instead of mechanical, for the fore-ordained harmony of Leibniz requires achievement in the neoclassical way, being at once its datum and its desideratum, its foundation and the end of its aspiration.

It is not hard to see how the terms of the neoclassical system are designed for the self. Such requirements as clarity, symmetry, propriety, unity of design, simplicity, restraint, order, reason, truth, and truth to nature are overtly geared for literary improvement, implicitly geared for moral improvement, and essentially geared to reflect, on the personal and social planes, the beauty, force, and light of the universal order. But how do we fulfill those requirements when restraint means restraint of impulses that are always with us, indestructible; as Pope suggests in the *Essay on Man*, man cannot destroy "what composes man." How do we live up to an order that is at once perceptible, and inscrutable? Donne, in *The Second Anniversary*, seems far less certain of the powers of reason and learning than does his contemporary, Bacon, in *The Advancement of Learning*. It is nearly inevitable that neoclassicism poses itself the twofold task of proving the veracity of order as its datum and the necessity of order as its desideratum, for neoclassicism is not only traditionalist but teleological.

The way in which particular texts approach this primary task should afford us some understanding of the possibilities of the self in the neoclassical system. Within a generally unified framework definite discriminations will have to be made, according to the temperament and nationality of the writer and, perhaps more basically, according to the genre in which he is working. The self gets a more generous presentation in drama than in analytical or didactic poetry or in an expository dialogue such as Dryden's *Essay of Dramatic Poesy*; and it appears to get a little more latitude in narrative poetry and in comic drama than in tragedy. For our purposes a good cross-section of neoclassical writing is provided by two tragedies, Corneille's *Polyeucte* (1643) and Addison's *Cato* (1713), two comic works, Molière's *Tartuffe* (1664) and Pope's *Rape of the Lock* (1714), and two analytical and didactic poems, Boileau's *L'Art Poétique* (1674) and Pope's *Essay on Criticism* (1711).

The Exaltation of Self in "Polyeucte"

Polyeucte may at first seem somewhat anomalous, with a classical form encasing a statement of extraordinary energy and will. It reminds us that the eminently correct Boileau as an old man found fault with Corneille for seeking to excite admiration instead of purging the emotions of pity and terror in his tragedies. In a way, Corneille secures a response of admiration by failing to provide the degree of knowledge and sympathetic engagement which would be indispensable to the evocation of pity and terror. *Polyeucte* does not elaborate the Christian system as fully as it might, even within the form of classical drama. Greek tragedy, for example, by a sense of community partly derived from the Chorus, and by its careful building up of historical background, does much better in this regard. The fate of Oedipus is sudden in one way, terrifyingly slow and inevitable in another. The fate of Polyeucte seems by comparison intrinsically sudden, even if it is protracted; his choice is not only unexpected but unpremeditated, and we find the entire universe of the play continually shaken by random developments. It becomes a universe of contingency. And the question of how or where to discover a relaible *point d'appui* in this eruptive scheme of things takes on central importance. Our final estimate of Polyeucte's indomitability of will must, I think, take full account of this situation.

Three different responses to life's turbulence appear, and indeed compete, within the framework of the play. The answer of Felix is inveterate cunning and manipulation, the answer of a man who lives in ill-disguised terror of circumstances or "fortune," to use Corneille's own term; the answer of Pauline, the woman of "blind and quick obedience," complements that of Felix as daughter complements father—though she fails to be impeccably stoical, she can be recognized as one who lives in harmony with fortune; and, finally, Polyeucte's answer is the clean, decisive, active integrity of the man who can live in defiance of fortune, in that he lives for what fortune cannot confer or change. (Perhaps Sévère could be included in this schematization, as one who reflects on the merits of these answers and explains the ultimate value of fortune. He is in certain respects a Horatio to Polyeucte's Hamlet.)

Unlike the general run of Armenian Christians,[9] including Nearque, Polyeucte cannot be simply done away with and forgotten. By disregarding the logic of fortune, he converts himself from a potential subject of fortune into a critical element of fortune in the lives of Felix, Pauline, and Sévère. If we observe that there is no true force of evil in the play, it seems plausible to take it less as an individual tragedy, centering on Polyeucte, than as a collective tragedy precipitated by him. The equivalent of the tragic flaw might be seen in the deviousness, energy, and presumption with which other characters hold out against, not the good, but the highest good.

For the greater part of the play Pauline, Felix, and Sévère (and momentarily even Nearque) look on Polyeucte as some sort of self-seeking eccentric, as a singularly wilful man. But this reveals their characters more than his. Through conversion Polyeucte achieves enlargement and transcendence from which the Roman Sévère is, as his name perhaps implies, cut off. In this regard, something may be made of the hero's being Armenian, and presumably receptive to realities beyond the rationalism and efficiency of Rome. Christianity for Polyeucte proves upon baptism the "something whose Truth convinced at sight we find," truth which the other characters manage to see only with difficulty, and only as reflected in him. The faith that seems novel and alien to Sévère is new and eternal to Polyeucte. Is it not appropriate, then, to see his intensity and inflexibility as proof of the absoluteness of his self-surrender, rather than of his self-will?

Polyeucte fits neither of the two accepted categories for the Cornelian hero, being something other than a superrationalist or a reckless seeker of glory (in fact, it seems to be Sévère who on different occasions embodies these personalities). Far from having to reason, Polyeucte *knows*. For him *gloire* means not supreme honor but heaven, as though he brought to life a Miltonic shift from military to spiritual heroism. He shows that combination of orthodoxy and ecstasy which is peculiar to the deepest faith. Thus his heroism resides in his obedience to his faith and in his becoming the instrument of faith in others. That even Felix is admitted to the fold speaks well for the tolerant attitude of classicism as well as of Christianity; opportunism makes a better man of him after all. Polyeucte's obedience, his will to accept the infinite and eternal, breaks the hold of contingency over him and all the rest. The turbulence of fortune is controlled and transcended. Though Corneille claimed only a formal tidying-up at the conclusion of the play, this resolution strikes one as logically and dramatically fitting. As the tragic problem in the play has been collective, so the point of tragic composure and reaffirmation is collective. The idea of a system is upheld, but we must remember that the system in question, Christianity, works as a living system which both supersedes another and gains its prestige from its intrinsic value to individuals. While it is upheld, they are uplifted.

The Pathos of Self in "Cato"

A far more austere and passionless Augustanism offers itself in Addison's *Cato*, where the state, and not heaven, is at stake, and where the poetry, perhaps reflecting that fact, is more earthly than divine. As Dr. Johnson bluntly remarks, "Addison never deviates from his track to snatch a grace." The powerful impact of *Cato* upon audiences in England from 1713 and in America after 1760 was probably owing to extraliterary factors. Yet there is much to be learnt from a comparison between *Polyeucte* and *Cato*. On one level Polyeucte and Sévère have their counterparts in Addison's play in Caesar and Cato, though the sympathies of the English play are exactly reversed: Caesar, the figure of energy and will, is the secondary character and is in the main disesteemed as an assuming dictator, while Cato, the stoical protagonist, represents the unhappy end of a given order. The death of Cato conveys a sense of irreparable loss, rather than of incomprehensible prospect. Cato's body is but a barrier between his adherents and Caesar's wrath. Caesar sways the world, and Cato has not even died in a state of transcendent conviction. He dies in plangent doubt: "If I have done amiss,

impute it not!—/The best may err . . ." (act 5). Yet the principle of his approach to death suggests a perspective from
which Cato is able to enliven the appeal of classicism.

At a time when "pandaemonium" and "chaos" were still
truly evocative myths, and not synomyms for incidental disarray, the structures of classicism provided a stay against disaster. Wild Belinda's rage was not unknown to Pope, only
Pope's mastery over rage was unknown to Belinda. Cato's
coldness, in other words, is intense, inverted heat, his courage
a conquest over abiding fear. His life, and not just his death,
has been a response to a "secret dread, and inward horror,/Of
falling into nought. . . . Why shrinks the soul/Back on herself,
and startles at destruction?" (act 5). In short, while seeming a
positive, and perhaps clinical, display of neoclassical values,
Cato makes its deepest appeal on behalf of these values *from
negation*. It is true that in act 3, speaking as a generous counsellor, Cato champions a deliberate, stoical piety:

> Remember, O my friends, the laws, the rights,
> The *gen'rous* plan of power delivered down,
> From age to age, by your *renowned* forefathers. . . .
> O let it never perish in your hands!
> But piously transmit it to your children.
>
>   [italics added]

But in a situation of personal crisis, even an intimation of immortality, as opposed to dread of annihilation, gives Cato
pause: "The wide, th' unbounded prospect, lies before
me;/But shadows, clouds, and darkness rest upon it" (act
5). Beyond the chartered world, annihilation and immortality somehow image each other; and so the champion of
classicism makes his ideal of the possible, indeed of the
likely, then seeks to win for it all the devotion that spontaneous individuality might be capable of.

In their particular ways *Polyeucte* and *Cato* may be taken
as realizations of a neoclassical point of view, as dramatiza-
tions (the endowing with human life and motion) of neoclassical precepts. It is noticeable, though, that even as

Englishmen with their constitutional monarchy rejoice that they were not "born to serve" under an absolute ruler like Louis XIV, the English play is more chillingly performed to prescription than the French. It seems odd on the English side that *Cato* managed to serve the prejudices of Whig and Tory alike—was the Duke of Marlborough limned in Cato or in Caesar? And it seems equally odd, on the French side, that Boileau should have had reservations about Corneille. Perhaps these are the problems of classicism at work, the problems of imitative classicism which must have helped to call forth the machinery of analysis and criticism to channel more surely its own fluctuations. The critical writing of men like Boileau, Rapin, Le Bossu, Dryden, and Pope offers itself as both the image and the foundation of true neoclassicism.

Designing Selves in Augustan Criticism: Boileau and Pope

But even analytical neoclassicism has its designs for, or on, the self. As we can discover from Boileau's *L'Art Poétique* and Pope's *Essay on Criticism*, it purveys not only a conceptual model for the better self but also, in the figure of the poet-speaker, an actual model thereof. Our own resistance today to prescriptive and compartmentalizing criticism such as *L'Art Poétique* springs up so promptly that we may think it natural, when it is only fashionable. We look for imaginative interpretation and understanding, and, finding Boileau busy with the naming of parts, we feel with the romantic poet that he is murdering to dissect. Yet to Dryden, in "A Discourse Concerning the Original and Progress of Satire," Boileau was "the admirable Boileau, whose numbers are excellent, whose expressions are noble, whose thoughts are just, whose language is pure, whose satire is pointed, and whose sense is close." The difference between these two viewpoints is not fully accounted for if one says that we have lost the ability to see convention as inspiration, and order as emancipation. Our problem seems to lie in the fact that we see Boileau breaking down a work of art, or breaking it up, pretending that "inexplicable miracles" are just "ingenious mechanisms" which

any self-respecting Japanese schoolboy might study and reproduce. But isn't Boileau working the other way, building
up the work of art? He certainly knows that the whole is
greater than the sum of the parts and knows the difference
between the formal and the spiritual genesis of a poem. He
holds up the rules not as any open sesame but as the likeliest
passage into greatness. He may, like Aristotle before him,
avoid pronouncements on the merits of a single work, but he
has much to say of its purpose. He is silent about the Muse,
but much concerned with the poet's moral state. And, pedan-
tic as the whole performance may seem, he seeds *L'Art
Poétique* with suggestions of a character whose heart, like the
romantic Wordsworth's, "was social."

The opening couplet of the poem suggests that Boileau is
talking of more than poetry: "C'est en vain qu'au Parnasse
un téméraire auteur/Pense de l'art des vers atteindre la
hauteur." Soames, putting these lines into English, tells the
unqualified writer it is a "vain presumptuous crime/To under-
take the sacred art of rime." In words like *presumptuous* and
sacred he brings out, albeit in a heightened way, Boileau's
sense that the poet acts, even as poet, in a moral universe. It
is not by chance that Boileau's summing up of a poem reflects a definition of the cosmic harmony:

> Each object must be fixed in a due place,
> And differing parts have corresponding grace;
> Till by a curious art disposed, we find
> One perfect whole of all the pieces joined

The poet as maker has his patent from on high, and so the
first poetry was simultaneous with the beginning of civilization and virtue, with the sloughing off of "la grossiere nature."
As it did then, so now poetry may usher in "une gloire
nouvelle," provided reason, sense, and nature are honored.
The poet, working according to a past excellence, works
toward a new glory, and becomes one of its shining points:

> Que votre âme et vos moeurs, peintes dans vos ouvrages
> N'offrent jamais de vous que de nobles images.

Here it turns out that the poem written to prescription contains the poet and is written about him. The self is always there; the poet must only make sure he realizes its nobler possibilities.

Inevitably, in *L'Art Poétique*, Boileau has both shown and taken the path to excellence. His piety toward the values of the past and concern for a greater and better future, his awareness of the spiritual whole of the cosmos and his desire for order and harmony among the parts, his conviction that to be good as a poet demands potential goodness as a man, all bespeak the ideal he is describing. At the end of the poem he is within his rights in taking the personal stance of the friend; his rationalistic habit of analysis is meant to make known his felt commitment to a higher, rather than a grosser, nature and stands as a model of the commitment he asks the practicing poet to make.

If *L'Art Poétique* is a kind of handbook for poets, Pope's *Essay on Criticism* must resemble a handbook for critics, dealing less with works of art than with people who deal with works of art. Actully the two, poet and critic, belong together for classicism more intimately than later times have acknowledged. It is no accident that Dryden, Pope, Swift, and Johnson are at the forefront of analytical as well as creative literary activity in their period. Poets and critics emerge as sharers in a synergistic task of codifying and vivifying (the Horatian *Prodesse et delectare*) the relation that must obtain between creative freedom and moral obligation. The poet speaks to, and for, the man, and thus has a claim on the critic. Pope is unmistakably using Nature in what John Dennis called "a larger signification," as a cosmos reflecting the order and harmony of the Divine Mind. The *Essay on Criticism*, with its well-documented pattern of pristine excellence (part 1), contemporary degeneration (part 2) and envisioned recovery of excellence (part 3) is a treatise on criticism, in verse, but it is also tacitly a moral treatise, imaging in criticism the prototypal pattern of creation, sin, and restoration or redemption. Thus it is that pride (the cardinal sin) gets continually asso-

ciated with bad criticism. Pope contends that the critic "ought
to show" Morals, and lists as necessities for the critic attributes which are both intellectual and moral: candor, modesty,
sincerity, freedom.

So unquestionable is this moral/social force—the tribute the
individual owes to categories and types—to the working of
classicism that it served inadvertently to undermine the classical scheme. Wit, once an instrument of classicism, began to
seem a self-aggrandizing attribute, and so rapidly lost ground
to humor, which appeared more modest and humane.[10] Classical catholicity thus was put at odds with classical severity of
standards,[11] and despite the magnificent holding action of
Pope and Johnson, a hospitable catholicity was to prevail and
high classicism decline. This by the way. For present purposes
it is enough to observe the interpenetration of self and system in creative and critical works of the period. The neoclassical dramas, *Polyeucte* and *Cato*, embody the order of a
universe in the lives of their protagonists. The neoclassical
treatises, *L'Art Poétique* and the *Essay on Criticism*, inculcate
in ostensibly literary terms the order of a universe and inconspicuously illustrate it in the character of the poet-critics,
who are representative, not singular, who stand for a class,
not a personality. In these works the reality of the self is inseparable from the validity of the given. In the two pieces
now to be considered, *Tartuffe* and *The Rape of the Lock*,
the question of the self in the neoclassical system takes on
peculiar piquancy. The chief figure in each work is very much
a creature of the present—vain, opportunistic, and expert at
manipulating for personal advantage whatever system passes
current. In short, the question here is not how well the neoclassical view can hold up in the world of affairs, nor how attractive and necessary it can be made to seem by a process of
analysis. The question is simpler and more basic than that:
can it cope with the actualities of a distracted and perhaps in-
hospitable world, with no one to live its meaning, and no one
to expound it?

The Comedy of Self and Neoclassical System: Molière and Pope

The comic disposition of *Tartuffe* and *The Rape of the Lock* makes for portrayal of the world as it is, relatively unvarnished by art, relatively unalloyed by preconceptions. Egotism and pride get ampler play here, as the initial order of value suggests nothing so much as naturalism. Molière, of course, took as his motto the phrase "Follow Nature," and it is clear that nature did not include for him any just standard, divinely bright, or even Erasmus's instinct to excellence. The two persons with real power in *Tartuffe*, before the King steps in, reveal an eccentric, a problematical stripe. Tartuffe is an accomplished hypocrite, and it offers small consolation to think of hypocrisy as the tribute which vice pays to virtue. There is no clear standard of virtue to receive such tribute in the play. Orgon has his measure of virtue, but his is that curiously intense piety which reaches neither mysticism nor serenity. Quite apart from our knowledge of Tartuffe's duplicity, we may wonder whether Orgon is acting within reason, or with responsibility when he makes his *directeur de conscience* the director of his household and property; surely competence in one function is far from conferring competence in the other. We may wonder, too, whether his foisting of Tartuffe on his family reflects the intensity or the intolerance of his devotion. Dorine's presentation of the state of affairs at the outset of the drama invites us to suspect that something is amiss with Orgon as well as Tartuffe. Beneath Orgon's sincerity and Tartuffe's hypocrisy, a rigid concern with outward forms unites them; they complement and are necessary to each other. It is striking that Tartuffe is often effectively present on the stage not in himself, but through Orgon. Thus Orgon's sanctimonious formality would appear as an instrument of Tartuffe's hypocrisy, and as no less reprehensible. Though Molière himself was excommunicated from the Church and the intercession of Louis XIV was required to get him burial in consecrated ground, this play at any rate seems to fall within the realm of orthodoxy; it never approaches the piety of *Polyeucte*, but it is creditable that *Tartuffe* contains a tacit rejection of fake devotion and of the presumptions that unbalance true devotion, showing their frightening possibilities for the individual, the family, and the state. The King, in tidying up affairs at the end, acts as something truer than a deus et machina; he is but an agent under God, to whom a purer devotion has been due, and in whom resides the origin and end and correction of any human authority. Even so, the bias of the play remains negative; we get a troubling picture of what happens when the complex, divine order of the universe is perverted, but we find no intimation of a way to a better orientation.

With the latitude of the narrative form, Pope in *The Rape of the Lock* presents a more intricately detailed and more satisfactorily resolved picture of the clash between neoclassical absolutes and headlong actuality. The genius of the poem is to acknowledge and even to indulge Belinda's vanity, her social and aesthetic merits, and yet not compromise its own fundamental moral position. In a sense *The Rape of the Lock* brings the poised mind and spirit of the *Essay on Criticism* to bear on the context of society.

As a mock-heroic poem it binds together the world of social phenomena and that of philosophy, the world of everyday and that of epic, making the tension between them a primary source of evaluation. According to the nature of the mock-heroic (which is anything but *anti*-epic), the inflated pettiness of the everyday order stands out glaringly beside the true magnitude of the epic order. A subtler effect may also be recognized; the comparative terms of the poem imply that the everyday is a poor and confused copy of the epic, and lead us to imagine the everyday order as weakly, perhaps unwittingly, striving toward the condition of the epic order. Clarissa's catty speech at the beginning of canto 5 contains sound sense and morality which, to their detriment, neither she nor her audience adequately sees. She is right, but can get

little credit, being so purblindly at best. She is among the
first to grapple with her man in the free-for-all, and some
may think she is well matched with the fatuous, monosyllabic
Sir Plume. Again, Ariel is right in warning Belinda of the
Baron, who with his readiness to work by "force or sleight"
could remind us of Satan's recourse to "force or guile" in
Paradise Lost; Ariel bears comparison with Raphael in this
regard. But this also is accidental and ignorant worthiness.
Unlike Raphael, Ariel does not warn Belinda of herself;
rather he seems like Satan as he tempts Belinda with the
words, "Thine own importance know."

The simple fact is that Belinda can be like Eve, but like Eve
cannot be like God. She has her fiat—"Let Spades be trumps!
she said, and trumps they were"—but it is a far cry from *Let
there be light*; her cosmetic powers may suggest God's cosmic
powers (the two words have the same root), but we know,
though Belinda is enchanting, that God makes the universe
and Belinda makes up her face. It is possible to be half in love
with her achievement of beauty (perhaps she is not putting
on a face, but bringing out a sort of Platonic idea on her
face); still her neglect of the idea of her soul should preclude
our loving her wholly, in much the same way as we resist the
seductive surface, of beauty or sorrow, with which Moll
Flanders confronts us. The inherent difficulties of Belinda's
situation are graphically brought out in her "rites of Pride."
She is in her way a creatrix, and a certain worship might seem
due. But it can only come through the mirror, where suddenly
the creatrix has become the devotee, and the created thing
the object of worship. Reality anomalously worships an
image. The face Belinda prepares to meet the faces that she
meets ultimately provides a very uncertain shield against the
world, and an equally uncertain seal for a Cave of Spleen. It
is tempting to think of her face as artificial (the poem makes
it an opponent of nature), and to see as natural the Belinda
Umbriel sees, with "her eyes dejected [not rivalling the sun],
and her hair unbound [not binding men]." This natural moment is terrible for her, with chagrin, a sense of dishonor,

frustration, and rage building up to a confession less of secret sexuality than of wild passion and confusion: "Oh hadst thou, cruel! been content to seize / Hairs less in sight, or any hairs but these!" Albeit compassionately, *The Rape of the Lock* exposes the radical fault in the aesthetic bias, that under the guise of self-expression it glosses over and suppresses the undisciplined nature; and time holds in store both the loss of beauty and eruptions from the Cave of Spleen, which represent the inner tortures of the unregenerate self.

Yet, since Pope is far from being puritanically wary of beauty, it is well to observe that Belinda's comeuppance involves a principle more fundamental than that fleshly beauty is vulnerable and mortal. The first four cantos of *The Rape of the Lock* can be read in terms of a temptation and a fall. Only this will account for the delicious suggestion in the poem that the guardian sprites, though they seem so subject to scissors, might have withstood the Baron had Belinda kept her thought pure:

> Swift to the Lock a thousand Sprights repair,
> A thousand Wings, by turns, blow back the Hair;
> And thrice they twitch'd the Diamond in her Ear;
> Thrice she look'd back, and thrice the Foe drew near.
> Just in that moment, anxious *Ariel* sought
> The close Recesses of the Virgin's Thought;
> . . . .
> Sudden he view'd, in spite of all her Art,
> An Earthly Lover lurking at her Heart.
> Amaz'd, confus'd, he found his Pow'r expir'd,
> Resign'd to Fate, and with a Sigh retir'd.
>
> [Canto 3, 135-46]

The fate of which the poem continually speaks is not to be equated with a system of inexorable occurrence. It involves something like the Greek *Ate*, and is a factor of one's consenting in and implicitly willing a particular situation, and hence inevitably all its consequences. Belinda is beautiful, but also proud; she operates in a context which, ostensibly aesthetic and social, is basically moral. Not only does she play with fire, but she covertly consents to be burned. The poem furnishes exquisite hints that she has actually set her cap for the Baron, though she makes him too unsure of her, and of himself, to hope to damage more than the outskirts of the fortress, the hair instead of the heart. Indications of danger alternate with moods of self-indulgence and gaiety in the poem, and reveal Belinda as reckless, self-infatuated, and ripe to be victimized by Clarissa and the Baron.

The question is whether, after Belinda's temptation and fall, a redemption can take place. Does the poem complete its moral pattern, or to put it another way, can neoclassicism, besides predicting temptation and fall, produce a redemption? It seems to me that canto 5, like part 3 of the *Essay on Criticism*, at least offers the means to redemption. Belinda's fall, the personal ruin, has typically led to general chaos (the battle royal of the sexes); this is the unavoidable domino-effect of living in society. And the means to redemption, though specifically aimed at Belinda, will apply to society at large. Clarissa's address to Belinda, irrespective of Clarissa's dubious character, implies a better world, and the narrator, in his interested but uninvolved way, offers as present consolation a view of a cosmic light for Belinda instead of her cosmetic gloss. It is altogether like him to consider at once her unlearned state and an absolute truth, as he first appeals to her vanity ("Not all the tresses that fair head can boast,/Shall draw such envy as the Lock you lost"); and then, having doubtless won her ear, he moves her mind and soul, not cleansing them of vanity but raising their vanity to higher and eternal values, toward the eternal world: "This Lock, the Muse shall consecrate to fame,/And midst the stars inscribe Belinda's name." Sensuous and flighty Belinda becomes ascetical, if we accept the definition of asceticism as the choice of a greater over a lesser good. Accordingly, though we do not see Belinda, let alone Clarissa or Thalestris, actually giving up egotism for neoclassicism, we may say that the viability of the neoclassical way in their world is proven in the character and personality of the narrator.

It is easy to take the narrator of *The Rape of the Lock* for granted. The semidramatic character of the story and the sensuous vividness of its incidents certainly preoccupy our attention. But the narrator must be acknowledged at the end of the poem, where his position seems crucial enough—he sets the tone of the ending, governs the feeling with which we come out of the poem. Since his presence here causes no sense of abruptness or intrusion, we might well wonder whether he has not impressed himself upon us before and what his impact might be in the poem as a whole.

We can recognize his individual impress in the structure of the poem. Clarissa's fine moral chiding of Belinda is undercut by her own eager and sensual entrance into the fray; but the morality her speech expresses is not undercut. This distinction results from the narrator's ability to let even the hypocritical Clarissa enunciate legitimate and necessary values, knowing that they are secure even if she is confused. In effect, it is not enough to be a spokesman, one must be an exemplar of moral and humanistic values. In showing this about Clarissa, the narrator furnishes an important clue for our perception of his role. He is the exemplar of classical values, giving personality to their abstraction, as a man of knowledge and insight and understanding, devoted to order but aware of the possibility (and the possibilities) of passion, as a man of wicked wit and forgiving grace, as a man troubled but also moved by the problems of turbulent time, and eager, without truculence or intolerance, for the order of eternity. Whether we look, then, at Polyeucte or Cato, at Boileau or at Pope, the neoclassical position is that the self is best in the system, the system is best for the self. The self here designated must, however, be understood in Leibnizian terms as naturally rational, the system as essentially divine. On this basis Boileau can contend that reason's yoke, far from hurting, makes the mind divine; for reason, on the human plane, corresponds to the intuition of the angelic order, and to the omniscience of God. And yet we can hardly fail to see that this rationally regulated self, while it stands as the most conspicuous term of the Augustan equation, is partially offset by another sort of indebtedness to Greece and Rome, in the concepts of the sublime and the epic. In the epic, Dryden says, the poet "may let himself loose to visionary objects, and to the representation of such things as depending not on sense, and therefore not to be comprehended by knowledge, may give him a freer scope for imagination." In the same vein Boileau approves of the fact that "pour nous enchanter tout est mis en usage." Enchantment, captivation, and ecstasy seem proper to the epic. The terms proper to the sublime are congruous with these: elevating, transporting. But the prospect of an engaging new world of self-intoxication to counterbalance the world of self-discipline turns out to be deceptive, as the neoclassical mind proved more adept at analyzing than at generating the epic or the sublime. Oddly, though, what the spirit of communal achievement failed to do, the sense of danger did: in neoclassical satire, in Dryden's *Absalom and Achitophel* and Pope's *Dunciad*, for example, a conception of disorder and threatening dissolution produces something like a negative version of epic and the sublime. The concluding lines of *The Dunciad* make this quite clear:

> In vain, in vain,—the all-composing Hour
> Resistless falls: The Muse obeys the Pow'r.
> She comes! she comes! the sable Throne behold
> Of *Night* Primeval, and of *Chaos* old!
> Before her, *Fancy's* gilded clouds decay,
> And all its varying Rain-bows die away.
>
> [Book 4, 627–32]

After Fancy, let us recall, Wit expires, then Art after Art, Truth, Philosophy, Religion, Morality, Man, and for man the awareness of God, in the tremendous inclusivity of annihilation. It is the epic and the sublime of the antiworld:

> Lo! thy dread Empire, Chaos! is restored;
> Light dies before thy uncreating word;
> Thy hand, great Anarch! lets the curtain fall;
> And universal Darkness buries all.

It is significant that this apocalypse of a shattered state spreads from the smallest unit, the individual mind with its faculties of fancy and wit, outward to embrace the total complex, the universe. Hence two inferences can be drawn concerning neoclassicism and the self. The first is that neoclassicism is hardly a chartered, protected system autocratically bent on enlarging itself; rather it resembles an attempt to fend off chaos and pandemonium in a time when it was more than a slang metaphor to think of all hell breaking loose. The second is that, far from undervaluing the individual, it was intensely occupied with him as the one in whom the power of grace found realization (think of Polyeucte), or in whom the possibility of disorder and evil had its inception. This latter is presented as a frightening possibility for the self and for the system. The idea of the banality of evil belongs to the modern mind, whose peculiarity it is to be interested in more things for their own sakes than neoclassicism may have been interested in, but to be truly affected by fewer.

VOLATILE SELF AND SYSTEM IN
THE ROMANTIC COMPLEX

One may look upon the neoclassical regimen, whether we imagine it in terms of a Great Chain of Being or of Leibniz's foreordained harmony (the *Monadology*, 1714, falls in the thick of the neoclassical period) as what gives skill and aim to the raw force of a Polyeucte, as what gives meaning to the activity of individual will. It is otherwise in romanticism. If we recall the terms "mind" and "place" and Satan's confusion of them, we see at once that the problem for romanticism was to unperplex them, and that the relation of mind and place, as frequent and various as it is, functions according to an orthodoxy which is not known, or at least not foreknown; no rules are broken, no order violated, in that none exist but what are found by the way. There is particular latitude, then, as never before, for the mind to make its own place, if not to be it. The final stanza of Keats's "Ode to Psyche" enthusiastically depicts the fruits of this latitude. But the mode of the poem, which is marked by a fanciful and not un–self-sceptical nostalgia (aching for home, for place) forbids us to treat it as more than a moment in Keats's career, let alone in the romantic way. Blake brings us closer to the problems of the case as he limns the enormous and agonizing work of making a place intrinsically for and through the mind, with Golgonooza in *Jerusalem*. But it is more than a matter of hardship, after all. *Sleep and Poetry*, clearly bent on creating and celebrating the mind's peculiar place, nevertheless shows the insecurities and uncertainties of place, *and hence of mind*, in Keats and as well in romanticism. The amniotic illusion that the self is all that exists for sure encourages the invention of the romantic bower, but the bower is ineluctably borne, as in Coleridge's "This Lime-Tree Bower My Prison" or "Reflections on Having Left a Place of Retirement," into the world whose elements it would abstract for itself.[12]

Perhaps "Kubla Khan" provides the most articulate picture of the mind/place problem that we can find in a brief compass. Whether Kubla Khan is regarded as a political figure or as a creative God-surrogate or as God himself,[13] it is clear that he is making a place to suit himself *outside of himself*. The mind as it were challenges the intransigence of place in itself, and gets the better of it. But it is a circumscribed achievement. The deep romantic chasm not only represents place as beyond the imposing power of the mind, it represents a self-active place which sublimely carries the mind beyond itself and which, subliminally, addresses itself to the mind's arena, imposing on the mind: "And 'mid this tumult Kubla heard from far,/Ancestral voices prophesying war!" The meaning of the circle Kubla has drawn is itself ambiguous. It declares his power, within limits, and even so it is a power over space rather than place. At the same time it sets off the power of nature, intensifying, if it does not bring on, the eruption of nature (as though there were being administered an indirect cuffing and correction). Thus it comes to seem a check on his fiat, as the triple circles serve to check the power of the poet in the concluding section of the poem.

It is for the poet, of course, as the ground of meeting of

aimless, if overwhelming, natural power and purposive but narrow human power, to resolve the poem's position on mind and place. And he is irresolute, unrealized. What he has a mind to, what is in his mind, is precisely an absolute place of his own devising, which would recall and yet transcend Kubla Khan's specific place, as invention transcends the issuing of a decree. But his absolute proves to be hemmed in with contingency; it cannot create but only represent, and that uncertainly. It cannot begin apart from the damsel with a dulcimer, insofar as she and her song stimulate and enable his will; it cannot occur without an access of power in him and this is not forthcoming; and it cannot work, all else taken for granted, in the face of the apprehensions of "all who [hear] ." The effect is to suggest a place for the poet that is not only unavailable, but somehow inconceivable, or conceivable only as impossible, to the mind.[14] And if we look again at the deep romantic chasm *as place*, we find that it also partakes of indefiniteness and instability. Its greatest extremes are of ceaseless turmoil suggesting the earth in labor, and a final lifelessness, but it includes as well the contrast of hugeness and littleness, winter and high summer, in "rebounding hail" and "chaffy grain," and the contrast of romance and history in the demon-lover and the voices of war.[15] Its inaccessibility, perhaps physical but chiefly intellectual, is confessed in the speaker's resorting to similes as a means of orienting himself and enlightening us, but the similes on the whole prove his amazement, not his command of the place.

If we bring in the idea of the *genius loci*, and try to associate it with the *genius poetae*, a kind of repellency results. This for two reasons, one that the poet cannot execute his imagination and take his place, the other that the genius of the place is obscure, fascinating, forbidding, and in sum capable of being encircled, as space, but not comprehended, as place. Whether we look at the poem from the perspective of Kubla Khan's authority, the manifestations of nature, or the aspirations of the poet, we find that a mind/place dualism persists, not because place cannot be eschewed, as in the

Renaissance, but because it cannot be settled ultimately, which may be another way of saying the mind cannot reach a settled position.

No definitive declaration on mind or place can be taken at face value when the problem of *relation* (of encounter in situations that perhaps should be termed versatile) is perennial for romanticism; in fact the more insistent the declaration about the mind and its place, the more suspicious we have a right to be of its veridical status, for the more the poet insists on his declaration about the mind and its place, the more the poetry itself seems to recoil toward scepticism or a surprising dissatisfaction, as in *Sleep and Poetry*.

The Prometheanism of the romantic imagination, rightly stressed by Thorslev and by Bloom, actually involves a situation of uncertainty for the mind, and differs from Renaissance "satanism" not in demonstrating a greater freedom or potency for the mind, but in putting the mind in the ultimate jeopardy of dependency on a world without legitimate or secure definition. Hence Byron's Prometheus, as already brought out, can force nothing but a negative determination on the world (which is in its way as bad as Satan's case). His is, as Paul Ricoeur would say of our Titanic nature, "the lowest degree of freedom,"[16] and appeals to us only because the world he occupies exhibits the lowest degree of order. Shelley's *Prometheus Unbound* offers a more promising situation, with the protagonist breaking out of this negative determination, but in its turn it proceeds by the unfolding of a spontaneous universe which the mind cannot securely keep but must discipline itself to maintain. Demogorgon's sober summation of the principles of the play strongly suggests that the amplitudes of practical existence, though they extend both to the remote fixation of the barren rock and to the central fecundity of the marital cave, really occur *between* these two extremes, depending on how truly and how well we withstand the gravitational pull of the one and realize the aspiration to the other. And we must note that Prometheus does not necessarily see the rock in a true light—he can attach himself to it and think it good—and note also that the Earth, who furnishes the cave, does not necessarily understand, when Prometheus gives up his obsession with Jupiter, the freedom and advantage of his act. The point is, finally, twofold: (1) that the idea of a definitive place, even in the mind, is subject to qualification by the definition of the self, and (2) that place has no fixed significance and, even if it did, we might well not know if we were there. "The goal of the . . . unknowing guest . . . is the return to the home . . . [which] turns out to be where [one] has been all along, without knowing it."[17]

An ineluctable uncertainty invades both mind and place in the romantic order. In some respects it is this very uncertainty that makes room for a new dogmatism of the individual, as Blake, for example, comes to regard any system but one he creates as an enslavement, rather than as a possible stay or fulfillment. Fichte is a most vigorous spokesman for such a view:

> My system is the first system of freedom; just as [the French] are tearing man loose from his outer chains, so my system tears him loose from the fetters of the Ding an sich, from any external influence, and establishes him in his first principle as an autonomous being. . . . My system came into being by means of an inner fight with myself, against all rooted prejudices; not without their collaboration—it was their *valeur* which set my aim still higher and released that energy in me which was required in order to conceive it.[18]

But to react is to be influenced. Fichte willy-nilly acknowledges the power that the systems he is casting out have over him; "it is not without their collaboration" that he defines his autonomy. Then again, besides the oddity of generalizing the autonomy of the individual,[19] we are dealing with the oddity of a dogmatism that takes the form of projection, or with a philosophy that works as exhortation rather than definition. The terms of the individual's autonomy are conditioned by the encounter with the world, so that the very uncertainty of the world which gives rise to the dogmatism of the individual obliges him to know the determination of the world, much as a cell, though individualized, cannot be indifferent to the constitution of the body.

Thus, if the mind/place dualism encourages the dogmatism of the individual, it also like a wheeling telescope brings out *contra individuum* the cryptic insistence of the world, including the world of other men. Fichte himself, though given to what Coleridge calls a "crude *egoismus*," proves susceptible to system, if not to "*nature*,"[20] and has come to seem a forerunner of totalitarian German philosophy; putting men in society, he sees perfect freedom in perfect obedience. In like manner Schelling, whose proclamation of the ego competes with Fichte's, leaves man autonomy in relation to "the objective world" only to lose him, qua individual, in theological postulates and the idea of mankind as "a single consummate person" obeying the "law of freedom," and achieving "identity with the Absolute."[21] And Hegel, while also concerned with saving man from materialism and "all alien objective existence," construes the struggle of the individual as taking place between his "finite self-consciousness" and "the absolute self-consciousness," and with neither hesitation nor apology absorbs the individual into the collective body, and the collective body into the idea of Spirit, the idea of History.

> ... At a time when the universal nature of spiritual life has become so very much emphasized and strengthened, and the mere individual aspect has become, *as it should be*, correspondingly a matter of indifference, when, too, that universal aspect holds, by the entire range of its substance, the full measure of the wealth it has built up, and lays claim to it all, the share in the total work of mind that falls to the activity of any particular can only be very small. Because this is so, the individual must all the more forget himself....[22] [italics added]

Hegel indeed is the man who conceives of any instance of individuality as an abstraction, rather than as a concrete existence, on the strength of the pun that it is removed from the total body to which it belongs; his individual is "Das allgemeine Individuum."[23]

On this reading it is secondary whether the self is set in contrast with the world as nature or as society, or with an Absolute Idea. The paramount fact is that romanticism, in fundamental terms, is involved with negotiating a relationship between a certain, or rather an uncertain, self and an equally uncertain system. The positiveness of the Fichtean ego and the positiveness of the Hegelian concrete universal cannot be gainsaid, nor substantiated. What can be substantiated is the fact that romanticism was prepared to declare both, and in its poetry to search their ways. To that search, and especially the manifestations of will in it, we may profitably turn our attention, since our interest is not in what the period believed so much as in what it realized, in its philosophy felt in the pulses. As Schopenhauer remarks, "Dogmas concern idle reason; conduct in the end pursues its own course independently of them, usually in accordance not with abstract, but with unspoken maxims, the expression of which is precisely the whole man himself."[24]

The course that conduct pursues, and its implicit maxims, cannot be approached without a special caution. Romanticism presents a poetry not only in but of crisis (neoclassicism seeks to forestall crisis by homiletic reason or by satire, as in Pope's *Dunciad*, book 4). Crisis orientation in romanticism is typified in the Byronic tale or the Keatsian ode, in the *Visions of the Daughters of Albion* or "Resolution and Independence" or "Christabel." At the same time an impulse toward an elaboration of moments produces the kind of analytic dilation that we have come to recognize in the narrative of the period. In effect then, a possession by the moment—the crisis tendency—is counterbalanced by an abstraction of the moment, in terms of typicality, as in Wordsworth, or by means of analog and allusion, as in Byron.

Much the same dichotomy manifests itself in questions of will, where the self-subsistence of particular incidents must submit to incorporation into matters of recurrence-and-variation that have an evaluative bias of their own. As the self is ambiguous in the system, so is the moment ambiguous in the comprehensive scheme. The moment as such, though having an integrity of its own, is oblivious of the scheme and would appear to come under its influence only in retrospect, by virtue of an interpretive abstraction. But momentary presence and evolutionary meaning constitute alternatives of understanding, rendering what is possible to fine poetry if not to physics, a simultaneous grasp of the position, and the pace and destination of the subject.

MOMENT AND PATTERN IN WORDSWORTH AND BLAKE

Wordsworth's *Prelude* and Blake's *Jerusalem* offer paramount examples of this interplay of moment and scheme, pivoting around the question of will. On the surface, it is only fair to acknowledge, *The Prelude* would seem a poem that tends to self-knowledge, or to consciousness-as-knowledge, rather than to will. The home concern with the growth of a poet's mind explicitly governs its movement, and in one way or another Wordsworth comes, like a veritable Antaeus, back to the question of knowledge as the ground of his undertaking:

> Yet should these hopes
> Prove vain and thus should neither I be taught
> To understand myself, nor thou to know
> With better knowledge how the heart was framed
> Of him thou lovest; need I dread from thee
> Harsh judgments . . . ?
>
> [1, 625–30]

Or again we have Wordsworth's lesson and self-consolation upon encountering the "blind Beggar" with his "upright face "

> Wearing a written paper to explain
> His story, whence he came, and who he was.

> Caught by the spectacle my mind turned round
> As with the might of waters; and apt type
> This label seemed of the utmost we can know,
> Both of ourselves and of the universe;
> And, on the shape of that unmoving man,
> HIs steadfast face and sightless eyes, I gazed,
> As if admonished from another world.
>
> [7, 639–49]

If anything, we see not only knowledge but a certain decorum of knowledge as a crucial feature of these lines.

What, though, if we inspect the "admonition" in the lines,
in the very scene, and the character of the blind Beggar, "upright" and "steadfast" as he is, and a clear cousin-german to
the Leech-gatherer? Doesn't the context of agitation and
anxiety that serves as a foil to the encounter with the Beggar
present Wordsworth developing an attitude and not just coming to a conclusion about knowledge? Knowledge serves as
the fulcrum of the episode, but its intrinsic weight is directed
at Wordsworth's state of mind, perhaps his state of being, in
terms of the regulation of his desire and need. And the issue
becomes one of self-regulation, which is heavy with implications for the individual will to project itself continually and
variously through *The Prelude*.

FRUITFUL FAILURE AND INCIDENTAL CAUSE: THE WILL IN *THE PRELUDE*

The very opening lines of *The Prelude* contain the kernel of
Wordsworth's interest in self-regulation and will:

> O there is a blessing in this gentle breeze,
> A visitant that while it fans my cheek
> Doth seem half-conscious of the joy it brings
> From the green fields, and from yon azure sky.
> Whate'er its mission, the soft breeze can come
> To none more grateful than to me; escaped
> From the vast city, where I long had pined

> A discontented sojourner: now free,
> Free as a bird to settle where I will.

While these lines signal the major topic of freedom in the poem, the terms of freedom have an air of subjectivity and volition that becomes all but characteristic; but before developing this idea, it may be well to indicate how idiomatic and pervasive the terms of will seem here at the outset of the poem:

> Content and *not unwilling* now to give
> A respite to this passion, I paced on
> With brisk and *eager* steps, and came at length
> To a green shady place, where down I sate
> Beneath a tree, slackening my thoughts *by choice* . . . .
> [1, 59–64; italics added]

The indices of the will in the opening lines are only less conspicuous than this. Wordsworth's response to the gentle breeze is more than an expression of bursting emotion. Its spontaneity is not as simply sensuous as it appears, but arises from a clear principle of judgment and evaluation of personal will (*spons*). His desire to be free informs the opening exclamation and the superlative ("none more . . . than . . . me") as well as words like *blessing, joy, grateful*, which define an individual position as well as describe particular feelings. Wordsworth makes a singular identification of himself ("to none more grateful than to me"), and the appositive phrases that follow come to seem explanatory, indeed causal: telling us that when he is confined or forced to a place, he pines and is discontented, whereas when he is free, and can choose his own place, he is elated. The issue is only secondarily one of place, city versus country; first it is one of freedom, *felt and willed*. The phrase Coleridge uses in "To William Wordsworth," "chosen Laws controlling choice," is not only an outside conception of Wordsworth; it is in Wordsworth's own awareness, here in the first verse paragraph of *The Prelude*, where he gives himself up to a "chosen guide," sure that he cannot miss his way. The end, albeit undefined, is willed, but not the means; as Plato says in *Gorgias*, "If a man acts with some purpose, he does not will the act, but the purpose of the act." But it appears that the assurance is problematical, or premature; the verse paragraph ends with a restatement of open or radiant possibilities, now in a faintly troubled, interrogative mood:

> whither shall I turn,
> By road or pathway, or through trackless field,
> Uphill or down, or shall some floating thing
> Upon the river point me out my course?
>
> [1, 27–30]

This dualistic mood of confidence and questioning which recalls the "quickening virtue" of the "correspondent breeze" somehow "vexing its own creation" and which continues even after Wordsworth takes "the road that pointed to the chosen Vale," suggests something basic about the will: it is at once positive as to present being, and obscure, contingent as to becoming, as to the process of time. As Wordsworth himself says, " . . . My days are past / In contradiction; with no skill to part / Vague longing, haply bred by want of power, / From paramount impulse not to be withstood." As it pertains to the writing of the poem—and this is a subject on which Herbert Lindenberger has written tellingly in his *On Wordsworth's Prelude*—the question of will is salient enough. But the beginning of *The Prelude* clearly associates two aspects of will, one being the poet's, the other the personality's, the person whose activity and nature the poem pursues and records. And the will of the personality has not, to the best of my knowledge, been extensively studied, though its presence is indirectly noticed by Geoffrey Hartman, for example, where he points out that in "Nutting" the "child's wilful consciousness matures into the sympathetic imagination."[25] There is room for a fuller presentation of the will in *The Prelude* (and in "Nutting," "Peter Bell," "Resolution and Independence," "The White Doe of Rylstone," and "Hart-leap Well," among others), and a need also to show how the will matures and what part it may play in the process of maturation. Though

Wordsworth sums up *The Prelude* as a narrative "of intellectual power, fostering love,/Dispensing truth, and over men and things/Where reason yet might hesitate, diffusing/Prophetic sympathies of genial faith . . ." (12, 43), such a definition excludes the way of the poem in favor of its destination, though of course destination, once reached, draws retroactive energy and resonance from its way.

The tension between destination and way is chronic in Wordsworth's poetry, and would seem to be part of a larger tension in romanticism. It is a tension that hardly stands out in the neoclassical era. If we treat the Snowdon episode in *The Prelude* and the last fifty lines of *Windsor Forest* as visions of unity and a human ideal, the difference in respect of destination and way should be evident. Pope makes the fleet the destination of the trees, and the furthest regions of the earth the destination of the fleet, and universal sway the destiny of England, possessor of trees and fleet (the phrase "Earth's distant ends" seems in context as much teleological as geographical). The recurrent "shall" of the lines reinforces their sense of inevitability; the way to perfection is a combination of clear principles, and high values, and time. So sure is Pope of what "shall" betide that he offers prophecy as a reflexive version of memory: "And naked youths and painted chiefs [shall] admire/Our speech, our colour, and our strange attire!" The passage centers on Windsor but translates itself via the fleet to remote climes; it celebrates the English, but embraces "all mankind." The sea lanes of English commerce become the backdrop for Pope's abiding sense of national and philosophical destination in the "scene of opening fate."

The Snowdon episode is also all-encompassing in vision, but it is obviously blind and erratic in process. Even nature proves less stable or perspicuous, at first encounter, for Wordsworth than for Pope, since the former cannot plan effectively so much as one step ahead, and loses his guide. Nature for Pope is absorbed into and takes the shape of commerce and sway. For Wordsworth it has the shape of surprise. But in the final analysis nature proves more definite and revelatory for Wordsworth than for Pope. What it reveals is the ultimate interpenetrating unity of all things, despite surface separation and division. All "waters" come together at the foot of Snowdon; mist becomes earth, "in headlands, tongues, and promontory shapes," and further becomes the link (not the barrier) between water and sky; the "one voice" of the waters covers "earth and sea" and reaches the responsive heavens. When all things come together for Wordsworth, the resulting unity represents an ideal of the mind, not of society as with Pope. They come together not in response to an abstract ideal of patriotism or universality, but according to their own properties in natural, even seemingly casual, relationship. An inevitability of nature rather than purpose manifests itself; where Pope disingenuously proffers memory in the guise of prophecy, Wordsworth cleverly pursues memory into revelation.

And yet Wordsworth's is not entirely or even basically a world of casual developments. Almost without exception, a decisive advance in Wordsworth's consciousness in *The Prelude* is associated with an act of will that, though abortive, becomes a cryptic, psychic cause of revelation. Three episodes—the rowboat venture in book 1, the Simplon Pass-Como sequence in book 6, and the ascent of Mount Snowdon in book 14—can be used to illustrate the complex and evolving contribution of will to the growth of the poet's mind.

The rowboat episode, even if the editorial parenthesis ("led by her") suggests a clear sense of direction, is internally blind, and on one level shows the confinement of Wordsworth's "horizon" and, by implication, the confinement of his knowledge of the world and of the sources of his own happiness. The episode is reminiscent of the opening lines of *The Prelude*, in its manifest concern with freedom[26] and in the personality of its concern. But this episode is not a mere matter of circumstance; it is contrived by the actor, who projects and invests himself in it. At the same time, it is expansive and dramatic (where the opening of the poem is specific and lyrical), and moves as much to the fulfillment of its own, as of his, terms. Perhaps even in the description of the boat (which is "tied," and then "unloosed") it is a depiction of the over-coming of restraints and the attainment of romantic freedom in the universe. The boy is momentarily checked by con-science ("an act of stealth / And troubled pleasure"), but soon shakes this off, giving himself with mounting elation to the force of his own activity. Such phrases as "Proud of his skill, to reach a chosen point," "elfin pinnace," "Lustily" "Heav-ing . . . like a swan" reveal his conception of himself as a romance hero, indulging in a romanticized will. But again, in the alternating pattern of restraint and bursting free that marks the episode, an obstacle looms in the form of the mount. The boy's "I struck and struck again" is what we now call a counterproductive gesture; the faster and farther he goes, the larger and mightier the cliff, so that the element of restraint quickly gains dominance and reverses, literally, the direction of the action. That the scene is operating in terms of will emerges sharply in the description of the huge peak "as if with *voluntary* power instinct," and seemingly "with *purpose of its own*" (italics added). This is not mere personi-fication, or a mere metaphor of the time of writing, but a genuine recovery of the young boy's apprehension. Against the will he has been exerting, a contrary will has arisen.

What is the nature of this will? Can it be intrinsic to the "huge peak, black and huge," or is it a sheer imposition of the rower, of his reluctance to believe that his great will and conception of himself could fall before "a soulless image" (6, 526) of brute matter? Perhaps neither, in any simple way. The dramatic thrust of the episode and the extent to which it encases definitions of the boy's self-understanding and self-activity cannot be caught with the cleft logic of the peak's will, *or* the boy's. The kind of separation which prevails be-tween Wordsworth and Mont Blanc in book 6, and which obliges the poet to distinguish between "soulless image" and "living thought," has no place in the rowboat episode. The Mont Blanc encounter is static, indeed touristic, affording an experience of the object without encouraging that experience of the self in relation to the object which is the keynote of the rowboat episode. A certain passivity, perhaps an atrophy of "soft luxuries" (6, 557), marks scenes like the beholding of Mont Blanc; the rowboat episode partakes of Wordsworth's "underthirst/Of vigour" (6, 558-59)[27] and involves his essential position as a vital agent in being.

Thus, if the boy's excitement and ego-lust are transmitted in some measure to the peak, it is also true that that very action begins to reveal the peak's capacity for receiving such emotion. More, the boy's heightened passions entail a heightening of his sensibilities, of his susceptibility to dimensions and terms of experience unapprehended in the ordinary walks of his day. (Though it was Coleridge's commission to bring home the exotic to everyday, we do Wordsworth an injustice by overlooking how surcharged and singular his ordinary moments can be, and how far he was willing to go to put himself in the way of such moments.) A crucial feature of the scene, and of Wordsworth's approach to experience and poetry, escapes us unless we grant its peculiar combination of the singular and the predictable. Chateaubriand shrewdly remarks that "moments of crisis produce in man a heightening of life," but however rare it may be in itself the capacity for such heightening is never wanting. Thus a modern philosopher, H. Wildon Carr, remarks that

> consciousness . . . [which] in its special form of knowing or awareness, illuminates our activity at the central point of progressing action . . . *is concentrated in a focus of attention when the activity is intense and the situation is novel.* [But] it is dispersed and relaxed when the situation is familiar and the action automatic. [italics added]

In other words, it is ordinary enough for Wordsworth to have extraordinary perceptions and intuitions in so "concentrated" a moment. "New and unwonted" cases[28] elicit unexpected powers.

But it is important to stress that the rowboat episode involves more than knowing, unless we recognize Carr's definition: "Knowing is not awareness of what is or is not, but

the grasp or apprehension of becoming."[29] This idea of becoming, of making a critical step in the development of the
self, is very much involved in the rowboat episode, and it will
be useful here to turn to a superb analysis of a classic example
of revelatory crisis in religious history. The following quotation is drawn, without supererogatory comment, from
Erich Auerbach's *Mimesis*:

> From the humdrum existence of his daily life, Peter is
> called to the most tremendous role. . . . Because his faith
> was deep, but not deep enough, the worst happened to
> him that can happen to one whom faith had inspired but
> a short time before: he trembles for his miserable life.
> And it is entirely credible that this terrifying inner expe-
> rience should have brought about another swing of the
> pendulum—this time in the opposite direction and far
> stronger. Despair and remorse following his desperate
> failure prepared him for the visions which contributed
> decisively to the constitution of Christianity. It is only
> through this experience that the significance of Christ's
> coming and Passion is revealed to him.[30]

As long as we recognize the "voluntary power" of the peak
for what it is, a *negative* power, the justification of the literal idea comes readily to hand; it is not in the nature of the
peak to conspire with the boy in the maintenance of his pride,
nor to contribute to his false sense of the definition of the
actual world. As Byron says in another context, "whatever is,
is," and in being itself generates a certain insistence that must,
where one is in effect learning to come to terms with oneself
and with the world, make it seem "as if" endowed with
voluntary power—the episode claims no more. Wordsworth
implicitly learns of the will that inheres in the way of things,
and his knowledge is less analytical than metaphysical
("modes of being") and less definite than potential, as the
modes are still "unknown." The action of *The Prelude*, over-
all, revolves around the occasions and means and results of
discovering these modes of being,[31] with the will (as in the

rowboat episode) serving the crucial function of setting the
scene and the tone of the scene and exhibiting the crucial
capacity to be chastened without despairing—for the stubborn
persistence of "a darkness" and of "huge and mighty forms"
in Wordsworth's "mind" and "dreams" represents not only a
penalty exacted (he labors under their burden), but an energy
exerted in his struggle to grasp and inhabit new modes of
being (he labors upon them), and a singular joining of forces
(he labors in alliance with them—2, 259). As he writes himself, with weighty fusion of helplessness and unyielding purpose and subtle collaboration:

> after I had seen
> That spectacle, for many days, my brain
> *Worked with* a dim and undetermined sense
> Of unknown modes of being.
>   [1, 390–92; italics added]

The difference between the "stealth" with which the boy
gets the scene underway and his timorously "stealing" his
way home gives one measure of the shape and import of the
episode. The action ends where it begins, in the cove by the
willow tree, having as it were a completed pattern of denial.
But cancellation of the gain made by the lad originally committed to an "unswerving line" does not mean defeat. There
is a chastening or rectifying rather than a crushing of the will.
Contrariwise, though it appears that an expansion of knowledge is taking place, from the rocky cove to the craggy cliff
to the huge peak, the assumptions or foundations of knowledge itself are undermined. In effect, classical reason—the
power to predict and choose within a given framework of action and consequence—goes by the board. And personal will
encounters its own inadequacy—the universe of the actor is
not *the universe*, and his action within familiar assumptions
carries him willy-nilly into another strange dimension (so also
his emotional keenness and elevation enhance his susceptibility to the import of that dimension). The scene, for all its
overt purposiveness, proceeds by surprise. What Wordsworth

learns is that he is ignorant. Accordingly he retains

> No familiar shapes
> . . . , no pleasant images of trees,
> Of sea or sky, no colours of green fields. . . .
>   [1, 395-97]

Both his understanding and his will stand suspended, where both have been presumptuously active. But both also stand at a threshold, where they have been circumscribed.

Much of Wordsworth's experience at Cambridge (book 3), as well as his sense of himself in "Summer Vacation" (book 4) and his sense of education and society (book 5), involves a more or less obscure projection of purpose, and failure, and intimations of recovery. The vividness of the rowboat episode (or the skating, or the springe-raiding, or the cliff-hanging episodes) is not maintained, but the sense of self-engagement persists in a muted key, as befits the onset of "a regular desire /For calmer pleasures" (2, 49-50). It is as though the aftermath of the rowboat episode, certainly the outstanding early example of Wordsworth's personal will and its wake of upsetting effects, had for the duration blunted the sharpest edges of a need for self-projection and assertion, leaving Wordsworth in a position where he "could dream away [his] purposes" (2, 192). For he has obviously not drawn any axiom of behavior from his discomfiture. To the contrary, he is "working with" something which yet necessarily remains "dim and undetermined."

Still there appears no *direct* correlation between his activity and what develops. The exultation he seeks concretely in the rowboat befalls him, in "fleeting" and "shadowy" form, afterwards (2, 312-13), and it seems immediately valid to read, as an incipient gloss on the obscure impact of the rowboat episode, Wordsworth's estimate of such momentary "mo

> that the soul
> Remembering how she felt, but what she felt
> Remembering not, retains an obscure sense

Of possible sublimity, whereto
With growing faculties she doth aspire,
With faculties still growing, feeling still
That whatsoever point they gain, they yet
Have something to pursue.

[2, 315-22]

This quotation not only incorporates a pervasive activity of the will, it also anticipates the great utterance concerning "something evermore about to be." It introduces us explicitly to Wordsworth's sense of an emergent relationship between the will and time, the relationship I have tried to define with the phrase "blind teleology." In Wordsworth's case the relationship has a biographical basis, since he is dealing with time according to the pattern of an individual life, and not of, say, a society or a cultural epoch. As the quintessential case of the will in action in the boyhood phase of his life, the rowboat episode initiates the time/will relationship and sets up, with the ignorant anticipation of its conclusion, an awareness of "something to pursue" that must always be unattained, since both its terms keep changing in themselves and in relation to each other.

In books 3-5 of *The Prelude*, then, we may observe a transitional phase (calling the rowboat episode one of the crucial phases) in the development of the will, as Wordsworth seeks to define his position in adolescence and early manhood. In relation to nature that position proves almost a discursive counterpart of the structure of the rowboat episode, being at once forthright and assertive and also, paradoxically, ambiguous and passive. Wordsworth portrays himself in two postures. The first is active and self-determining, where he is "coercing all things into sympathy" and imposing his "own enjoyments" on "unorganic nature" (2, 390-92); here, with "consciousness not to be subdued," he gives "a moral life" to every natural form, down to "the loose stones that cover the highway" (3, 130-32). The second is, as he says himself (in the very act of proclaiming "a plastic power," "a forming hand," "a local spirit of his own"),

> for the most [part] ,
> Subservient strictly to external things
> With which it communed.
>
> [2, 366-68]

We can only conclude that the dramatic impasse of the row-boat episode remains to be resolved; neither self-determination nor self-abnegation characterizes the emerging will, where nature is concerned.

At the same time, another factor is gaining prominence in Wordsworth's story of defining, or *realizing*, himself. It comprises man and society and introduces the significant variables of Wordsworth's image of himself in other men and his image of his place among men. In this context, which our interest in nature has perhaps led us to undervalue, Wordsworth makes few positive claims for himself. If he is involved with nature, he seems aloof, or at best tentative, with men: "I was not for that hour,/Nor for that place" (3, 81-82). Clearly, though, aloofness is not a simple condition, but a problematical choice for him:

> Though I had learnt betimes to stand unpropped,
> And independent musings pleased me so
> That spells seemed on me when I was alone,
> Yet could I only cleave to solitude[32]
> In lonely places; if a throng was near
> That way I leaned by nature; for my heart
> Was social, and loved idleness and joy.
>
> [3, 227-33]

He charges himself simply with "indecisive judgments" and "submissive idleness" (3, 215-632), not just describing his behavior but revealing his inner state as an "independent" being. In a sense he gives a picture of choice, not spontaneously settling on its object as in the case of the boy ten years of age, but somehow blankly expectant and unengaged. Choice is now "random" (3, 374), or inert and imaginary:

> Look was there none within these walls to shame
> My easy spirits, and discountenance

> Their light composure, far less to instil
> A calm resolve of mind, firmly addressed
> To puissant efforts.

[3, 346-50]

Yet it is necessary to see that his "regrets" (4, 307) imply a frustrated form of the will and differ from his rapturous boat ride chiefly in his knowing the resistance of the world to his self-ideal and in his readiness to blame the world (especially the world of Cambridge) for that. Even so, his failure to articulate the educational panacea alluded to in book 3, 371-401, should not count against him; he is venturing or vaunting a personality position, not undertaking a philosophy, and in the deepest sense the poem—dramatic, reflective, autobiographical, celebrative, argumentative—becomes his philosophy of education.

It is striking that Wordsworth, already denied the fulfillment of his romantic wilfulness, is also denied the satisfaction of his discontents; that is to say, he neither triumphs nor has opportunity for indulging himself in self-justifying denunciations. In effect we may begin to suspect that the postulates of the merely personal will, whether optimistic or sulking, always stand to be corrected. Wordsworth's regrets meet with what he himself strongly calls "chastisement" (4, 307), after the night-long grange party where so naturally, and yet unexpectedly, the "morning rose" where "vows / Were . . . made" for him, and again, also following a night of "strenuous idleness," when he meets the serenely companionless ex-soldier and finds, in his character and the complex act of benevolence he occasions, a "quiet heart" once more (4, 309 f., 370 f.). The figure of enormous spiritual power cased in a fragile senility carries deep metaphysical valences in Wordsworth's poetry; characters like the Leech-gatherer and Old Cumberland Beggar replace Shakespeare's kings as ultimate and paradigmatic beings. This discharged veteran is set apart by his "ghastly" aspect, which makes him seem to operate across the threshold between death or spirituality and material reality.[33]

It may be argued, of all these instances, that the intellect stands corrected, rather than the will. And no doubt the intellect, as presuming it can know what may be good or bad for someone, is put into its place. But more than intellect, it is commitment, positive as aspiration and negative as resentment, that stands out in fact. The intellect becomes, in a distinct revision of the classical scheme, an element of the self-will, which is truly at stake, the intellect only recognizing the uncertainties, the unpredictability of the situations in which the self wills or would will its answerable conditions.

Two features of the correction of the will involved in the event of vow making and succoring of the veteran require special attention. The first is its explicitness in Wordsworth's mind, and its positiveness—he recognizes the "chastisement" as a good. It is important to observe, though, that the good in question has rather an uncertain value for the long run. The vows are felt, and not here really known, so that their force and aim remain as "dim and undetermined" as the product of the rowboat episode. By the same token, the quiet heart is local and self-contained, rather than permanent and influential, in the ordinary passages of his life. This is important to keep in mind, inasmuch as the gain in knowledge we can measure here really confirms Wordsworth in his understanding of uncertainty. Even if incidental knowledge, up to and including knowledge of possible principles, is increased for him, his vital will remains unresolved. In fact his knowledge of vital unfulfillment is greater in book 4 than in book 1, without any remarkable development of saving measures. Wordsworth avows his hope—and certainly more than study is involved—for a way to uphold "intense desire through meditative peace" (4, 306), and we cannot but be impressed with the separation of the vow making (intense desire) from the quieting scene with the veteran (meditative peace). As will and time meet as it were on a slipping plane, a fault line, so do desire and peace for Wordsworth, who thus experiences Saint Augustine's dilemma without having his recourse to an organized faith. Some will see it as the dilemma of the present as well, and it may be that the form the answer takes for Wordsworth, as his situation unfolds, will have an interest independent of the autobiography of his mind.

As regards the correction of the will, the second notable feature of the vow-making and ghostly-veteran scenes is the structural chiasmus which links them underneath: the one moving from people to a consummation in nature, the other from nature to a resolution through man. In the case of the vow making, Wordsworth appears to be removing himself from the press of men as instinctively and decisively as in the ice-skating episode (1, 425 f.), but in his typical way he is not "leaving the tumultuous throng" in all its terms. Rather he returns to man, as decisively and spontaneously as he leaves, in such episodes as that of the ghostly veteran. A second tendency of the poem seems to emerge along with the tendency to the correction of the will, namely, a self-distrust or self-irritation among men that enhances Wordsworth's contact with nature, while this enhanced contact with nature generates a keener and deeper human feeling:

> Nor less do I remember to have felt,
> Distinctly manifested at this time,
> A human-heartedness about my love
> For objects hitherto the absolute wealth
> Of my own being and no more. . . .
>   [4, 231–35]

But, as already indicated, a deep uncertainty enters into the reciprocity between man and nature. It appears as event, not law, and indeed bears intimations of no law save that of the will, since event, as history, can contain no other law for the participant, as self. This may seem a strange declaration, but the earlier discussion of the will and necessary patterns of biography in "Tintern Abbey" should have prepared for it. The principle at work has been well described by Charles Altieri, who writes that Wordsworth "accepts his identity as a being in process . . . and . . . learns to accept himself as a creature whose identity is not a set of contents but a centered lawful process of experiencing varied contents."[34] Though the "contents" are given, the centering takes place around the will, in accordance with Yeats's brilliantly paradoxical assertion, "The lot of life is chosen." And it is clear that Wordsworth, encountering such obviously significant events, is in no position to say once and for all what they signify, partly because the time is premature and partly because the will is unready: the position he elects toward them must weigh heavily in the ultimate resolution. Nor is this just a matter of inference. Wordsworth himself in book 4, 256 f., declares his sense of making progress without quite securing a destination, his sense of things happening that contain essential elements for his being, if he could only determine himself firmly and clearly enough in relation to them. It is a Heisenbergian situation in the biography of the spirit.

The lines in which Wordsworth tries to come to grips with his situation—biographically, not poetically as at the end of book 1—are so much a reflective, metaphorical reprise of the rowboat episode that they will well stand quoting in full:

> As one who hangs down-bending from the side
> Of a slow-moving boat, upon the breast
> Of a still water, solacing himself
> With such discoveries as his eye can make
> Beneath him in the bottom of the deep,
> Sees many beauteous sights—weeds, fishes, flowers,
> Grots, pebbles, roots of trees, and fancies more,
> Yet often is perplexed, and cannot part
> The shadow from the substance, rocks and sky,
> Mountains and clouds, reflected in the depth
> Of the clear flood, from things which there abide
> In their true dwelling; now is crossed by gleam
> Of his own image, by a sunbeam now,
> And wavering motions sent he knows not whence,
> Impediments that make his task more sweet;
> Such pleasant office have we long pursued
> Incumbent o'er the surface of past time
> With like success, nor often have appeared

Shapes fairer or less doubtfully discerned
Than these to which the Tale, indulgent Friend!
Would now direct thy notice.

[4, 256–75]

Though on the surface the lines seem general in application, covering "past time" and future "shapes," it seems just to regard them as a generalization of the poem's present; they do not speak definitively for the poem, but aptly for where it has reached and what it can avow. We must not forget that one example of genius in *The Prelude* is its simultaneous obedience to the power of the mature poet and accommodation to the circumstances of the growing youth. The metaphorization of the rowboat episode takes on no small importance, indicating as it does that Wordsworth is beginning to gain distance on it (it is no longer a bemusing "object over near"), but *also* that it is beginning to achieve the status of necessary, primal, radiant subject in his mind. In fact, given the cluster of images and elements it shares with the three paramount episodes of will in *The Prelude*, this extended metaphor may be accorded, if not equal billing, more than a background role in the present argument.

The "slow-moving" boat, I propose, should be taken as the reflective analog of the "elfin pinnace" of book 1; the "solace" on the "breast" of the water as a modification of two features of the earlier episode: its pursuit of ecstasy, and its abrupt encounter with the "masculine" cliff; the litany of objects ("weeds . . . roots of trees") as the counterpart to the tale of sense-deprivation consequent upon the earlier episode ("no familiar shapes," etc.), while at the same time a basic uncertainty of judgment persists ("Yet often is perplexed") and indeed becomes explicit as a matter of self-conception: "and cannot part/The shadow from the substance," or part "gleam of his own image" from "a sunbeam." Wordsworth unmistakably has returned, via the metaphor of imagination, to the scene of his most vivid and vital discomfiture, not so much to seek meaning as to find orientation. The return is less an intellectual than a psychological act, or perhaps rather an ontological impulse directed at a recovery and establishment of the self vis-à-vis what has worsted it. In other words, tempered by reflection and a modest aim of solace, the will is making a second essay at the water and the mountain, and the effectual self. The picture is clearer, somewhat, than in the rowboat episode, but the position not materially improved.

The agitation that persists in Wordsworth's spirit, betraying his awareness of inadequacy to do or be what he would, comes out sharply in the most "intellectual" part of the poem, devoted to "Books" (5). The opening words speak for themselves:

When Contemplation, like the night-calm felt
Through earth and sky, spreads widely, and sends deep
Into the soul its tranquillising power,
Even then I sometimes grieve for thee, O Man. . . .

And the concluding cry of the first verse paragraph shows how much of a personal statement, and how much a statement of baffled will to invariable power, is involved here:

Oh! why hath not the Mind
Some element to stamp her image on
In nature somewhat nearer to her own?
Why, gifted with such powers to send abroad
Her spirit, must it lodge in shrines so frail?

At the risk of seeming churlish, one must remark that the claims for man and mind are more of a prayer than anything else in the experience of the poem to date. There have been no "palms achieved," nor has there been decisive proof of powers to send the spirit abroad. In point of fact, book 5 itself bears ampler witness to the fragility than to the honor of the products of man and mind. The dream of the Arab (5, 56 f.) introduces Shakespeare and Milton as needing to be saved from a felt peril, not praised. And thus is set the tone of the book, for all practical purposes. Twin themes of beginnings and guides recur throughout the book, but the beginnings (say, "Poems withal of name") bid fairer than the developments measure up to, and the guides (the Arab himself, the mother) ominously disappear or ("the keepers of our time") prove foolish and oppressive. In the long run, book 5 must be taken as a book of invocation, meant to enunciate as hopes for mankind Wordsworth's hopes for himself. But what he says of the modest "covenant" of study again holds good as a general principle: "Nor were we ever masters of our wish" (5, 470, 476). Instead the real advance of the condition of large wishing in the book is a clear act of faith, at once superbly moving as utterance, and poignantly vague as substance:

>   when we first begin to see
> This dawning earth, to recognise, expect,
> And, in the long probation that ensues,
> The time of trial, ere we learn to live
> In reconcilement with our stinted powers;
> To endure this state of meagre vassalage,
> Unwilling to forego, confess, submit,
> Uneasy and unsettled, yoke-fellows
> To custom, mettlesome, and not yet tamed
> And humbled down—oh! then we feel, we feel,
> We know where we have friends. . . .
> . . . *then* we feel
> With what, and how great might are ye [dreamers]
>   in league,
> Who makes our wish, our power, our thought a deed,
> An empire, a possession—ye whom time
> And seasons serve; all Faculties to whom
> Earth crouches, the elements are potter's clay,
> Space like a heaven filled up with northern lights,
> Here, nowhere, there, and everywhere at once.
>   [5, 513-33]

More than an act of faith, this is finally an act of will, a reflex of being "unwilling to forego, . . . mettlesome, and not yet tamed." But it has its price in sheer exhaustion, as Wordsworth is fain to "relinquish . . . this lofty eminence" for "humbler" ground. All this means, though, is that the topical will is in an eddying motion. As book 5 draws to a close, the essential will reasserts itself in terms of the literary execution of "airy fancies" (567), writing becoming the indomitable act of will that exhibits

> that most noble attribute of man,
> Though yet untutored and inordinate,
> That wish for something loftier, more adorned,
> Than is the common aspect, daily garb,
> Of human life.
>
> [5, 573-77]

The man who will not accept "taming," we must note, leaves the door open for "tutoring" and "ordination." And it is well to remember here that taming and tutoring have been alternatives from the start, and nowhere more graphically than in the rowboat episode. Taming crushes, but tutoring secures, the will; at this stage we know that the former is not about to happen, but like Wordsworth we cannot know how the latter may come about.

It is the Simplon Pass-Como sequence that most clearly resumes and advances the situation of the rowboat episode, not only in terms of the presumption of knowledge, the pursuit of a selfish goal ("trophies" as Wordsworth says), a sharp failure, and a revision of opinion and posture, but also in specific detail: the guide (in the rowboat episode, the immediate cliff) whose presence and function evade ordinary definition; a mountain, against which his prowess is somehow to be measured; a body of water, whose relation to him and the mountain proves less simple than appears; and in general a physical world more complex in structure than at first believed. This is, as already suggested, almost an idiosyncratic setting for crucial episodes in the poem.[35]

The very approach to the climbing of the Alps betrays a material similarity to the rowboat episode, in terms of motive energy, if not of overt ecstasy. Wordsworth describes illicit pleasure, resistance of convention overcome, a romantic anticipation of great doings:

> Nor had . . . the scheme been formed by me
> Without uneasy forethought of the pain,
> The censures, and ill-omening, of those
> To whom my worldly interests were dear.
> But Nature then was sovereign in my mind,
> And mighty forms, seizing a youthful fancy,
> Had given a charter to irregular hopes.
>   [6, 329-35]

The actual climb (6, 557 f.) is dramatically understated and, once more illustrating a gain in knowledge without a corresponding spiritual assurance, is explicitly offered as an example of a disappointed will ("an underthirst/Of vigor" in Wordsworth becomes the "source" of "sadness" for him). But the intensity of his mood can be measured by the depth of his grief; he had had "hopes that pointed to the clouds." It is striking that he (and Robert Jones, of course)[36] cannot find the peak after his somewhat petulant objection to its mere materiality a few lines before (6, 523 f.). The irony of crossing the Alps unawares remains, however, incidental, even if it is mortifying. A more basic irony lies in Wordsworth's ignorance of where to place his hopes (an ignorance as decisive in character in the twenty-year-old as in the ten-year-old) and in his ignorance of how to achieve them. The ultimate irony, also consonant with the rowboat episode, lies in the fact that his immediate practical failure proves a source of revelation impossible without it. The will to achieve high hopes by ascending lofty mountains proves at once vulgar and ludicrous, in conception, and ennobling, in effect. The will causes, in its limited way, more than it can know.

The immediate effect of this failure, that celebrated statement on the imagination, may well seem to leap away from the actual scene into quite another dimension of experience; it is certainly treated that way as a rule.[37] That conclusion doubtless arises in large part from the rhetorical disjunction, singularly cataclysmic even for Wordsworth in *The Prelude*, between one verse paragraph and the next, between *"we had crossed the Alps"* and "Imagination. . . ." By contrast, the shift at the end of the rowboat episode, from "huge and mighty forms . . ./ . . . moved slowly through the mind/By day, and were a trouble to my dreams" to "Wisdom and Spirit of the universe!" seems smooth and natural; we may well believe that one thing contains intimations of the other. The question, then, is whether the substance of the verses on imagination upholds the initial rhetorical impression of abrupt transcendence. There would seem to be grounds for arguing that it does not.[38] Indeed, the way the imagination is described suggests that Wordsworth is taking it, *at this stage*, as the name of the obscure activity that is set off in his mind—the same that went on in his mind just after the rowboat episode—and that activity, beyond being named, seems hardly less obscure now.

The emphasis of the lines on imagination, as far as the occasion itself is concerned, falls unmistakably on obscurity and bewilderment; "glory" is a retrospective label of the *man writing* years later as opposed to the man climbing. Here is what Wordsworth says:

> Imagination—here the Power so called
> Through sad incompetence of human speech,
> That awful Power rose from the mind's abyss
> Like an unfathered vapour that enwraps,
> At once, some lonely traveller. I was *lost*;
> *Halted without an effort to break through*;
> But to my *conscious* soul I *now* can say—
> "I recognize thy glory." . . .
>   [6, 592–99; italics added]

It seems clear that the passage works as a deft combining of anticipation and retrospection. The imagination is named, *but not grasped*, as the thing working upon him out of his very failure. Leslie Brisman has justly observed that the statement accumulates a lot of abstractions and falls short of "adequate expression." Perhaps, though, this feature does not so much succeed in avoiding the definition that would "limit meaning" as avoid a definition that would immediately and prematurely establish meaning.[39] While these lines represent an advance over the end of the rowboat episode, and over the reminiscent metaphor of book 4, they amount to much less than the statement that will arise out of Wordsworth's final failure, to see the sun rise on Mount Snowdon. The after-episode here (621 f.) strikes one as a truer *actualization* of the imagination, without achieving a *realization* of it; it remains prolepsis rather than presentation. The formal definition Wordsworth gives here looks ahead, and again is hopeful and invocative, so that the imagination becomes in effect a special "trophy" replacing those he renounces (610).

In the renunciation of trophies the merely "particular will" is of course much reduced. This goes well with the pattern of toning down the aggressive will in favor of an accommodated or rectified will that the poem exhibits. But the will hardly goes by the board. As already suggested, the imagination virtually turns into an object of the will now, if it has not been implicitly so all along, with Wordsworth's obsessive dwelling on the rowboat syndrome. We may recall, too, that the articulated statement on imagination does not *fully* anticipate a consummation. There remains in the lines a subtle negative bearing, or at least an inexplicable promise rather than full realization—the fertilization of "the whole Egyptian plain" (616) is potential only, "Tumult and peace, and darkness and the light" (635) stand essentially unreconciled. The continuity from the material to the mythical that Wordsworth will traverse in book 14 he remains somewhat shy of now.

Wordsworth describes himself in book 8 as "seeking knowledge . . ./Far less than craving power" (599-600), with some hint of power as a subsidiary object; but it seems that his quest for power is in positive terms complete by book 6, and that, even as he begins to dip back into his past for sustenance, he is trying to analyze and apply the definitions he has now drawn, from experience and reflection, in situations (such as London and the French Revolution) where they do not ordinarily thrive. A tacit will can be argued here, but on the whole it appears passive or inert. Wordsworth is involved not only with "objects over near" (9, 337) and hence hard to see straight and in perspective, but also with massed humanity, which has proven treacherous and unwieldy for him all along. In terms of himself as subject, these books represent the narrowest dimensions that could be imagined as viable.[40] Wordsworth appears less than an actor, less than a "sojourner" (that favorite word); he is a member of a class (Englishman) and even if celebrated as such he seems not to count, but to pass along a path of tenuous contact with the scene.

> I was unprepared
> With needful knowledge, had abruptly passed
> Into a theatre, whose stage was filled
> And busy with an action far advanced.
> [9, 92–95]

His moments of intensest engagement seem curiously anachronistic, as when pleading for the preservation of the Convent of Chartreuse, or evanescent, as in his "memory of the farewells of that time" (9, 267 f.). He is unusually prone to invest his energies in generalization and in identification with the crowd (10, 155 f.), though not without self-skepticism (10, 191 f.). He plainly confesses his sense of insignificance, if not irrelevance (10, 146–54). Nor is this a casual or superficial judgment. It is clear that Wordsworth wants a role, as artist and man, but that the ego-feeding will of the rowboat and Simplon-Como episodes has little if any play. The juxtaposition of the "Romish chapel" scene (10, 553 f.) and the news of Robespierre's death, though structurally reminiscent of numerous passages where an action or scene emblematize an emergent value, clearly shows how little he is making happen, how little in a positive sense is happening to him. It seems almost an act of escapist self-consolation—the will indulging itself rather than pursuing an object as before—that Wordsworth gives loose play to gaudy tricks of poetic imagination. Indeed, he seems aware that he is making a wanton use of the "plain Imagination and severe" with his pyrotechnics on the fox-glove (8, 365 f.). And it must be considered in any judgment of the autonomous or apocalyptic imagination in his work that he tended to see it as involving "a wilfulness of fancy and conceit," that is to say, not a free and spontaneous tendency, but an artificial and primed one. The quasi-apocalyptic moments at conclusion of the rowboat and Alps-crossing episodes, as I have already suggested, represent a somewhat baffled movement into an enriched reality, rather than an abrupt revelation of a natural tendency away from reality.

It is not insignificant that the Grotto of Antiparos (8, 560-89) resumes the imagery of searching into an obscurity that the rowboat episode established in Wordsworth's mind. The physical setting is changed in this instance, boasting neither water nor mountain, but the grotto (cognate with crypt) takes every advantage of the freedom of the metaphor to confirm the implications of the previous scenes. Not now a pursuit of "power" but a pressure to act must be recognized in Wordsworth, perhaps in reaction to the very standstill which the outward situation occasions:

> It might be told . . .
> . . . that, seeing, I was led
> Gravely to ponder—judging between good
> And evil, not as for the mind's delight
> But for her guidance[41] —one who was to *act*,
> As sometimes to the best of feeble means
> I did, by human sympathy impelled.
>   [8, 518-24]

In this light we may well read his nightmare of pleading before unjust tribunals as a personal, and not a political, point: his dream projects him, at last, into the thick of the action, and he is for whatever reason powerless to make a difference. The despair he feels reaches beyond the impossible state of things for man in general and reveals his impotent sense of himself—it is the nadir of the will, though its full intensity may not come home once and for all till the failure of the Godwinian redemption: Wordsworth "yielded up moral questions in despair" (11, 305).[42]

Now should we fail to note that the will emerges as a central and vital concern for Wordsworth in the later stages of his time in France and upon his return to England. Wordsworth cannot see how to engage his will in the cause of the French Revolution, and laments his return from France as an overruling of his (albeit unapplied) will: "Dragged by a chain of harsh necessity,/So it seemed" (10, 222-23). In each case the failure of his own desires for action, or often merely passionate faith in principles (e.g., 9, 518-41; 10, 153-90; 10, 437-70), throws him back upon himself in terms of will. This can best be recognized in his pursuit of Godwinism, as the failure of "principles" and "events" makes him deliberately seek "elsewhere" for "safer" terms "of universal application" (11, 194 f.). In effect, he is using his will to offset not only a disappointment but a sense of animal duress; his mind, he says, was "let loose and goaded," but being a person

> somewhat stern
> In temperament, withal a happy man,
> And therefore bold to look on painful things,
> Free likewise of the world, and thence more bold,
> I summoned my best skill, and toiled, intent
> To anatomise the frame of social life. . . .
>
> [11, 275-80]

But the remedy ("reason") entailing its own failure, and reducing Wordsworth to the "soul's last and lowest ebb," he does not blame it so much as the will that had elected it. This point deserves every emphasis, as proof of a bias and preoccupation couched so simply at the heart of the poem as to run some danger of going unnoticed. Here is Wordsworth's plain declaration:

> This was the crisis of that strong disease,
> This the soul's last and lowest ebb, I drooped,
> Deeming our blessed reason of least use

Where wanted most:[43] "The lordly attributes
Of *will and choice*," I bitterly exclaimed,
"What are they but a mockery of a Being
Who hath in no concerns of his a test
Of good and evil; knows not what to fear
Or hope for, what to covet or to shun;
And who, if those could be discerned, would yet
Be little profited, would see, and ask
Where is the obligation to enforce?
And, to acknowledged law rebellious, still,
As selfish passion urged, would act amiss;
The dupe of folly. . . ."
                              [11, 306-20; italics added]

Here, if we but add the recurrent word *presumption*, is a virtual summary of the career of the will in the poem, but it is proof of its indispensability that no final renunciation follows. Rather, paradoxically, Wordsworth wills a suspension of the will, according to the dichotomy prevailing in the Arab dream: abstract science and poetry. The former, as he says, gives "no admission" to "the disturbances of space and time" that derive "from human will and power" (11, 330-32), and the latter, in the form "of pastoral Arethuse," gives special admission and consolation to "a glad votary" (who may, however, in this respect need to be "willingly deceived" [11, 465-70]).

Perhaps, though, what we are witnessing is a biasing of the will finally away from practical individual power toward "intellectual[44] power," toward the evocative, *made* products of man. Certainly it is a bias built into the writing of the poem which, as an experiment in the new epic and an essay at the *opus maximum* of a life, is both contextually and personally bound to a conscious aesthetics. Previously in the poem—witness the movement from book 5 to book 6 where Wordsworth proceeds from anxiety to dignified emulation vis-à-vis his great predecessors—aspiration and self-transcendence (or gains in self-authority) have accompanied this bias. At the end of book 11 self-protection and bold wish fulfillment would seem uppermost. Sounding startlingly like the man who makes up for his failure to cope with reality with a supercilious "Above-all-I'm-an-artist-and-an-artist-is-above-all," Wordsworth gives out with his final assessment of himself: "A sensitive being, a *creative* soul" (12, 207). But the qualifying phrase, "In Nature's presence" (12, 206), sufficiently tempers the subjective arrogance of the claim, and gets a substantial boost from the following passage on the "spots of time" (12, 208 f.).

It is odd that the initial effect of these lines is to convince the reader of the mind's natural and predominant force;[45] perhaps this effect derives from an illusion of versification, in the visual emphasis of the distich:

> The mind is lord and master—outward sense
> The obedient servant of her will.
> [12, 222-23]

For the ultimate weight of the passage is unsettled. The material event, the spot of time, proves the source whereby the mind is "nourished and invisibly repaired." All the same, an "efficacious spirit" seems to "lurk" within the material event, so that spirit and incident enjoy in turn a seesaw ascendancy. This condition is summarized in the core statement of the passage, concerning the knowledge

> *to what point, and how*
> The mind is lord and master. . . .
> [italics added]

The determination of that point and of the means of mastery is hardly possible within the statement, and no more so in the illustrative anecdote of the pitcher-bearing girl in the strong wind (12, 231 f.). Wordsworth, it must be recognized, calls it an "ordinary sight," evidently pushing the conclusion that the "visionary dreariness" of the scene depends on "the mind." And so it does, but not simply or entirely, since the set of the mind, its readiness and pitch to work on the ordinary scene in that extraordinary way, depends on the antecedent scene: inexperience as a rider, the lost guide, the rough and stony moor, the infamous gibbet-place and "monumental letters" of the murderer's name. The pool and beacon and girl-with-pitcher bucking the wind cannot be separated from the ominous forescene any more than the vow making can be separated from the nightlong revelry or the rearing mountain from the ecstatic rowboat.

This is not to imply that Wordsworth does not know what he is talking about. A legitimate acceptance of his statement offers itself if once we take it to cover the character or integrity of the mind, and *not its arbitrary freedom.* In other words, the mind's mastery of outward sense does not extend to making of it whatever may seem commodious, but rather involves its innate ability to withstand being mechanically determined by the circumstances of outward scene. Its "will," then, is the will of its integrity, its drive to maintain its being and not be overwhelmed from without. This is, in Blakean terms, to avoid falling into a philosophy of Experience because of the pressure of experiences. This drive, of course, has implicitly a positive element, in terms of what the mind may recognize in what it encounters. We may well recall the opportunism of the mind in response to such emergencies as the rowboat episode and the debacle of the Alps climb, as well as its maneuvers to stave off the disaster of the French Revolution, with Godwin, and then the compound disaster of Godwinism, with art. In sum, "the mind is lord and master" makes not only an imprecise but a polemical assertion in which the possibilities of the poem and, more, the viability of the poet are put to the proof.

It is one of the peculiarities of books 12 and 13 of *The Prelude* that they suspend the action and apparently seek to substitute a gospel for a life, that is, they tend to give a detached theoretical answer to a pressing autobiographical question. The answer, in short, has one less dimension than the problem. How to restore imagination and faith includes and yet remains less than how to restore Wordsworth's imagination and faith, just as abstractions include and yet lack the specific density and shape of their cases. The peculiar intensity of conviction and weight of illustration in books 12 and 13 do not quite produce satisfaction that the problem—of "death-like" desertion in the soul and eventual "despair"—is being met, let alone solved. And yet the poem offers no true precedent for solving problems. For one thing, it is not enough, Antaeus-like, to return to the ground of memory. And for another, every calculated maneuver of self-enhancement or self-restoration, from the jaunt in the rowboat to an imaginary dip in pastoral Arethusa, fails either in its own terms or in terms of the scepticism of its very exponent. In this light books 12 and 13 appear a statement of knowledge or consciousness separated from means or will. They represent an impasse in the poem: Wordsworth cannot be contented with merely knowing what he knows—such knowledge in a practical case is otiose faith—and yet he cannot jump in a boat or stride up a hill and count on transcendence and epiphany. Perhaps he knew better before he came upon the Alps; his "lingering" about till the guide and the rest of the party were forced to go ahead (6, 566 f.) may be reminiscent of the sensuality of restraint, as in "Nutting," but it seems likelier to betray misgiving in sensuality. The temptation to follow

> an invitation into space
> Boundless, or guide into eternity

has hardly been extirpated from his being, but somehow it has been defused and made suitable for a hearthside philosophy, enjoying but the homeliest of manifestations (13, 142-68). Not an *o altitudo* but the secret humanity of the mundane bears witness to his undying adventurousness. And thus the ascent of Mount Snowdon, instead of a triumph on the Alps. The man who cannot find his ultimate light will settle for a sunrise.

In relation to will, the thrust of the poem has been toward a rectification based on its evident failure, a cautionary effect Wordsworth reminds us of as late as the end of book 12, where the death of his father seems to him to have "corrected [his] desires." But there also has appeared a catalytic effect— the presence of the will to "power" or "trophies" precipitates

gains that otherwise seem not to come. It is, I think, in keeping with both tendencies—to need and withal to play down
the will as will—that the resolution of the poem and the ultimate restoration of Wordsworth's spirit develop in the
Snowdon episode. The rowboat episode gives us the will ex-
travagant, the Simplon-Como sequence the will acquisitive,
the Snowdon episode the will compensatory—to see the sun
rise seems a modest good for a man who has gone through
despair; and the bland, really neutral statement gives little
scope for egotistic purposes. It is just another excursion
("one of those"), on the face of it. If it takes on distinction,
it is in a negative way. The phrase, "westward took my way,
to see the sun/Rise, from the top of Snowdon" (14, 5–6) has
the smack of a viaticum; the enjambed stress on "rise" is
hardly enough to offset the ominous resonance of "westward."

The play of will in the Snowdon episode seems slighter
than it is because in fact the disjunction between purpose and
result which so wrenches Wordsworth in the rowboat and
Simplon-Como episodes does not occur. We forget, or blithely
ignore, the fact that Wordsworth again fails, this time to see
the sun rise, because the conversion from failure to success,
from the equivalent of *"we had crossed the Alps"* to "Imagination . . ." has a smooth physical continuity and is made—
in fact, not in logic—so plausible an unfolding of the possibilities of the climb. The conscious local aim, to see the sun rise,
has given way in a continuous line to the vital, permanent, if
also elusive, aim of the poem: for the poet to know and be
and express himself in a total life and universe.

It is necessary to stress, however, that the vocabulary of the
episode ("adventurous," "undiscouraged," and especially
"with eager pace and no less eager thoughts") specifically
recalls the will-oriented opening lines of the poem, and suggests the volitional atmosphere of the rowboat episode. The
basic will and drive of the actor operates even on this unpre-
possessing occasion. Its operation is reduced to a basic level
of self-preservation (as opposed to self-aggrandizement) in a
"wild place" on a forbidding night. The overtones of death in

the passage have already been mentioned, and may be noted again in this connection as Wordsworth resists (what in the rowboat episode he as it were insists on) the invitation of the mere earth: "With forehead bent/Earthward, as if in opposition set/Against an enemy" (14, 28-30). The impulse of aspiration, the will of life itself, is implicit in this quotation, resounding as it does with the terrible alienation of Wordsworth from the generous earth. It is the ultimate irony of the will that this night, so full of mystery and premonition, should yield full resolution for Wordsworth, where the open, towering promise of Mont Blanc yielded a dramatic letdown. Perhaps Wordsworth recognizes this; the emphasis on "chance" in the description (14, 34, 65) indicates as much, and is certainly unprecedented.

The action of the Snowdon passage displays that complex of elements that I have called idiosyncratically Wordsworthian: the ambiguous guide, mountain, water, effort, failure, revelation. Wordsworth is again *primed*, by a condition of the will, to receive what he wants, and hence what he gets, however surprising it may prove: "When at my feet the ground appeared to brighten . . . /. . . a light upon the turf/Fell like a flash, and lo! as I looked up/The Moon hung naked . . ." (14, 35-40). And what he gets, despite the element of surprise and the possible intimation of a Manichean order, is clearly total and one, without the cleavages in experience, in time, or in understanding that have marked earlier episodes. The baffling failure to tell things apart in book 4, in the passage that metaphorizes the rowboat episode, is resolved into a reality of recognition of how things interfuse among themselves:

> and at my feet
> Rested a silent sea of hoary mist.
> A hundred hills their dusky backs upheaved
> All over this still ocean; and beyond,
> Far, far beyond, the solid vapours stretched
> In headlands, tongues, and promontory shapes. . . .
> [14, 41-46]

By the same token the bemisted and bemusing abyss of book
6, in the Alps-climbing scene, is at once literalized and resolved
into intelligibility and communication, as the voice of the
waters is carried through the mist to be felt in the heavens.
All waters are one, all things between the waters and the sky
are one, the sky is one under the one "sovereign" Moon, and
on the other axis the Moon gazes on the ocean of mist and
seemingly heeds the anthem of the waters from their "fixed,
abysmal, gloomy breathing-place."

But even if the episode, and the poem, would appear here
at last to have removed itself from the will, kicking over the
stool from which it has soared into imagination, it is striking
that Wordsworth's explication preserves many terms of the
will:

> it appeared to me the type
> Of a majestic intellect, its *acts*
> And its possessions, what it has and *craves*,
> What in itself it is, and *would become*.
> [14, 66–69; italics added]

There is, also, a suggestive contrast between bending earth-
ward, as if in opposition to an enemy, and the scene resting
"at [his] feet." The former puts the man up against it, the
latter puts him in a position of receiving tacit obeisance from
nature. But he is no *dominus tyrannus*. Rather a mutuality of
lordship and dependency emerges in the numerous terms of
will that penetrate the passage. The idea of "mutual domination" (81) and "interchangeable supremacy" (85), as well as
phrases like "cannot choose but feel" (86) and "Willing to
work and to be wrought upon" (103) suggest a dimension of
will in the very modes of perception and conception of the
world. In the construction of the poem the very placement of
the Snowdon episode, giving metaphysical value precedence
over chronology as it does, must be seen as an act of will.
And yet it properly looks like a simple act of description.
The active, specifically purposive will is rectified, scaled
down, in *The Prelude*, but initiates and seasons vital episodes;
and the metaphysical will as it were supervenes, maintaining

the harmonious and fruitful contact between the absolute self and the absolute universe.

This position of mutuality—a Spanish sword affording a sharp advantage to the self and the other at once—strikes me as characteristic of Wordsworth, and stands up even in the face of the claims for individuality he makes in the peroration of *The Prelude*. Wordsworth writes:

> Here keepest thou [Man] in singleness thy state
> [14, 211]

and again he declares:

> The prime and vital principle is thine
> In the recesses of thy nature. . . .
> [14, 215-26]

But these utterances must invariably be measured against Wordsworth's fear of

> The tendency, too potent in itself,
> Of use and custom to bow down the soul
> Under a growing weight of vulgar sense,
> And substitute a universe of death
> For that which moves with light and life informed,
> Actual, divine, and true.[46]
> [14, 158-63]

For Wordsworth, as positive as he sounds, retains a sense of "the incumbent mystery of sense and soul" (14, 286), and while he leaves nature a "handmaid" with but a "secondary grace" (14, 260, 315), the mind recognizes, not invents or imposes, its intrinsic use. Wordsworth, a champion of the ontological will that is the "sentiment of Being" (2, 401), speaks of and for the indomitability of the spirited self. Of its *dominance*, in any sense of arbitrary freedom of encounter, he seems to offer little proof. Indeed, as Hartman says, he shied away from that dominance in the form of apocalypse. I have tried to indicate that he shied away from it as a form of unreality, and, quite apart from conspicuous traumata like the death of John Wordsworth, it is only necessary to remember

Raisley Calvert clearing "a passage" for Wordsworth so that his "stream / Flowed in the bent of Nature" to see that arbitrary freedom is not at issue. Calvert does not create the will, or the ability; those are given. But he removed a "hazard to the finer sense" and thus gave space for will and ability.

It is striking to see Wordsworth saying as much. He had withdrawn "unwillingly from France" when "a youth [Calvert] "

> in firm belief
> That by endowments not from me withheld
> Good might be furthered—in his last decay
> By a bequest sufficient for my needs
> *Enabled me to pause for choice*, and walk
> *At large and unrestrained*; nor damped too soon
> By mortal cares.
>   [14, 349-62; italics added]

Wordsworth's proclamation of the diviner "quality and fabric" of the mind includes a confession of the divinity of "this frame of things" and basically works less as a law than a gesture of faith, a formal postulation of the principle of the apprehending and willing self over against the solidified systems of education, social organization, or politics, or the emergent and liquid system of experiences. But that self, identifiable with the moon hanging splendid, sublime, and unique in the firmament, nevertheless is reached via the lower world, without which it shines on vacancy. And without ceasing to be a self it has clearly ceased to be arrogant or aggressive or singular: the growth of the poet's mind has given way to the recognition of the mind of man.

BLAKE'S *JERUSALEM*: A SELF WITHOUT SELFHOOD, A SYSTEM AGAINST SYSTEM

The cabalists make a distinction between the serpentine path of actuality and the straight projections of the intellectual will. Some accommodation between these two would seem to be a major object of *The Prelude*, and would seem to be claimed as a definite accomplishment by Wordsworth in the "Ode to Duty," especially in the cancelled stanza on "the second will more wise." This will is clearly that of reconciliation rather than projection, of acceptance rather than aspiration. It is a *retrospective* will, and so may seem mildly paradoxical, for the will ordinarily goes to the present or future. But the real problem with it lies not in its revision of the past (prayer in one of its dimensions has accustomed us to that) but in its disguising of local effect as general principle. That is to say the second will, however authentic it may be for the completed situation, in no way reduces the uncertainty of the case in progress. The Simplon letdown and the Snowdon epiphany are alike unpredictable, for Wordsworth's conviction of the divinity of man gives no guarantee of the terms of its manifestation. In this connection it is important to note that the relation between purposive acts and meandering actuality in *The Prelude*, while it pivots around the self, is less and less devoted to the ego (or, as Blake might say, the selfhood). For the self comes to operate as a medium or principle in the text, and not as an idol or goal.

This would seem an essentially abstract treatment of the self. What gives it special energy and immediacy is the dramatization of its coming about. By contrast, *The Excursion* presumes the state of abstraction and wearies us with its recitation of the conclusions and consequences of the will, rather than its vital economy and intrinsic action. Or again, "Hart-Leap Well," after *The Borderers* an unusual (almost Coleridgean) example of wilfulness carried near obsession, lacks the biographical articulation and spiritual depth that would make it penetrating, as well as striking. It is, in a sense, this very sophistication on the question of will in a poem like the "Ode to Duty" that takes hold in Wordsworth's later work and deprives it of the élan that marks the subject in *The Prelude*. Wordsworth seems to have come to talk in abstractions from knowledge, instead of talking materially of life. The material is canned, its sonorities imposing but no longer infectious.

At the same time the tendentiousness that marks Blake's

Jerusalem makes it clear that the open developmental mode of *The Prelude* is not the only way that the matter of will can be plausibly rendered in a romantic context. For Blake immediately, bluntly, and uncompromisingly gears this poem to the satisfaction of the will of Los. It is as though Wordsworth had, instead of settling for (and struggling with) his failure, infinitely delayed and variegated a passage to triumph for the boy in the rowboat episode. And yet, on deeper analysis, it becomes clear that the will of Los is more explicit only, and not more effectual, than that of the Wordsworthian actor. The conversion from biographical time to mythic time accounts for this explicitness, but it does not eliminate the complexities, indeed the perplexities, of the process of realization so notable in Wordsworth. In a sense these perplexities are intensified. The predetermination of the ultimate states makes their seeming unattainability the more frightful. The memory of ultimate states as real and proper makes their absence the more grievous. For while Wordsworth is sifting memory for a possible revelation, Blake is bending conscience to a necessary recovery. The paradox is then that the process in Wordsworth comes to seem so natural and inevitable in retrospect, while remaining in Blake so accidental and elusive in prospect.

This is mainly owing to the fact that the will of Los is a form of terror and is implicitly, in spite of its stated goal, as susceptible to outward influence and to self-doubt as any terror. But the terror is understandable enough. Once the mythic structure has made for the explicitness of goal already cited, the remoteness of the goal and the resistance it engenders generate a burden not really experienced in the Wordsworthian scheme till he is driven to give up "moral questions in despair." The analogous cry in *Jerusalem* occurs from the very outset in Los's "Yet why despair?" In like manner the furnace and the building of Golgonooza appear at once, and tendentiously, while the Snowdon ascent occurs by the way, and late, though centrally.

It will at once identify the enormity of Los's terror and

focus on the primary presence of the will in *Jerusalem* if we take the opportunity to compare the given situation with that of Pope's *Dunciad*, book 4. In *The Dunciad,* if we set aside the latent cautionary and hortatory influence of the satire, the action takes place in the brief moment as everything worthwhile tips over the precipice of Darkness and annihilation. This is precisely the moment which, on the face of it, the action of *Jerusalem* has reached. But while Pope submits us to the consummation of the moment, Blake invokes its breadth and power and engages us upon the necessity of escaping *and utterly reversing* it. The horror of the inevitable in Pope becomes the terror of the impossible in Blake. On the other hand, the elimination of the will in the face of inevitability in Pope is counterbalanced by its exaggeration in the face of impossibility in Blake. But the latter includes also an element of need, that is, an idealistic insistence on the return of a lost "remembered" perfection—as of childhood, though of course it substitutes for the nostalgia of biographical memory an elaborate reconstitution of mythical vision.

That substitution, of vision for memory, proves the basis for a complex confrontation of self and system in *Jerusalem*: complex because Blake in rejecting "selfhood" and "system" nevertheless idealizes a self and imagines a system that so interpenetrate as to be at once neither and both. Memory, in the form of obsessive canonizations of past occurrences, is the real form of the bugbear of selfhood in *Jerusalem*. And the real form of the bugbear of system is the interpretive logic of memory, the trap of necessity framed on an institutionalized reading of the remembered event. This is, in effect, a raising of information—the localized past—over nature, or the implication of universality:

Phantom of the over heated brain! shadow of immortality!
Seeking to keep my soul a victim to thy love! which binds
Man the enemy of man into deceitful friendships,
Jerusalem is not! her daughters are indefinite:

By demonstration, man alone can live, and not by faith.
My mountains are my own, and I will keep them to
    myself. . . .

[1, 4:24-29]

For it is not things (mountains) but being that belongs to
man, and whatever diminishes his being must be resisted.
Hence, at a basic level, the emphasis on will in Los, and on
the expression of the force of being defending and affirming
itself:

I labour day and night, I behold the soft affections
Condense beneath my hammer into forms of cruelty
But still I labour in hope, tho' still my tears flow down.
That he who will not defend Truth, may be compelld to
    defend
A Lie: that he may be snared and caught and snared and
    taken
That Enthusiasm and Life may not cease. . . .

[1, 9:26-31]

It is notable, too, that the Spectre of Urthona introduces
the idea of will into the relationship with Los, and seeks to
pervert or cancel that radical function of Los's being. The
speech that begins "Wilt thou still go on to destruction?"
makes this clear enough. The repeated "wilt thou" is more
than a future declarative, it is implicitly a charge of wilfulness
and works as a logic-chopping attack on the will of Los,
though it comes disguised as an argument for altering behavior which is presumably senseless, ignoble, and harmful
(1, 7). The response of Los makes no bones about the fact
that the will is the basic instrument of the "contention" between himself and the Spectre:

I know thy deceit & thy revenges, and unless thou desist
I will certainly create an eternal Hell for thee. Listen!
Be attentive! be obedient! Lo the Furnaces are ready to
    receive thee

I will break thee into shivers! & melt thee in the furnaces of
    death;
I will cast thee into forms of abhorrence & torment if thou
Desist not from thine own will, & obey not my stern
    command!

                                                    [1, 8:7-12]

But the explicitness of the will and its focus on persons
may suggest a contradictoriness that the poem does not at
first seem able to expel. For Los, the great champion of freedom and *caritas*, uses the Spectre coercively and without
mercy. It might even seem that he becomes a Lambro figure,
"stung . . . from a slave to an enslaver," and that he has
erected a principle of behavior to suit the situation: "I must
Create a System or be enslav'd by another Man's."

We may readily observe, however, that the Spectre is less a
separate identity (and therefore not to be coerced) than a negative or self-destructive possibility of Los's own nature. The
Spectre represents selfhood—good deeds measured by a strict
arithmetic of reciprocity, bitter suspicions of being used and
imputation of the meanest motives and conduct to others,
fear of being a laughingstock and dupe, vindictiveness, paranoid anxiety about the limits of knowledge, since one can
become a victim of ignorance (1, 7). And Los cannot be
guilty of dictating to a part of his constitution; the preservation of his more generous and more magnanimous self depends on his manipulation of his selfhood, just as the preservation of the romance world depends on Caliban's obedience.

A greater difficulty in the wilfulness of the position Los
takes resides in his creation of a system "to deliver Individuals
from . . . Systems." On the surface, surely, this has the same
tune as the kettle calling the pot black. The pity that leads
Los to oppose "the system" has seduced him into counter-
proposing only another system. The question has to be asked,
how is he different from Urizen? The answer ultimately is
given in the action of *Jerusalem*, but two clues may be identified right here. First, the paradox lies not in the system that

counters systems, but in the system that serves individuals. Thoroughgoing, conservative, monolithic: these are terms ordinarily associated with systems, and Blake is trying more to break the associations than to institute a state of atomic incoherence. The whole must hold together, but as versatile substance, not rigid form. That is why Blake's statement on system, in the positive sense Los adopts, stresses individualism and creativity: "*I* must *Create* a System. . . . *My* business is to *Create*" (italics added). In short, a new definition of system, as something responsive to the entirety as well as the individuality of creation, vital not mechanical, versatile not repetitious, is propounded by Los.

On the face of it, Los wills this unusual system. But how far, we may ask, can such a system be susceptible to will? As far, we may answer, as the domination of the Spectre and the construction of Golgonooza, a building which is at once the material-metaphorical embodiment of Los's ideal and a projective fantasy of perfection. Occurring this early in the poem, it sets a standard of expectancy, but also works as a measure of difficulty and loss. The architecture of Golgonooza—really its constitutive elements, for it has, significantly, no architecture—must be regarded as the product of a negotiation of Los with himself. But the deliverance of individuals, which is the ultimate form of Los's will, depends on a multiplicity of other negotiations[47] in which Los's part may be limited to the atmosphere of possibility generated by his will to perfection. His will continues in the poem, by and large, as a positive force of possibility, comparable to the force of the "willing" (and somewhat shadowy) Friends who "endur'd for Albion's sake . . . " (1, 19). But the realization of his will remains as subject to contingency as Wordsworth's.[48] The negotiations that give the poem the coherence of a slowly developing mosaic do not immediately answer to his will, and in the final analysis it may be that they are resolved by virtue of the poet's will; but this is a question to take up later.

These negotiations organize and focus the poem, and must be carefully followed for best understanding of its character.[49] They may have all the Blakean blatancy of a "dialectical" struggle of "mutually negating opposites,"[50] but they also exhibit the subtlest gradations of evolution, including a bewildered division among friends. It is not Los and the Spectre, but instead Albion and Los, or Albion and Vala and Jerusalem, who are involved in the most critical negotiations. Where they are concerned, realism contends with the reality of which it is properly a part, self-image with the ideal self; freedom shackles itself, and love and friendship deed themselves away. The colloquy of Vala, Jerusalem, and Albion which brings the first book to a close graphically illustrates the strangling involutions of the case. In particular the role of Albion must be scrutinized, for in it the pervasive, if subtle, function of the will and the interplay of self and system take shape.

Albion, briefly seen before as a brooding and skeptical logician (1, 4), emerges now as an important and dogmatizing Job: "I have no hope/Every boil upon my body is a separate and deadly Sin" (1, 21:3-4). Where the poem espouses pity, Albion opts for self-pity. Where it espouses forgiveness, he takes his stand on remorse. Vala seeks to move him, indirectly, by describing her plight and confusion (1, 22), a recapitulation in fact of the horrors with which the Spectre of Urthona had tried to unman Los. Vala is, of course, an ambiguous quantity, being at once "the lilly of Havilah" and a dangerously winsome agent of a limiting naturalism. In the present situation, though, she represents a degree of hope for a melancholic and inverted Albion. But Albion is wooden and curt in response:

I brought Love into light of day, to pride in chaste beauty
I brought Love into light & fancied Innocence is no more[.]
[1, 22:17-18]

We may readily note, even so, that Albion is passing a judgment on himself by invoking a strict interpretive scheme of action/motive/consequence: I brought/to pride/I brought . . . and Innocence is no more. In effect, he has willed the action joyously, according to one set of presumptions, and it has borne him abruptly into an area of consequence which argues another framework of rules. It is to adapt to the way of things that he repudiates his former ways. He seems to think that decency and the logic of survival demand it.

Jerusalem, however, goes beyond Vala's indirect effort to move Albion, and challenges him point-blank. She sees his position as a case of indulging a will to atomistic logic: "Why wilt thou number every little fiber of my Soul/Spreading them out before the Sun like stalks of flax to dry?" (1, 22: 20–21).

Albion responds in kind. With the issue of the will in the open, he makes the gesture which serves as a motif of decision and will in the poem; he "turnd his face toward Jerusalem." Inevitably we recall his turning *away* from the voice of the Savior at the outset of the poem, and instinctively we construe the change of direction as an index of hope. But Albion is frankly discountenancing Jerusalem and, as it proves, his very self, with a series of subjunctives that confess the limits of his power, not his will:

Hide thou Jerusalem in impalpable voidness, not to be
Touchd by the hand nor seen with the eye: O Jerusalem
Would thou wert not & that thy place might never be found
But come O Vala with knife & cup: drain my blood
To the last drop! then hide me in thy Scarlet Tabernacle. . . .
                                                                [1, 22:26–30]

He is soon more explicit about this will: "I came here with intention to annihilate thee!" (1, 23:3). Clearly he hopes, by annihilating her, to have done once and for all with the attributes of hers which he experiences in himself. This is a familiar psychic transference and delusive shortcut to a desired resolution. But the point is that, if Jerusalem were dead, she would have to be recreated or replaced by Albion, since his need for her to exist is no less real than her existence in itself. By the same token Albion would be recreated or replaced if he could truly annihilate himself. This, basically, is what Blake means when he speaks of states. Individuals exist intrinsically, but also representatively as constituents of the irreducible universe. Even while Albion denies and thwarts himself, he exists as memory and image for Los et al.

Jerusalem recognizes Albion's bent, and suffers under it, but also opposes it. She will not "hide . . . in impalpable voidness," nor let him—in pretentious sacrifice and sterile self-glorification—"hide" in Vala's Scarlet Tabernacle. Rather Jerusalem meets Albion squarely, maintaining both her temper and her attack. She identifies the will to death in Albion and places him in the most elaborate order of death-dealing, war, while at the same time presenting an alternative avenue of will which, at least momentarily, stirs his sense of possibilities other than death. The veil forgiveness weaves "with Wings of Cherubim" (1, 22:35) has put an imperfect effect on Albion's imagination, in that he conceives of a seductive "Veil" of nature—Vala's appeal—and not of Jerusalem's higher and purer state. Moreover, in proportion as this veil operates in his imagination to revive the appeal of "every ornament of perfection and every labour of love" (2, 28:1), it revives his sense of the consequences thereof ("Innocence is no more"). Thus his parting from Jerusalem at once declares the finality of his will never to err again and the logical necessity of continuing in a state we recognize as error:

> He felt that Love and Pity are the same; a soft repose!
> Inward complacency of Soul: a Self-annihilation!
>
> I have erred! I am ashamed! and *will* never return more:
> I have taught my children sacrifices of cruelty: what
>   shall I answer?
> I *will* hide it from Eternals! I *will* give myself for my
>   Children!
> Which way soever I turn, I behold Humanity and Pity!
>   [1, 23:14–19; italics added]

The upshot of this first negotiation is, on a subordinate level, an evidencing of Albion's susceptibility, and at the same time, more urgently, a hardening of his resistance to "every ornament of perfection and every labour of love." The will of Albion appears in a second phase of his turning away, now not from the Voice of the Saviour, which effectively, as an appeal to hearing, expresses a force outside of himself, but from "the Divine Vision" (2, 29), an implicit product of the collaboration between its existence and his apprehension of it. It is hardly accidental that the syntax of the lines suggests a causal relation between this aversion and the appearance of the Spectrous Chaos:

> Turning his back to the Divine Vision, his Spectrous
> Chaos before his face appeard: an Unformed Memory.[51]
>   [2, 29:1-2]

It is important to observe that things go counter to the will of Albion here, as well as in his bringing of Joy to light. He gets chaos when he wants the literal reduction of life—both personal and natural—to the ultimate metaphoric assurance of rock:

> All these ornaments are crimes; they are made by the
>   labours
> Of loves: of unnatural consanguinities and friendships
> Horrid to think of when enquired deeply into; and all
> These hills & valleys are accursed witnesses of Sin
> I therefore condense them into solid rocks, stedfast!
> A foundation and certainty and demonstrative truth:
> That Man be separate from Man, & here I plant my seat.
>   [2, 28:6-12]

But he embraces the contradiction of a confounded foundation sooner than "return again," that is, sooner than rectify his path and turn once more *in humility and love* toward the true Jerusalem. Accordingly, Vala may now broach him directly, repudiating Jerusalem and redefining the order of the world so that her command, "Know me now Albion: look upon me," seems a grace instead of a menace.

This is the brief but momentous negotiation (2, 29:25-

30:15) where the feminine will asserts itself over the masculine will—a perversion for Blake—and the masculine will can respond only with a mixture of reverence and named, but not understood, images of "eternal fear." The contradiction of rock-hardness by Chaos is complemented by another contradiction, of femininity supervening upon over-masculinity. Los, who hears "the contentions of Vala" with mounting agitation, sees the "Female Will" as a product of Albion's wilfulness: "O Albion, why *wilt* thou Create a Female Will?" (italics added).

In this way Los's relation to Albion changes, as he now sees the latter's condition as his intention and undertakes a negotiation of combined words and—what is new—overt action to bring Albion back to his true self. The idea of Albion's making a radical choice in turning away is repeated frequently (2,33:12-34:3, 34:7, 35:14, 38:15), and with it a positive appeal to turn back (34:30). Between these extremes the gesture of following (33:11, 34:10) first suggests a tutelary activity in Los and the shunned Saviour alike, and it is this tutelary activity that culminates in the desperate, ill-conceived, and self-doomed effort to hustle Albion to safety, as if a capture of his body were a recovery of his spirit. But the will is either free or false; the attempt to force the will of Albion cannot solve his problem, but does show, again, the explicit awareness that his problem resides in the will:

> *With one accord* in love sublime, &, as on Cherubs' wings
> They Albion surround with kindest violence to bear him
>   back
> Against his will thro' Los's Gate to Eden. . . .
>   . . . but Albion dark,
> Repugnant, rolld his Wheels backward into Non-Entity.
>   [2, 39:1-6; italics added]

The narrator advises us that the will must be essayed again, "in the day of Divine / Power" (2, 39:18-19). For now forcing seems to revert to following (39:20), but not without dramatic alterations springing directly from Los's "violence,"

which is proper as regards his own Spectre, but sinister in relation to Albion. The terms on which Los operates, and the
grounds on which he may meet Albion, have inevitably
changed, so that we must see the attempted "rape" of Albion
as a crisis in the pattern of negotiations we are following in
the poem.

Los has put himself in a most vulnerable position,[52] while
at the same time Albion's hand of resistance is strengthened
with an impulse of indignation and righteousness. It is as
though the impulse to violate Albion's will betrays a self-
violation in Los's own will, since Los grows "sick and terrified" when he returns to the Furnaces that have been his
mainstay and the expression of his will against destruction
and cannot face what they contain without the special intercession of "Divine Power" (42:1-8). And Albion, as though
sensing Los's discomfiture, attacks and makes unprecedented
demands of him (42:9-16). And it appears that the indefat-
igable Los, whose constant will has seemed to stave off ultimate destruction, has become an instrument for something
outside himself, even if that thing is Divine Vision. Without
"the Divine hand . . . upon him" (42:56), he seems unable to
stand. Is this then a shift toward a separate transcendent
power of divinity in the poem, a power that, though it inter-
cedes in the affairs of life, does not belong to life implicitly?
Is the will of Los a surrogate for Divine Power, and no substantive thing?

Perhaps the answer to these troubling questions is best approached by comparing Albion's response to the appeal of
Jerusalem, already discussed, with Los's response to the imminent threat of death. Albion hardens himself against the
appeal; Los, by implication at least, accepts the saving, vital
force. In effect, the irreducible vitality of Los's nature enters
into the efficacy of the Divine Power, just as the wilful rigidity
of Albion nullifies Jerusalem's virtue. The Divine Power, in
short, is not an independent, gratuitous agent, but a source—
half-spontaneous, half-induced—of Los's continued efforts on
behalf of perfection. When it seems, analytically, that Los

cannot go on, it proves, vitally, that he cannot give in. A will to life prevails over the deathliness of any of its moments.

It is not surprising in these terms to find that, while the Divine Vision remains conspicuous as a re-source, the action of the poem continues to rest with Los and Albion in the main, with special emphasis on the condition of will they sustain. In fact the action resumes, after the debate over "dominion" or conflict of wills, in such a way as to maintain the *presence* of the Divine Vision and at the same time the effectual activity of Los, once again "following Albion" (2, 44:20). The autumnal beauty of Vala which Albion so adores (2, 29:29-34), and which portends his consumption in death, must be contrasted here with the sunset light (2, 43:1-5) which creates the atmosphere for Los's continued endeavors *without portending night.* For Albion has given himself over to the mechanical succession of time, whereas Los has given himself to a fight against mechanical succession, against material time, in the knowledge that the true Albion is not subject to it. Jerusalem has shown the same perception in an early address to Albion:

Wherefore *hast thou shut* me into the winter of human life
And *clos'd up* the sweet regions of youth and virgin
   innocence,
Where *we live.* . . .

                   [1, 20:5-7; italics added]

Clearly the actions of "shutting" and "closing" represent Albion in terms of his fallen state and mechanical succession, and belong in a historical past, but the verb *live* addresses itself to the essential Albion, and occurs in an eternal present. Los's function, in this light, is to reveal the perpetual high noon, whose traces only appear in the time-bound sunset.

And Los, after the crisis of will in the Furnaces has been overcome, proceeds at once more lucidly and more variously with his work of salvation. His hectic, even monomaniacal labors no longer preoccupy him, nor does he merely follow Albion, as it were waiting to pounce. He invokes the Divine

Power (2, 44: 21 f., 46:9); and, being careful not to provoke Albion to "turn his back" explicitly again (2, 45:2), he seeks to discover Albion's disease from within, rather than curing it from without (2, 45:3 f.); and, perhaps most important of all, he begins to conceive of his role as more than a holding action, "hindering" destruction, and extends it into creative action, "persuading" the Sons of Albion to the right (2, 45:29-38).

And yet with awful suddenness, in spite of the superior scope and depth of Los's labors, Albion utters his *"last words Hope is banishd from me"* (2, 47:1). For Los has rectified his own will, without touching Albion's in its extremity. If the Saviour in receiving Albion "in the arms of tender mercy" and building him a "sublime . . . Couch of repose" (2, 48:1-5) is answering Los's prayer (46:9), it would seem a sentimental comfort, not an effectual one, with Albion apparently deceased. "Hope," it would seem, "is banishd" from the poem, and not only from Albion. This is the nadir of life in the poem.

But it remains a nadir, and is not an annihilation. Something at the root of life, we may infer, remains unaffected within Albion, who himself has lamented the fact that death and annihilation are not the same. And we note that, for all his scouring in the interior of Albion's bosom, Los has not reached "the interiors of Albion's fibres & nerves" (2, 46:4). Besides, intimations of resurrection occur in the scene following Albion's last words, and explicit mention of his "Eternal Individuality" carries word that his is no conventional death. The fact that he reposes on the Rock of Ages also associates him with quintessential (as opposed to merely actual) life, and redeems the idea of reducing all to deadened rock which he had made his refuge before. Erin's funereal oration (48:53 f.) presents both the consequences and an accurate rendition of the nature of Albion's "death": he is not in any significant way himself, his proper self is effectively dead. That oration also includes a prospectus of renewed perfection (49:65 f.), and a suggestion that "a Refuge can be found" (48:59). Albion, it would be fair to conclude, dwells in a world of death, and is not conventionally dead himself (like Blake, who professed to have "died several times since" birth). This proves to be the case as viewed by "those [enlightened ones] who disregard all Mortal Things" (3, 55:1). Albion resides among "the Dead," retaining "his awful Strength" but to no effective purpose. And it is paramount to see that the act of the merciful Savior in receiving Albion on the Rock of Ages is in a sense proleptic and *is not consummated* until Albion himself "fled" and "came to the Rock of Ages" and "took his Seat upon the Rock" (3, 57: 15-16).

But the direction of focus of the poem, now that its low point has been reached, clearly changes with plate 55, constituting a "reversal of perspective" which is distinct without being obtrusive.[53] Where attention has been largely devoted to the threat of destruction and the efforts—very vigorous but still negative in orientation—to stave it off, a positive emphasis now develops, as we begin to see what has been fought for, more than what has been fought against. In one sense the negative impulse, consummated in the peculiar death of Albion, is also exhausted there, and a sort of reaction expresses itself in the positive movement. But in a deeper vein, a lucid choice of what is positive is taking place, a choice that has been adumbrated by Los after *his* worst moment of dismal opportunism and force.

Nothing so effectively indicates the change in the poem's weave as the shift from the Sons to the Daughters of Albion as the motivic figures, at the midway point. A positive role for women, embryonic in the person of Jerusalem up to now, begins to emerge articulately, and a milder, more generous, almost more humorous temper can be discerned. It is a shift from an activist and attacking mode, headstrong and local in orientation, and preoccupied enough in the moment to become a little headlong, to a conservative, comprehensive mode, drawing on the nourishing *matrix* of the whole organism and aware that time is its instrument and ally, for the sap in winter recedes and concentrates without leaving the naked tree for dead. To use the metaphors of the poem itself, it is a shift from the mechanical austerity of the Furnace to the intimate grace of the Loom. The antiphonal exchange between Los and the Daughters of Albion (3, 56) seems meant to establish the values I am describing.

Los, to begin with, presents himself in a different light, pursuing a different, really a more feminine and fundamental, rather than aggressive and specific, course of action, though what he does has the same end in view: Albion must be restored. He is, proleptically, enlarging himself, readying himself for Enitharmon, and implicitly readying us for the reunion of Albion and Jerusalem. This is the dominant note of his utterance, and should check the centrifugal suggestion that he is indulging in some eighteenth-century sexist dogma. We must recognize irony in his opening sentences: "What may Man be? who can tell! But what may Woman be?/To have power over Man from Cradle to corruptible Grave" (3, 56: 3-4). But the irony is directed less at Woman than at the cliché conception of woman so far prevailing in the poem. By the same token, Los's apostrophe to Albion, "why didst thou a Female Will Create?" (3, 56:43), works counter to the ominous effect of the original form of the question (2, 30:31). It is a measure of how far both Los and the functional status of Woman have changed in the poem that, now, the presence and activity of the female will is associated with Albion's resurrection, with the loving faith of those who cannot accept this death of his:

> Look back into the Church Paul! Look! Three Women around
> The Cross! O Albion, why didst thou a Female Will Create?
> $$[56:42-43]$$

These are uneasy lines; indeed the entire passage calls for the most scrupulous weighing. Let me suggest, in line with the reading which recommends itself to me, that Blake is using the vitally hopeful image of the women around the cross to convey the complemental relation of man and woman in what he sees as the true church, in contradistinction to the antifeminism of "the Church Paul." This all but monoecious unison of man and woman was so in and from the beginning, if we "look back." Deep in the Church, in its background as it were, we can descry ("Look!") a complementary trinity of women. The momentous presence of woman at the birth and death of Christ entails the idea of her importance throughout. Her "power over" man (56:4) is not concrete but contributory, and is tempered by the evident irony of Los's view. Certainly the marks of this power are equally marks of service (56:7 f.), as will emerge in the course of this analysis. And it should be clear that the service is free and creative, though Los in addressing the Daughters echoes his speech to the Spectre of Urthona: "and/You must my dictate obey" (56: 30-31). The Daughters, however, obey from their "gold-beam'd Looms" (56:31) and their "response"—the word may suggest participation in a religious dialogue—reveals how precious their service is when the Eternal Man has become "subservient to the clods of the furrow!"

> We Women tremble at the light therefore: hiding fearful
> The Divine Vision with Curtain & Veil & fleshly Tabernacle.
>
> [56:35-40] [54]

The actual terms of the female will, at this juncture, involve nothing but beneficent service, summarized in the following lines:

> Entune: Daughters of Albion, your hymning Chorus mildly!
> Cord of affection thrilling extatic on the iron Reel:
> To the golden Loom of Love! to the moth-labour'd Woof
> A Garment and Cradle weaving for the infantine Terror:
> For fear; at entering the gate into our World of cruel
> Lamentation: it flee back & hide in Non-Entitys dark wild
> Where dwells the Spectre of Albion. . . .
>
> [56:11-17]

It is clear, by analogy, that Albion need not have so stub-

bornly "turnd away"—the equivalent of "flee back & hide"—
if he had availed himself of the unperverted female will. Its
natural cooperation and goodness can be inferred from the
difference between Los's commands to his Spectre (1, 8:9-15)
and his command to the Daughters of Albion. The latter,
though it uses the idiom of compulsion ("must my dictate
obey"), is couched in a context of banter and lilting music
which transforms it into a species of imperative appeal:

> I mind not your laugh, and your frown I not fear, and
> You must my dictate obey. . . .
>
> [56:30-31]

Here, in sum, is a negotiation of will predicated on graceful
respect and cooperation. It contains as well a prophecy of rectification of Albion's will, but the poem proceeds obliquely,
if not cagily, to that point. The radiating efficacy of this
negotiation immediately appears only in the way the Cities
change and seem active and purposive (3, 57:1-7).

It is not, then, a case of things in *Jerusalem* suddenly going
all the other way. The activity of Los, against extinction, gets
a needed qualification and enlargement, so that we feel its
positive prospects more definitely than before. At the same
time the situation of Albion hardens beyond the previous
evidence; it is the immediate effect of this hardening ("But
Albion fled from the Divine Vision," 57:12) that appears in
plate 58, which seems predominantly Urizenic on its face.
This extreme negative impression, we must note, is one that
the poem checks almost at once, with a new sense that good
may be fashioned out of evil (3, 59:2-7), and life born of
death:

> The Habitation of the Spectres of the Dead, & the Place
> Of Redemption & of awaking again into Eternity[.]
>
> [59:8-9]

Thus we should recognize still a continuing positive *idea*, even
in the teeth of apparent negation. There is presently a continuing positive *impulse* associated now with the Daughters
of Los, in the following chaste and poignantly lovely lines:

Endless their labour, with bitter food, void of sleep,
Tho hungry they labour: they rouze themselves anxious
Hour after hour labouring at the whirling Wheel
Many Wheels & as many lovely Daughters sit weeping

Yet the intoxicating delight that they take in their work
Obliterates every other evil; none pities their tears
Yet they regard not pity & they expect no one to pity
For they labour for life & love, regardless of any one
But the poor Spectres that they work for, always
    incessantly.

They are mockd, by every one that passes by, they regard
    not
They labour; & when their Wheels are broken by scorn &
    malice
They mend them sorrowing with many tears & afflictions.

[3, 59:30–41]

In effect the positive alternating so swiftly with the negative is put in confrontation with it; the battle is fully engaged, and a hopeful outcome grows more and more plausible.
Something like a pattern of such alternations begins to emerge
in the colloquy of the Divine Vision and Jerusalem (3, 60–62),
and with it a confirmation of the feminine precedence in the
initial work of recovery. Jerusalem, whom Albion's deathly
status affects even to her will ("Why wilt thou" recurs in the
description of her alienation), nevertheless keeps some orientation toward and obscure apprehension of the Divine Vision,
because she senses that her present false convictions are temporary and delusive. The promise of redemption receives
special emphasis with the insertion of plate 61 into the
text,[55] as Blake's version of the Joseph-Mary relationship
builds on the idea of the *felix culpa*:

if I were pure, never could I taste the sweets
Of the Forgiveness of Sins! if I were holy! I never could
    behold the tears
Of love! of him who loves me in the midst of his anger in
    furnace of fire.

[3, 61:11–13]

The passage further uses Jehovah's message to imply, beyond the forgiveness of sins, the unreality or delusiveness of sins; Jehovah reassures the agitated Joseph that Mary "is with Child by the Holy Ghost" (61:27).

The movement of alternation-as-confrontation culminates in plates 64, 65, and 66; here nothing is left but "to decide Two Worlds with a great decision, a World of Mercy and/A World of Justice, the World of Mercy for Salvation" (3, 65: 1-2). Not that the poem is rushing to a conclusion—its conclusion, as Frye remarks, is so gradual as to seem strangely imperceptible. But in fact this is proper and effective in a work whose linear narrative commitment—the visible progress of action—must defer to a radiant conceptual principle, namely, that individual cases (narration) pass within a permanent structure of states (principles). The action properly may not—cannot—end till the conception is complete, and so chapter 3 winds up, having set the battle raging (65:29), with an access of explanatory fervor that elaborates the content and value of the datum of action: "the Starry Heavens are fled from the mighty limbs of Albion" (75:27). But these lines also contain a crucial suggestion of the self-punishment, if not self-negation, of the destructive will (65:74-75, 66:38) and renew, in the midst of apparent negation, the idea of the creative role of the feminine in any true state of goodness (69:16 f.). In short, the momentum of redemption instituted in plate 55 is not exhausted, but disguised.

The ostensible concern with the destructive will (4, 80-82) paradoxically serves to bring out its self-weakness and, eventually, to confirm its inability to withstand absorption into the positive frame. Unexpected, but unsurprising, a sweet sobriety and chaste triumph inform the utterance of the formerly frantic Los:

Let Cambel and her Sisters sit within the Mundane Shell:
Forming the fluctuating Globe according to their will.
. . . sometimes the Earth shall roll in the Abyss & sometimes
Stand in the Center & sometimes stretch flat in the Expanse,
According to the will of the lovely Daughters of Albion. [56]

Sometimes it shall assimilate with mighty Golgonooza:
Touching its summits: & sometimes divided roll apart.
As a beautiful Veil so these Females shall fold & unfold,
According to their will the outside surface of the Earth
An outside shadowy Surface superadded to the real Surface
Which is unchangeable for ever & ever. . . .

                                                          [4, 83:33-48]

This declaration indicates not just a new knowledge, but a
new position toward knowledge, a new mood. Such details as
the wilfulness and secrecy and wandering of Jerusalem (4,
86:30, 32, 41) and Enitharmons perverse defiance (87:12-
88:21) become symptomatic of a temporary derangement,
where at the start of the poem they had represented a final
threat of destruction. Union is recalled by the very presence
of division: "Two Wills they had; Two Intellects: & not *as
in times of old*" (4, 86:61; italics added). In a sense the materiality which dominates the earlier part of the poem has abated
enough for the poem itself to escape the obsession of materiality; its metaphors (agents of materialization), whether of
furnace or loom, lose much of their insistence, and its faith
and will come securely to the fore. The "blow" and "swing"
—the material dimension—of Los's hammer are complemented
by its "force" (88:50), which I take to be a spiritual dimension involving purposive and expressive will, a sort of *en-
telechy*; as Los confesses, "I have tried to make friends by
corporeal gifts but have only /Made enemies: I never made
friends but by spiritual gifts." (91:15-16).

In these terms it is not necessary to have a graphic reversal
and resolution in the poem. *Jerusalem* is not geared to pursuing an action, but its action to exhibiting a complex condition of spirit. And in the terms of the poem this condition
—inherently conflictive between *and within* its representatives—cannot have a final resolution. The crucial factor is a
matter of mode or mood of vision, or what one makes ontologically of oneself and one's situation. The will, as I have
tried to bring out, enters vitally into the case. The poem involves not a position, but a disposition, which gradually

moves toward the affirmative, despite the constant presence of doubts and retardations.

The redemptive function of the Breath Divine (94-96) may
make it seem that arbitrary grace, rather than will, is responsible for the concluding affirmation. But in fact Albion is as
responsible for the salvation of the Breath Divine as the latter
for his. In a sense he even saves himself, as it turns out that
his will to save others manifests—is informed by—his will to a
creative self-restoration:

> Albion stood in terror: not for himself but for his Friend
> Divine, & Self was lost in the contemplation of faith
> And wonder at the Divine Mercy & at Los's sublime honour
>
> Do I sleep amidst danger to Friends? O my Cities &
>   Counties,
> Do you sleep? rouze up, rouze up! Eternal Death is abroad!
>
> So Albion spoke & threw himself into the Furnaces of
>   affliction
> All was a Vision, all a Dream: the Furnaces became
> Fountains of Living Waters. . . .

[4, 96:30-37]

The Empedoclean leap of Albion here does produce a salvation, because where selfhood is an evil, self-abnegation proves
a good. But as long as Albion's restitution means the coming
of Jerusalem, the consummation of the world's perfection, a
clash seems to arise between the chosen values of the poem
and the characters of the persons in it. The resolution seems
foreordained in an arbitrary way, within the terms of a conceptual preference, but the persons seem free and doubtful
and confused and perverse. In this regard the conflictive action comes to resemble an excrescence in relation to the radical conviction of inevitability in the visionary world. Indeed,
what we see in the poem as encounters of individual will
Blake expressly defines as an opposition of states. The poem,
gradually, emerges as a system of mutual responsibility and
influence even while it recommends two antisystematic free-

doms: freedom from institutional forms, and freedom to be authentically individuals.

It is something, though perhaps not enough, to be able to respond to this dilemma with a primary sense of an intense individual life in the persons of *Jerusalem*. Nor will it quite do to say that individuality petrifies into solipsism without the kind of communicativeness that makes for mutual responsibility and influence. The main thing to recognize is that the system Blake espouses arises out of the activity of individuals, and does not determine it. The states exist for individuals, who may occupy them in turn, being in no way categorically bound to states. As Blake puts it, mildly correcting a Johnsonian love of generality, "General Forms have their vitality in Particulars" (4, 91:29). This is the key idea of the fourth book, and it extends our grasp of Blake's renunciation of system by contrasting system not with anarchy but with life (vitality). Systems that work by imposition, as dead weight crushing individuals to a uniform shape and station, will not get by Blake, who refuses to mistake a formal similarity for natural coherence. The latter bears witness to the vitality of individuals, and graces general forms, whereas the former overbears individuals and disfigures life. Individuals, then, are not illustrations or even representatives of a system they may belong in. Rather the system belongs to them, and they are its substantiation.

In the final analysis, the problem generated by *Jerusalem* revolves not around the relation of system and individual in the poem, but around the poem's "particular" system and the reader's frame of reference. For the poem, though it so massively alludes to social, historical, and political figures and events and ways, yields exceedingly little to them. Its business is to realize a point where "all was a Vision, all a Dream," and for those who do not consort with such a universe, or even enter upon it by speculation, Blake's portrayal of it as *olim et futurus* must create a sense of the anomaly of imagination masquerading as history, and "Visionary forms dramatic" (4, 98:28) as original historical entities. Blake is of course merrily candid about this; for he is for imagination as truth, not memory and natural discovery.

It would seem to follow from such an orientation that history is *ideally* for Blake a form of prayer or mystical invocation, and *actually* a form of degeneration. Whether it is necessary, or fitting, to object to that view need not concern us here; it may be a red herring in any case. Blake differs from the typical developer of a golden-age myth in his insistence on its inward reality, and thus proves invulnerable to the usual form of the objection. He is not asking us to remember and adore an ideal time, but to realize *this* as the ideal time bedaubed and bedevilled *almost* beyond recognition. The underlying will in the poem is focused then on the achievement of a quasi-Platonic reality in the face of an obscuring actuality.

The net effect, I would suggest, is to involve the poem deeply in the problematics of Blake's faith in art. We take that faith for granted,[57] as at first blush Blake himself seems to do. But it ought not to be taken for granted. The nineteenth century increasingly explored and was bewildered in the faith in art; and Los, verging on "despair," cryptically anticipates that difficulty before Albion gives him distracting or attractive work. Even apart from this, though, Blake poses the peculiar problem of one who, seeking to define the world, seems to opt for art. Thus we need to ask whether this led him to a consummate or a tendentious view of the world. In truth, it may be argued, he is the one with the need to face the question. This he does not do. By a self-justifying and self-fulfilling set of resolutions, he may make it seem that art will do, that Los is a version or a *virtus* of Albion. But the more successful his work, the more urgent is the question whether we are seeing the world of his art—sheer self-enclosed virtuosity—or the world through his art. To the extent that the art takes up the world to reconstitute it, the relation of one to the other falls into a troublesome imbalance. The poem, for all its urgency and force, runs the danger of succumbing to the pull of what seems physically a lesser body, the poet in the poem. He is an enigmatic figure—he is dedicated, righteous, inspired, but is it all merely subjective expression, tinged with an uncertain compulsion, and if not, what are the grounds of his authority outside of our willingness to indulge him? This enigmatic figure calls us to himself as much as to a vision that may be vouchsafed him, and ultimately makes himself the cause, and not just the medium, of the poem's action. With a sudden, and strange, access of knowledge of what is *outside* the poem, Enitharmon inside it notes that "the Poets Song draws to its period" (92:8), occasioning the suspicion that this matters more to how things get resolved than internal logic and movement.

No one wishes to challenge Blake's right to assert his status as creator or his faith in art. The foregoing comments tend rather to call attention to an issue implicit in his creative assertion, namely, the way the will of the actors in the poem extends to the will, the arbitrary will, of the poet, or the way the poem may serve to manifest the poet's will to art as an independent construct. Such independence, the merits of which are not to be gainsaid, entails a certain defect and isolation for any work, since the more a work is about itself the less it is likely to have about it of the power to sense, catch, crystallize, illumine, penetrate, measure, and convey the moving forms and meanings of things. Art is a secondary enterprise;[58] to strive to be primary is its arrogance and attenuation. Blake is probably not trying to make it primary, but the terms of his vision and his role in *Jerusalem* raise the spectre of this problem.

It is a problem of some moment for romanticism. None of the major poets was impervious to the lure of an arbitrary creativity and peculiar domain. Indeed it is almost a mark of the gathering force of romanticism that poets of the later eighteenth century begin to bend toward arbitrary self-determination in art, as Collins's "Ode on the Poetical Character" clearly shows. What I term the will to art—the deliberate fabrication of a world over against the world, the deliberate pursuit of the sort of sway over an audience which later gives rise to the Paterian axiom that all art aspires to the condition of music, autonomy, and irresistibility—this will to art develops decisively as a condition of romanticism, and needs to be deeply explored. Its occurrence is not naive, but conscious and indeed controversial, in that it proves subject to rebuttal by the propositions of actuality. If we may put this in terms of smaller categories than self and system, the issue becomes one of the play for dominance between subject and object. A poem thus may entail a problematical relation between expressive and mimetic modes[59] *existing simultaneously*. The problems of that relation will be the primary focus of attention in the ensuing pages, dealing first with the will to art in Keats, as the outstanding exemplar of this position, and then with the will to art in English romanticism at large.

3

THE WILL TO ART

Poetry is not like reasoning, a power to be exerted according to the determination of the will.

Shelley

She [the sonnet, the Muse] will be bound with garlands of her own.

Keats

With me poetry has been not a purpose, but a passion; and the passions should be held in reverence: they must not—they cannot at will be excited.

Poe

It is of use to conceive of romanticism not as embodying expressive modes of aesthetics, but as exhibiting a new and paradoxical tendency toward such modes. For this tendency is in itself incapable of being direct and pure. As it appears it conveys and subsists in a version of awareness that, while not perhaps reaching the ultimate stage of mimesis where a known character and condition and world are imaged forth in lucid and telling ways, nevertheless makes a basic claim to accuracy and justice and truth. The chief difference between mimesis and expression, between the mirror and the lamp, lies not in the origin of the image; in either case, let us recall, the content of what is presented is somehow *there*.

The classical view holds that it is possible to imitate nature, or to imitate Homer, who unmistakably imitated nature. Hence the rubric, "What oft was thought," implies a preexistent awareness, and "well expressed" presumes only a rhetorical setting forth of same. But Keats, though opposed to any straining after verbal or conceptual singularity, still removes himself from the Popean view. For him the poet's idea should only *seem as if* it had held a place in the reader's mind all along. This position is also maintained by Schopenhauer where he (1) cries out against the "impossibility and absurdity" of the assumption that "Shakespeare, for example, noted, and then reproduced from his own experience of life, the innumerable and varied characters of his dramas," but at the same time (2) insists on a certain creative fidelity to experience: "It is obvious that the man of genius produces the works of poetic art only by an anticipation of what is characteristic." Schopenhauer is denying at least the simplest version of mimesis without surrendering something that is *as it were* mimesis, "a prophetic anticipation of the beautiful."[1] In other words, what begins as individual and unprecedented apprehension develops, in retrospect, into common recognition.

This point is also plainly set forth by Coleridge in *Biographia Literaria*:

> On the *immediate*, which dwells in every man, and on the original intuition, or absolute affirmation of it, (which is likewise in every man, but does not in every man rise to consciousness) all the *certainty* of our knowledge depends; and this becomes intelligible to no man by the ministry of mere words from without. [1:168; italics added]

What Coleridge and Schopenhauer are getting at here contains the essential character and operation of the expressive mode, which makes general and overt what may at first seem tacit and peculiar.

On this reading the significant difference between mimesis and expression lies in the degree of light surrounding the image, its public versus its peculiar status at first encounter *only*; the lamp reveals to the holder what he is turn reveals to others. Keats puts it well when he says that "poetry should *surprise*," but with the restriction that it do so "by a fine excess and not by Singularity—it should *strike the Reader* as a wording of his own highest thoughts, and *appear almost* a Remembrance"[2] (italics added). What we find in fact in romanticism is a compromise, if not a compromising relationship, between expressive and mimetic modes. If we take the former to exist typically in prophecy, the latter in any effort to catch the given terms of the world, we will be obliged to accept a blurring line of distinction, as prophecy moves to secure for itself the status of true representation, or mimesis.

This is apparent enough in Blake's *Jerusalem* or *Milton* and in Shelley's *Prometheus Unbound*, the foremost prophecies of the romantic era. But the basic gesture of converting the peculiar into the normative offers itself with jewellike delicacy and definition in a smaller poem, Wordsworth's "She Dwelt Among the Untrodden Ways." Here Wordsworth pits against the whole fashionable world and a cynosure beauty surrounded with praise and love—against the standard mirror world, in short—the maid "whom there were none to praise / And very few to love." No one even suspects her existence, and *hence*, as the poem's logic proves, she is neglected. But it is a logic of metaphor and conviction, not of carefully staged analysis. Elliptical, ejaculatory, the images of the second stanza are images of bringing to light what had been out-of-the-way beauty ("a violet by a mossy stone")[3] and one unjustly neglected ("a star / When only one is shining"). They function in a revelatory manner, equivalent to the lamp, and tend to convert the reader from smug neglect to poignant appreciation, thus by implication converting common perception to revelation, mirror into lamp. The ostensible isolation of the girl and of the speaker—"And oh! the difference to me"—implicitly gives way to a new creative, rather than habitual, community of response. The lamp, as the mirror cannot, belongs to the holder, so that the scene is in a sense his. Still, what it discloses it also publicizes, or makes into common property.

We may go further and say that the lamp seeks to publicize, the expressive artist to popularize, what begins in singular vision. And yet the temptation of singularity—freedom from the constraints of community, a giddy autonomy and sense of the self as the world, or as taking its measure— exercised a profound force in the romantic spirit. The growth of humor and the countenancing of eccentricity, documented by Tave in *The Amiable Humorist*, may be taken as signs of this force. Its chief manifestation is not, however, in social terms; rather it occurs in the realm of art where a dissolution of genres and conventions, occurring in spite of Dr. Johnson's efforts to supply a conservative cement, led to two paradoxical effects: (1) it put an unusual burden of communication on the artist, who had, as Pierre Vitoux says of Keats, the "perilous responsibility of having more to invent and less to adapt";[4] and (2) it gave the artist, if he renounced or circumvented that burden, unprecedented license in creation. The interchangeable freedom and burden of the romantic position are written into the Preface to the second edition of *Lyrical Ballads* (themselves an instance of generic dissolution) and are formally declared in Wordsworth's later axiom that "the poet must create the taste by which he is to be relished."

The temptation of licentious creativity was strong enough to draw in writers as diverse in method as Byron and Wordsworth. In *The Prelude* Wordsworth, attributing it to "some rash Muse's earnest call," associates it with the first conscious cultivation of the "poetic faculty" (8, 365-425), and again with a reaction against the despair of the French Revolution (11, 461-70). In *Childe Harold* Byron also strikingly associates the temptation of singularity with the first access of poetry and with a reaction against grief and despair in human experience (canto 4, 3-6). We may note at least a wry criticism in the fact that inexperience or unbearable experience seems to account for the temptation in both poets. But it would be just to see its provocation, not its explanation, in this. If singularity in art were only a spontaneous manifestation in the novice, or only a conditioned, tendentious sign in a maturer man, perhaps it could be written off with despatch. But it is both spontaneous and conditioned, existing in the poet and in the experience of poetry, and so takes on a more considerable standing. He who can expatiate on it must have known what it is to be seduced by a vanity of singularity. But a perverse virtue appears in that seduction; not to know it is to know only the conventional. The only escape from the dilemma would come from validating or domesticating singularity, by showing its secret presence in humanity at large. In short, the problem of how to get away with an impulse to singularity, which makes for a manipulative aesthetics in romanticism,[5] is compounded by an opposite impulse in a centripetal direction, and the integration of the two conflicting impulses becomes a key issue for the romantic artist.

This, it may be stressed, is a conscious problem. Chatterton's forgery may reasonably be regarded as one solution, with its ingenious invention of a self and a community at one and the same time. And Wordsworth's sense of Chatterton—it is a patent projection of his sense of himself—in "Resolution and Independence" gives a clear picture through all its agitation of the way the will informs an artistic singularity. The artist wills his world in the face of the world, and wills his vision onto the world—this is the gist of the poem in its aesthetic phase, before the Leech-gatherer, hardly a helpless or passive man, asserts his independence and substance and raises the poem and the poet alike to practical philosophy. But this desire for arbitrary creativity, the desire to manipulate the matter of the world, reducing man himself to matter, still appears elsewhere in Wordsworth's work; a salient example has already been noted in *The Prelude*, book 8, 365-425.

What, then, accounts for the potency of the aesthetics of singularity? For one thing, the fact that it gives intimation of ultimate power, as Los shows in Blake's *Jerusalem*; but perhaps also the fact that it gives the occasion for overcoming ultimate danger, such as Shelley reveals in the fate of the poet in *Alastor*. In either case it is possible to recognize a radical new application of the aesthetic mode, one in which the object is not fine contemplation of the way of things but experience of superiority to their flux. It is no wonder that

Schopenhauer, in *The World as Will and Representation*, put aesthetics effectively on a par with sanctity as a source of transcending nature in its filminess and mortality. What the romantics did, going one step further with this notion of Schopenhauer's, was to look for a source of transcendence not just in the aesthetic object, but in the aesthetic act.

KEATS AND THE AESTHETICS OF REDEMPTION

Nowhere is this radical investment in aesthetic activity more apparent than in the work of Keats. The proportion of his poems that deals with poetry is unusually high, and seems scarcely to diminish as his powers grow. To the contrary, there is an increase, in complexity and depth, as poetry is asked or seen to do more and more. The new aesthetics runs its gamut in his work, from a heady autonomy ("Ode to Psyche") to an escapism that hints of thwarted power (*Sleep and Poetry*) and another that hints of thanatopsis ("Ode to a Nightingale"), to a personal perfection (*Endymion*) and an impersonal one ("Ode on a Grecian Urn"), to self-destructiveness (*Lamia*) to vision-as-representation (*The Fall of Hyperion*) to an ultimate lucidity of practical philosophy, where aesthetics and actuality ultimately fuse ("To Autumn").

It should not surprise us to find it so. Keats, more than any other romantic, willed himself to become a poet, in the sense that the primary will and engagement of his being was to turn quintessential poet,[6] and the gestalt of the poetic vocation— the things it is possible or obligatory to have in hand without scandal—included all the aforementioned possibilities. It does not seem that Keats amplified or revised the terms of being a poet, as, for example, did, Wordsworth, but it is his distinction that he engaged those terms more purely and persistently than any.[7] This engagement begins at once, and is at once (at least cryptically) complex. The poem "To George Felton Mathew" (1815) first announces the will and at once the ineffectiveness of the will in face of the world:

> . . . *fain would I* follow thee
> Past each horizon of fine poesy;
> . . . .
> But 'tis impossible; far different cares
> Beckon me sternly from soft "Lydian airs,"
> And hold my faculties . . . *in thrall.* . . .
>   [11–19; italics added]

It turns out, too, that poetry in the person of the muse has a will of its own, expressed through a necessary *locus*; thus even if the poet could cultivate his art, he would need to find another field:

> But might I now each passing moment give
> To the coy muse, with me she would not live
> In this dark city, nor would condescend
> 'Mid contradictions her delights to lend.
> Should e'er the fine-eyed maid to me be kind,
> Ah! surely it must be whene'er I find
> Some flowery spot, sequester'd, wild, romantic. . . .
>   [31–37]

At this stage, it is clear, Keats is aiming toward occupancy of a poetic place rather than command of a poetic state, as though the genius of the place would become his by osmosis. At any rate, something outside of himself, whether that something be Mathew himself (53) on the strength of his mute, if glorious, endowments (74 f.), or the "incitements" of the literary past (55–73),[8] seems indispensable for his purpose. The existence of the poem proves the human capacity to make a compensatory aesthetics of deprivation, but the intention of the poet is to draw on the primary power of aesthetics; and as long as he fails to do so he produces a consolatory, not a consummate, poetry. The will to art is baffled, because the would-be poet knows the locus of poetry and even some of its inhabitants, but only so much of its nature as to be able to say it includes the "gloomy" with the "bloomy". The weak rhyme and the prettified natural image hardly invite praise. The poet, whose will now defines him more graphically than his power, knows better than he *does*, and can fall back on nothing more than a candid cry for help, from Mathew or a landscape or a literary background. His will needs to borrow enabling power for its own sake, but also paradoxically at some sacrifice of its autonomy. On the other hand, it is inhibited in its usual setting—*in thrall*—and is making a sacrifice for freedom in poetry, not a sacrifice of freedom for poetry. His is not a Faustian bargain.

Much the same syndrome of relations occurs again in *Sleep and Poetry*: a will to poetry as paramount for the self-image, with that will dependent for realization on something singular outside, and also subject to a crippling influence of circumstances. But significant changes also occur. We see at once that the tentative eagerness of the earlier "fain would I" has modulated into a veritable fiat: "so I may do the deed/That my own soul has to itself decreed" (97–98). This is in fact a cardinal change, in that the will comes under its own domination; the quasi-reflexive verb, "to itself decreed," makes the seesaw position of the speaker quite clear. In like manner, the use of the verb "overwhelm" suggests both victimization and victory. In lines 61–62, "if I can bear/The overwhelming sweets," a finite and perhaps dubious capacity for poetry is confessed; the speaker may not be able to cope with poetry, which may prove too much of a good for him. But in lines 96–97, "O for ten years, that I may overwhelm/Myself in poesy," he intends and achieves the overwhelming, and remains on top of himself. This overwhelming is a form of fulfillment, but it occurs at best only in a cryptic vein. The position grows clearer near the end of the poem as Keats, facing the formidable challenge of his limitations as poet, accepts these limitations as a form of opportunity and motivation, and thus makes them a source of liberation and self-growth:

> though no great minist'ring reason sorts
> Out of the dark mysteries of human souls

> To clear conceiving: yet there ever rolls
> A vast idea[9] before me, and I glean
> Therefrom my liberty; thence too I've seen
> The end and aim of Poesy.
>
> [288-93]

In effect, Keats's experience of the way to poetry, and therefore his conception of poetry, is evolving into complex patterns and depths. We note at once here that more than sensuous pleasure and luxurious scenery are involved. An intellectual and indeed an epiphanic and celebratory force emerges in his present vision:

> Sometimes [poetry] gives a glory to the voice,
> And from the heart up-springs, rejoice! rejoice!
> Sounds which will reach the Framer of all things,
> And die away in ardent mutterings.
>
> [37-40]

This is a basic human response (41-46) raised to articulate power in the poet. And it is striking that Keats's praise of sleep is in part predicated on its refreshing the capacity to make this lucid and holy response:

> Most happy listener![10] when the morning blesses
> Thee for enlivening all the cheerful eyes
> That glance so brightly at the new sun-rise.
>
> [16-18]

It becomes clear that Keats is beginning to find poetry in fundamental experience. If he still clings to the exotic (63 f.), it too is growing articulate and serves as the source, but not the cause, of the verse that makes us "ever wonder how, and whence/It came" (70-71). Again, something of the exotic persists even into the visitation of the charioteer, following the recapitulation, in all its stubborn sensuousness, of the merely glamorous stage of poetry (101f.). But the dominant concern of the charioteer passage is with consciousness and will. The charioteer—as artificer he is Daedalus, as messenger,

Mercury[11]—reminds us of the usual heavenward life toward
which both sleep and poetry direct themselves; and, more, he
becomes the immediate cause of an evolution and elevation
in Keats's view of poetry: "*for* lo! I see afar" (125; italics
added). There is little need to comment on the change from a
closing, almost an arrested, luxury in the first stage of poetry
("In the recesses of a pearly shell") as compared with the activity and expanse of the charioteer lines; but it is well to
note that the expansion involves not just moral value ("nobler
life") but also moral choice ("I must").

No doubt a feeling of difficulty enters into this "must." It
reflects the transitional situation, rather than an inward reluctance. Even the charioteer seems to experience ambivalence
and difficulty in the "glorious fear" with which he acts. What
determines the quality of the occasion is the fact that the sun,
looked *to* earlier, here seems to look *on* and enhance the developing scene:

> and now with sprightly
> Wheel downward come they into fresher skies,
> Tipt round with *silver* from the bright sun's *eyes*.
>   [130–32; italics added]

Finally, too, since the enlarging motion of the scene entails a
certain transience, the relation of the aspiring poet to the charioteer resolves itself explicitly into one of the will and commitment:

> but I will strive
> Against all doubtings, and will keep alive
> The thought of that same chariot. . . .
>   [159–61]

This will is tested, of course, by the sheer magnitude of its
undertaking. But to make another, easier choice proves "impossible!/Impossible!" (311–12). Difficulty only confirms
the will and is presently itself forgotten as the new day—and
a new spirit—exhibits itself. Here Keats shows a jubilant will,

and one ultimately independent of its earlier stimulus, sleep
(he has had a "sleepless night"):

> ... the morning light
> Surprised me even from a sleepless night;
> And up I rose refreshed, and glad, and gay,
> *Resolving* to begin *that very day*
> These lines. . . .
>
> [399–403; italics added]

Perhaps indeed this jubilance of resolution is independent
also of the sun, and lies within itself and in its end, "these
lines" that in retrospect deal not primarily with the obstacles
to poetry, but with its indomitability in the face of obstacles.

It cannot be too strongly stressed that Keats's development
of the idea of poetry, his development as a poet, is bound to
the occasions of his will. The exhibited will is the informing
activity of a work like *Sleep and Poetry*, though a pattern of
artistic growth appears as the prevailing subject. The poem
proves an essay in the will as much as an exercise of a budding
art. The letter to Hessey in which Keats speaks of beginning
"to get a little acquainted with [his] own strength and weakness" makes it clear that the character of the poet counts
heavily in the expression of his gifts. He is speaking of *Endymion*:

Had I been nervous about its being a perfect piece . . . &
trembled over every page, it would not have been written. . . .
I will write independantly [*sic*] —I have written independently
without Judgment—I may write independently, & *with
Judgment* hereafter.—The Genius of Poetry must work out
its own salvation in a man. . . . I would sooner fail than
not be among the greatest.[12]

The qualifying force of "may write" is not to be blinked
here; and the concession to secret, if not naturalistic, growth
must be recognized in the statement, "The Genius of Poetry
must work out its own salvation." But no doubt remains that

Keats *"will* write independently," or that he *"would* . . . be among the greatest" (italics added). And ultimately this will is sure enough of itself:

> *When* every childish fashion
> Has vanish'd from my rhyme,
> Will I, grey gone in passion,
> Leave to an after-time
>   Hymning and Harmony,
> Of thee and of thy works, and of thy life;
> But vain is now the burning and the strife;
> Pangs are in vain, *until* I grow high-rife
>   With old Philosophy,
> And mad with glimpses of futurity.
>   ["On Seeing a Lock of Milton's Hair,"
>   lines 23–32; italics added]

The chiasmic relation between "old" and "futurity," on the one hand, and "Philosophy" and "mad" on the other helps to reveal the complexity of Keats's assurance. What is to come about in the fullness of time ("when," "until") would appear to depersonalize the individual with the immemorial wisdom of old philosophy, and in another respect to disestablish his being by pitching him into the anarchy of madness and the insubstantiality of the future. But these are effects of a falsifying separation of states, as well as falsely implying in the speaker a merely momentary intoxication ("high-rife," "mad") with overtones of passivity, or at least of being overcome. Keats's resistance to being overcome has already been brought out; it will appear again, graphically, in *The Fall of Hyperion*. Let us only observe that it is very much present here. Keats is no chance victim of philosophy or futurity; rather they are his targets, objects of his aspiration and his will. And the intoxication of the lines is both planned and logical, since he avoids the extreme dangers of depersonalization or disestablishment by pitting them against each other and inventing a *tertium quid*. He will be privy to philosophy and futurity at one and the same time, just as in the final stanza of the poem he is both "temperate" and "hot and flush'd." By combining philosophy and futurity in himself he is to become complete and free from either bias or defect.

Though by itself "On Seeing a Lock of Milton's Hair" cannot stand among the most accomplished of Keats's poems, it has long been recognized as pivotal in his *conscious* development as a poet.[13] But this development is usually seen to have an intellectual bearing. Even if *intellectual* admits of a broad humanistic interpretation, involving a riper and deeper understanding of human experience as well as a fuller grasp of books, much more is involved than the word can convey. The intensity of the attributives "high-rife" and "mad" at once warns us away from putting a purely intellectual construction on the lines. Their true focus is on the fusion of philosophy and futurity in what Keats intends for himself, and the fact of intention counts for as much as its content.

Keats, in sum, is imagining and willing a power of wisdom and prophecy. These are the powers he has to reconcile within the structure of *The Fall of Hyperion*, his most ambitious poem and the fullest statement he makes concerning his idea *and his experience* of himself as poet. Thus "On Seeing a Lock of Milton's Hair" takes on a critical position in the long view of Keats's career, representing the first substantive articulation of his will to poetry. It should not seem strained to contrast this small poem, to its advantage, with the more imposing show of *Sleep and Poetry*. For coming to acknowledge that one can be "high-rife with old Philosophy" is a way of correcting the denunciation of Boileau and preparing for the incorporation of Dryden, at least, into the pantheon-arsenal of authors through whom Keats will consummate and secure his own poetic position. And even "glimpses of futurity," by the same token, involve a quantum gain over the obscure and baffled excitement of the charioteer episode. Finally, to have overcome the facile opposition between Boileau and the charioteer, or between the worlds they represent, enlarges at once Keats's receptivity and his opportunity as a poet.

The question that remains, given this most articulate and

cogent promise to himself as poet, is whether it can be brought to reality. Without at all implying that Keats recognized the critical status of "On Seeing a Lock of Milton's Hair" and acted accordingly, we may observe that, though his poetic vocation was far from unruffled, nowhere after this poem does he write its sort of pre-tending poem about poetry. The sonnet "To Spenser" describes a delay of the act of poetry according to an unpropitious—winter—season, but it also confidently forecasts and wills the undertaking of poetry in due time:

> Be with me in the summer days, and I
> Will for thine [Spenser's] honour and his [Leigh
>   Hunt's] pleasure try.

Here the exigencies of rhythm no doubt play a part in the separation of the future auxiliary, *will*, from the main verb, *try*, but the setting off of *will* gives it a suggestive volitional force that can hardly be ignored. And "What the Thrush Said" reinforces the idea of an almost spontaneously prolific time, holding out a promise of good that carries consolation and assurance reminiscent of Christian parable:

> O Thou whose face hath felt the Winter's wind,
> Whose eye has seen the snow-clouds hung in mist,
> And the black elm tops 'mong freezing stars,
> To thee the spring will be a harvest-time.
> O thou whose only book has been the light
> Of supreme darkness, which thou feddest on
> Night after night, when Phoebus was away!
> To thee the Spring shall be a triple morn.
> O fret not after knowledge—I have none,
> And yet my song comes native with the warmth.

It is striking that these lines make little of knowledge as such—the answer to Keats's aspiration, as already suggested, lies elsewhere. Of more direct importance is the answer implied in what the thrush says. It is a naturalistic answer on the face of it: in due season, in the ordained course of things, growth and increase and fruitfulness come about. Is Keats's poetry but an aesthetic version of the genetically set organic pattern? Not, perhaps, if we put proper emphasis on the evocation of the birds-of-the-air and the lilies-of-the-field inherent in the lines. For this evocation does more than merely shift from an organic to a providential routine, either of which would leave the thrush-poet in a passive position. Rather, in place of a definite *action* it establishes an *act* of faith or purpose, with the sense that specific recourses may count less toward our objectives than the orientation of our inner being. The thrush in this respect offers himself as complex analog, not a simple model, for the poet. The "light/Of supreme darkness" is something the thrush can be aware of in the poet without ever experiencing in itself, just as to feed on that light, or that darkness, is beyond the thrush in fact. The intricate movement from oxymoron—light of darkness—to synaesthesia—feeding on light or darkness—is rhetoric for the thrush, truth for the poet. Thus the promise of harvest-time contains a cryptic reminder that the poet has sown viable seed, and now that action must be complemented with an act of faith. In like manner the promise of the triple morn is aimed at the poet's spirit, not his eyes; even his darkness, the thrush advises, has its eventual dawn; and it is such dawn as only the transcendentalist Thoreau can match with his conception of the sun as "but a morning star."

It is not necessary to draw on the fact that Keats is putting words to the thrush's inarticulate song to recognize the degree of vocational conviction and self-prophecy he is expressing. The difference that obtains in nature between the poet and the bird or the season takes two forms in the poem: (1) the fact that the bird at best exhibits patience whereas the man must achieve faith, and (2) the fact that man not only *prepares* the harvest both he and the bird expect, but also can conceive and presumably realize a morning beyond everyday, a triple morn. Taken together, these differences suggest an active, developing state of being in the poet, for which the emerging seasons or the "native" song of the thrush may serve as but a convincing sign.

The fundamental invocation of a limited analogy, rather

than a substantial identity between things in nature and the poet's state, appears graphically in a letter Keats wrote less than a fortnight after "What the Thrush Said": " . . . the rise, the progress, the setting of imagery should like the Sun come natural too [sic] him [the reader]. . . . If Poetry comes not [to the poet] *as naturally as* the Leaves to a tree it had better not come at all"[14] (italics added). The native gift of the poet is not just what he gets, but what he does, what he intends and abides by. The essential point of "What the Thrush Said," then, is more than an "it-must-follow-as-the-night-the-day" that the poet will come into his own. Rather, it is that the ontological will to poetry, pervasive in all the poet's being, may infallibly be trusted and should not be concentrated on any action (gaining knowledge, for example). That will realizes itself in its own sphere and its own terms, as properly as the spring returns and the thrush sings. The message ultimately becomes, stop trying—as by the pursuit of knowledge—to be a poet, and be it. What remains for consummation of the will to poetry is, as the spring coming or the thrush in song, a matter of manifestation.

The question may arise whether Keats is consciously or even explicitly saying this in the poem. I would not stipulate that he is, but perhaps, without trying to say the same thing disingenuously, that the poem is saying through him essentially what I have described. The poem, in other words, conveys an apprehension and through its metaphors a conviction that poetry is the natural manifestation of the poet, and it further says that the person addressed in it is a natural poet, even though Phoebus, the god of poetry, seems absent from him for a season. It is even tempting, given the absence of the god and the burdensome feeding on darkness in "What the Thrush Said," to speculate that the poem cryptically summarizes a peculiarly poetic "dark night of the soul" and the beginning of a recovery therefrom.

But manifestation for the poet proves not so simple as for the thrush. His nature is not so simple. Mere passage of time will not suffice to produce his song, since time, which is opportunity and potential guarantee for him, also gives him room for the very reflections, misgivings, and errors that "What the Thrush Said" seeks to combat. Thus the temptation to knowledge, echoing perhaps that aboriginal mistake in the Garden, continues to beset Keats even while he moves into his greatest poetic expression. A kind of *psychomachia*, between analysis-as-mechanical-guarantee and ability-as-vital-agent, between external calculation and intrinsic utterance, can be witnessed in him. In spite of his better nature, Keats was subject to the same impatience for logical truth and final resolution that he himself otherwise rebukes in Coleridge. Keats uses Coleridge to illustrate the absence of "*Negative Capability*, that is when man is incapable of being in uncertainties, Mysteries, doubts, without any irritable reaching after fact & reason. Coleridge, for instance, would let go by a fine isolated verisimilitude from the Penetralium of mystery, from being incapable of remaining content with half knowledge."[15] He was able to conceive of "taking hints from every noble insect that favours us with a visit" as having profound spiritual value and sustaining force ("sap will be given us for meat and dew for drink").[16] But his sense of "Indolence," of the integrity and efficacy of the "passive and receptive" state was at best inconstant. If he thought it as meritorious as giving and doing, and a near "neighbour to [certain] truths," he also suspected that this might be "mere sophistication."[17]

We should not be surprised, then, if he reverts to the elided ideal of philosophy ("Epistle to John Hamilton Reynolds," lines 71–82) after "What the Thrush Said." But in this very reversion we can see, more clearly than ever before, a paradox in the will to poetry, a paradox perhaps in the explicit will itself, in that the latter may either focus or distort its bearer. We may recall that Wordsworth equated beatitude not with an absence of will, but, like Jakob Boehme, with an absence of *particular* will. It seems to me that Keats, though he could express a will to being in poetry, as in "What the Thrush Said," also is beset by a will to poetry as an instrument of coming to be, evidenced in the "Epistle to John Hamilton

Reynolds." What emerges in a number of the pieces concerned with poetry is a condition of alternating ecstasy and
helplessness—"remembrances/That every other minute vex
and please"—with the implication that the personal will, the
integrity of the self, may need qualification, even conversion, before the artistic will can take effect. *Sleep and Poetry*
shows the will to art as something exercised across a boundary of sleep and romance; it is a boundary which Keats is
willing to cross, but its world remains remote—it descends to
him fleetingly and inscrutably, as does the voice of the nightingale, and he can no more pursue it than he can follow the
nightingale across the modest barriers of meadow, stream,
and hillside.

   In short, the early poems either enforce or encourage a loss
of personal will, without a corresponding development of artistic will—we see the artist *in potentia*, or the artist *manqué*.
"What the Thrush Said" represents a shift toward a fundamental conviction that the artist is ready and secure, but the
"Epistle to John Hamilton Reynolds" reverts to the division
between person and artist, and indeed makes this division a
matter of paramount concern. It is hardly surprising that the
poem betrays a degree of radical struggle and incohesiveness
in Keats's mind and strains toward wholeness without commanding its parts. It is well to look precisely at what Keats is
undergoing:

> Oh, never will the prize,
> High reason, and the love of good and ill,
> Be my award! Things cannot to the will
> Be settled, but they tease us out of thought,
> Or is it that imagination brought
> Beyond its proper bound, yet still confin'd,
> Lost in a sort of Purgatory blind,
> Cannot refer to any standard law
> Of either earth or heaven?

[74-82]

Apart from the rapid tonal movement from despair, to a

weary assertiveness (76-77), to unsettled interrogation (78-82), we may note the irreducible tension within each stage of Keats's feelings. Reason and love, will and intellect (thought), imagination and law represent a system of opposing faculties in a conflicted self. The subordinate oppositions between good and ill, heaven and earth, only go to show how deep is this pattern in the poem. And there emerges a strong contrast with the condition of the persona in "What the Thrush Said." In this poem the whole being of the persona informs and expresses his will, and thus promises can be made for him. In the "Epistle to John Hamilton Reynolds" a particular will reduces the power of the whole being and leads it into analytical quandaries. No doubt the conflicted mind is analogous to the "eternal fierce destruction" Keats witnesses in the sea (93-98). His response to what he obsessively calls "that most fierce destruction" (102) makes it clear that he owns it within himself as well as observing it without:

> Away, ye horrid moods!
> Moods of one's mind!
> [105-06]

But the form of exorcism is a sort of self-annihilation, the very antithesis of the self-realization of "What the Thrush Said." Here in the "Epistle" Keats writes (one is tempted to say wilfully):

> . . . I'd sooner be a clapping Bell
> To some Kamtschatcan Missionary Church
> Than with these horrid moods be left i' the lurch.
> [107-09]

In sum, the will to being in poetry is confronted with the will to be no more (than a clapping Bell at least). Poetry versus death: it is possible to trace these alternatives of Keats's vital will forward in his career, recognizing that the very continuance of the poems intimates a certain resolution, but without denying the force of its adversary. The essential will to poetry for Keats must conquer, by redefinition and finally by loving, lucid, poignant contemplation, a specious will to death.

We should take it not as a mark of struggling but as the mark of commitment that Keats took more than "moderate pains" with the composition of "Ode to Psyche." With this, the first of the great odes, he obviously comes into his own as a poet. Despite his "pains," we may recall, the poem was "done leisurely" and "in . . . peac[e]able and healthy spirit."[18] It is apparent that Keats *felt* and understood the poem to be a special forward step and fulfillment. It was for him both a necessity—"wrung/By sweet enforcement"—and a great gesture of freedom—"Yes, I will be thy priest, and build a fane." In short, whether in terms of Keats's experience or of its own content, the "Ode to Psyche" stands as a pivotal achievement in Keats's vocation and dedication to poetry.

One major index of the change taking place may be found in the relation Keats bears to his material. The preternatural encounter of the "Ode to Psyche" is reminiscent of a handful of earlier poems, most notably *Sleep and Poetry*. But in "Psyche," even as the "visionary" element is ostensibly increasing, the sense of a reality belonging, or at least available to, the poet breaks in on our attention: "Surely I dreamt today, or did I see/The winged Psyche with awaken'd eyes?" The poem does not pause to decide, but the idea is strong here that the dream offers a more lucid reality, if not an actuality, so that the brief and agitated ecstasy of the charioteer passage seems remote, like a part of another scheme of understanding. The "muddy stream" of "real things" has no place now, not because the poet is avoiding reality, but because he is perceiving it, and *himself*, differently. He is not dependent any longer on the momentary gift of a preternatural visitor. To the contrary, he has become the source of bounty, ready to supply the needs of the celestial figures and able to protect them from a world whose threat is only implicit and "far, far" away.

The question of the reality of the scene is resolved at the same time as the question of the role of the intrusive (perhaps voyeuristic) poet. For what he intrudes upon is more than sacred turf, it is sacred time:

> Yet even in these days so far retir'd
> From happy pieties, thy lucent fans,
> Fluttering among the faint Olympians,
> I see, and sing, by my own eyes inspir'd.
> [40-43]

Where at first the poet was faint "with surprise" (7), now the gods themselves, as images or as agents conscious of their fate, become "faint." And the poet, without explicitly referring back to the possibility that "dreaming" could sum up the whole experience, simply affirms: "I see." And it emerges graphically that his poetry is self-dependent; he sings as one who sees, not as one who is shown: ". . . by my own eyes inspir'd."

Thus what appears to be an appeal to Psyche, or a dialogue with her (44–50), turns out to be an assertion of power and a unilateral exercise of power on the part of the poet. "So let me be thy choir" does not really request a favor; it says that he can sing, *on his own*, and she needs someone to sing her divinity. Any lingering suspicion that the poet is not expressing ultimate self-confidence surely vanishes with his introspective decision: "Yes, I will be thy priest." This abrupt position would be arrogant, were it less generous. At the same time, the poet's generosity takes the form of making himself everything to the goddess he is ostensibly serving. To honor the goddess he creates a condign world; by creating that world he becomes a god. His utterly liberal creativity is of course the essence of the point I am making about Keats's realizing himself in "Psyche." He appears no longer the aspirant, dependent on this or that favoring circumstance. Even the landscape, which before he had looked to as a sort of surrogate muse, he now fashions to his own impulse and purpose. He has the freedom of poetry. He has, not to put too fine a point on it, his way with poetry in an expression of unchallenged will ("Yes, I will . . . ").

But one problem remains, relating to the world that the

poet converts into his own within the "Ode to Psyche." For all the skill and aplomb of the poem (which T. S. Eliot in *The Use of Poetry* regarded as the best of the odes), the world remains as a challenge and a correction to its formulas. The poet's invasion of time leaves him in a position where his final vows might seem "antique," and leaves the naturalistic architecture of his "fane" rather convenient than true. Overcoming the inner uncertainties and the inhibitions of his earlier work, Keats has proven that he can make a world in his poetry. What he can make of the world, how to overcome the difficulties and resistances it presents from without, remains at issue still.[19]

In this light it is significant that "Ode to a Nightingale," after precisely grappling with the force of the world, ends where "Ode to Psyche," circumventing that force, begins. This is to say, of course, that the "Nightingale" ends on a note of interrogation, of intellectual and spiritual irresolution, that stands at odds with the apparent declarative assurance of the first stanza. That irresolution images the state of the conflict between poetry, construed as uncontested, inexhaustible freedom and joy in being,[20] and the grim actualities of our creaturely shortcomings—pain, fear, drudgery, decay, confusion, death. The poem makes poetry *about* these latter things, but fails to make poetry *of* them, and so a tearing division remains.

But it is necessary to observe the seeds of division within the positive structures of the poem. The bird is more richly suggestive, but in itself just as inarticulate as the charioteer in *Sleep and Poetry*; what it elicits is the poet's desire, his projective will, rather than his power, or real will. The more it affects him, accordingly, the more it points up his ordinary removal from the state it induces in him.

Thus a sense of novelty, of something unfamiliar *and unbearable*, bursts forth even in the beginning of the "Nightingale," where happiness is not substantiated, but asserted, argued into place. The poet is experiencing himself in complex relation to the bird, and not, as would seem, straightforwardly empathizing with it. And what he experiences is excess, or drastic alteration ("My heart aches"), which he rather self-consciously makes analogous to death ("as though of hemlock I had drunk"). This is of course a dying *upward*, a going beyond the bounds of viability in the direction of fulfillment ("too happy in thine happiness"), rather than in the direction of deprivation ("to thy high requiem become a sod"). Death, then, is twofold, upward or downward, and means whatever goes beyond the usual boundaries of experience.[21]

But a deeper paradox than using the idiom of death to express happiness also takes place in the opening stanza of the "Nightingale." This second paradox grows out of the first. For in his very yearning for ecstasy the poet exhibits a reluctance to give himself over. In using the idiom of death the poet expresses a powerful will to continue as himself. It is not just what surpasses flawed mortal life but what threatens his peculiar economy that the poet apprehends in the bird's song. And in some measure though he wishes to enjoy ecstasy, he does not want *to undergo* ecstasy. He does not want the nightingale to bring it about in him, and so gives such an ambivalent statement, of glad welcome and latent reserve, in the first stanza. Nor is it long before the insistence on his own means, and hence his own will, becomes explicit.

With the second stanza of the "Ode to a Nightingale" the poet's response shifts from appreciation to emulation of the bird, and the bird's role from an ideal to a stimulus. The cry for "a draught of vintage" implies at least a partial rejection of the bird as agent of "transcendence." It may seem, of course, that the "drink" leaves the poet as dependent and passive as before. But the paramount fact is that the drink results from a concoction of essences, and expresses the poet's resources in precisely the same way as the "fane" of Psyche. Its power to intoxicate is entirely abstract and ideal; the initial realism of cooling in the earth quickly sublimes into myth (Flora, Hippocrene) and symbolic elements (dance, song, sunburnt mirth). In short, the poet calls not for an intoxicant, but for self-intoxication. In this respect, the poem suggests a state of lucid, even calculated, ecstasy.

This element of calculation, the poet's refusal to let go save on his own terms, intensifies *pari passu* with his rush to transcendence. He whips himself along ("away! away!"), and may seem to be taking on the bird's attributes ("I will fly"), but the activity of his own will, implicit in these very gestures, at once appears in his rejection of Bacchus[22] and his defiance of the retarding "brain."[23] The will, as it can make poetry in a draught that is a realization of essences, can go where poetry goes. Hence the abrupt transition-fulfillment of "Already with thee!" But the "Ode to a Nightingale" is insistently a poem of *relation*; if the grim world impels one to visions of relief, the transcendent world entails the anxiety of a relapse. It is with reference to this anxiety that the poet solicits his own death in the sixth stanza.

Happiness has been analogous to death at the start; here death becomes the source of a negative happiness—escape from pain—by virtue of the poet's opportunistic calculation. The meaning of death proves less than simple. Not only is the poet proleptically conscious of his death, which he stages as carefully as his earlier ecstasy, but he is conscious of his obsequies. Even though he calls himself "a sod," the high requiem (missa solemnis?) of the bird makes him a more considerable figure, and by his own conception. In general it is true that to imagine death is to imagine vital signs beyond death. But the poet in the "Nightingale" seems constitutionally averse to whatever would master, let alone annihilate, him. He is a powerful embodiment of what Shelley in his essay "On Life" calls the "spirit within [man] at enmity with nothingness and dissolution." Indeed, the burial that actually takes place involves not the nightingale lover but the nightingale's song ("buried deep") at last.[24]

The fact that the poem begins ("My heart aches") and ends ("do I wake or sleep?") with the poet helps to give focus to the preoccupation with self-identity and self-will it contains and imparts a singular sense to the poet's final insistence on his "sole self":

> Forlorn! the very word is like a bell
> To toll me back from thee to my sole self!

A crucial contrast, reinforced by homonymy, exists between the bird's "soul" generously poured abroad and the speaker's privately "sole" self. Giving primacy to that self, the poem moves on the strength of its imaginative spirit into two realms ordinarily impossible for the self: immortal ecstasy and mortal dissolution. It does so as a self-limiting series of speculations and experiments, and it is but a confession of this fact that the poet ends by asking seemingly unanswerable questions:

> Was it a vision, or a waking dream?
> Fled is that music:—Do I wake or sleep?

And yet a certain knowledge about the poet, the sole self, can be arrived at here, through the very paths of uncertainty. The distinction between vision and dream, between mysterious access to extraordinary truth and the ordinary play of mental images in sleep, begins to blur when the dream is a "waking" one, since "waking" means bringing to wakefulness as well as occurring while awake. Given the former sense, *either* vision *or* dream would leave the poet with a still unresolved access to the extraordinary, and his final question, though it implies a present self-confusion, only reinforces this access, since "waking" is possible even in sleep. As Keats had learnt from the thrush, "he's awake who thinks himself asleep" ("What The Thrush Said," line 14).

Wishing to be a poem of consummations, the "Ode to a Nightingale" remains a poem of problematical beginnings. It is a springtime poem paradoxically resentful of the spring because it is not summer; or, to put it another way, it expresses the poet's knowledge that he is a poet as well as his impatience with not being consummately so. To say so is no mere extrapolation from the unsettled and ambiguous position the poem results in. The contrast between summer and spring is explicit in the first and the fifth stanzas. The nightingale, we may recall, "singest of summer in full-throated ease," with the designation "full-throated" working to anticipate summer in the bird. But the poet can only "guess" about "the coming musk-rose" and the implied "summer eves." His summer seems less secure. Even more, the "dewy wine" of the musk-rose, which must remind us of his own quintessential draught, provides little consolation or delight, proving but "the murmurous haunt of flies." The wine of nature, earlier transcended by the draught of imagination, here seems poignantly unavailable. The fullest of summers for the poet, the summer of nature and of imagination, stays aloof.

But if the problem of the "Ode to a Nightingale" is how to attain full summer, the ode "To Autumn" faces the problem of how to retain it. At the same time, it must be recognized that the summer is not quite the same in both poems. In "Ode to a Nightingale" the summer is unrealized, and the task of the imagination is to realize it. In "To Autumn" the summer is all too forcibly realized and seems to have an independent substance of its own, so that the task of the imagination is to subsist where external bounty and cyclical process seem likely to exhaust the world. "To Autumn" represents Keats's intensest grapple with the force of matter in time, and it is because of this that the poem comes to reveal, more than any other, the intensest possibilities of the imagination. For the poem is structured in a pattern of diminishing sensuousness and increasing reflection, in such a way as to suggest that the speaker (implicitly the poet) is surviving and finally overcoming the onslaught of the material world. In other words, the poet comes into being as the overwhelming evidence of the world is sorted and shaped into a symbolic system of meaning and value. The poet *is*, whether the world threatens his being with bounty[25] or with death.

That the consciousness which develops in "To Autumn"[26] is a literary one grows clear in the third stanza; the question, "Where are the songs of Spring?," with its invocation of the *ubi sunt* theme, leaves little doubt of the aesthetic sophistication of the speaker's response. But more than aesthetics is involved, though the wonderfully prompt rejoinder seems merely to replace one music with another. For there is a boldness of decision in the cry, "Ay, where are they?/Think not of them, thou hast thy music too." This amounts to a revision of literary history by supplanting the *ubi sunt* tradition with a *hic estis* one, the nostalgic lyric with a poignant present lyrical meditation that is an articulation of music;[27] the poem engages itself to show the justice of that act of supplanting, through revelation of the season's music. As purveyor of the new song the poet is as independent and inventive as in the "Ode to Psyche," but here he remains entirely faithful to the terms he is given. Utter receptivity to what resides outside him proves consonant with utter assurance within. But this does not come about by happenstance. The poet chooses his conception of the autumn,[28] in the face of a contrary mythology—the very one embodied in the sensuous preoccupation of the opening stanza. And he chooses his poetry, in the face of the sort of landscape which, a few scant years before, he thought would never support his art.

In the final analysis the landscape, intractable nature, only fronts for the radical issue, namely that Keats in "To Autumn" is making poetry, by a perfect fusion of will and skill, out of what opposes poetry, that is, death. The forecast of death in the season and the presence of death in the poem have often been noted: the soft-dying day, the stubble plain, the wailful choir of gnats that mourn, the ephemeral existence of the wind, the swallows portending winter and lifelessness. But the sting of death, even the need of death exhibited in the "Nightingale," can find no place in the passage. The poet who consoles the autumn ("Think not of them, thou hast thy music too") safeguards the season against the very ravages of time that he indicates with the cornucopia reduced to "last oozings," and with the image of once omnipresent and multiplying autumn lost but to "whoever seeks abroad." Indeed, it may be that he is addressing himself, as well as the season, with the injunction against mourning for "the songs of Spring." The "mourning" of autumn in this regard is to the ear, and not of the spirit; there exists neither cause nor intention of mourning in gnat or lamb, let alone in the poet. As with "The Solitary Reaper" we must distinguish in "To Autumn" between the content and the state of the song, for where its content may be sorrowful its state is surely to life.

And yet this avoidance of negation in "To Autumn" is only a small part of the poem's incorporation of death into its own positive life. Every detail that portends winter proves indecisive, ambiguous, self-contradictory, and either reminisces or anticipates spring. What is descriptively wintry is affectively spring. The verb *bloom* (25) does not deny the fact of the "soft-dying day," but it makes the day die into life. The "rosy hue" on the "stubble-plains" (26) picks up the color of vitality—the day and the things of the day alike share in an experience of life. And more, the verb *touch* carries the color into inert objects, like Michaelangelo's God touching the finger of Adam.

The "wailful choir" of mourning gnats (27) seems on the surface an immedicable index of death. But besides the fact that sound in the gnats must prevail over meaning, the "light wind" (spiritus?) dramatically checks the tendency toward death by at least giving life equal time: "borne aloft/Or sinking as the light wind lives or dies." The gnats further establish in the stanza what can only have been cryptic before, a pattern of spatial imagery in which "up" signifies life and "down" death; the clouds and the gnats aloft are associated with life, the day at the horizon and the stubble-plains and the sinking gnats with death, and withal communication occurs between them.

So far from conceding to the death-drift he purports to describe, the poet is penetrating the life that lies concealed in death. And with the introduction of the "full-grown lambs" (30) a new ambiguity arises, creating doubts whether we are in prewinter or spring. The substantive idea in the phrase is "lambs," and hence spring, which no amount of qualification by terms like "full-grown" can alter. It is in fact a defiance of conventional language and understanding to say "full-grown lambs," but the statement stands in proof of something incontrovertible beyond conventional understanding. In keeping with this revision of the tendency toward winter, by use of winter's own evidences, the hedge-cricket and the red-breast remind us equally of spring.

But the final line of the poem moves us again emphatically toward winter: "And gathering swallows twitter in the skies." This is a departure ritual, and the statement by itself might seem to break once and for all the retarding energy of the foregoing lines. In context, its effect proves rather more complex and positive. We may note first that the phrase "in the skies" works as a consummation of the poem's spatial imagery[29] and carries the swallows up (and not *away*) into life. And second, we may single out the present participle *gathering* for special comment. For the present participle is predominant in the opening stanza, the statement of full summer, and the past participle in the second stanza, the statement of diminution and imminent winter. This contrast could hardly be systematic and invariable in the poem,[30] but it operates as an important signal by and large, as a signal of the permanence-in-the-teeth-of-destruction that Blake captures in *The Four Zoas*: "The fading cry is ever dying." The point is not to interpret *gathering* in terms of a grammatical abstraction; rather, it is to observe the particular working of this present participle as the poem comes to a close. *Gathering* indicates an action but it also describes a state, and nothing in the context of the poem forbids us to take both values, of action and state, to maximum extent (*sinking* cannot be treated as a state, being subject to the vagaries of the wind). If both action and state are kept in mind, the concluding line of "To Autumn" presents something like an active tableau, process without change, life going on (and never off, into winter).

This perception, this original intuition of life as permanent on the brink of death, is not only an act of consciousness but an articulation of will. The bees may be fooled by summer's largesse, but the poet is not fooled, just as the flies may be nourished by "dewy wine" where the poet is not nourished. The poet has known all along the transience of summer, along with its potency. He knows implicitly, too, something of his own transience, and his own potency. And he shows that his potency can affect the datum of transience in ways unavailable to summer. This is exhibited in his removing summer-autumn from the brief exaltation of mythology (stanzas 1–2) to the permanent modulation of reality (stanza 3). The poet does not come forward in the poem, but he comes through it. Its achievement is what he has set and willed himself to do, without tradition, without support: "Think not of them, thou hast thy music too."

The seeming effortlessness of the ode "To Autumn" is not inconsonant with the deep commitment and energy of will I have been discussing. Rather, "To Autumn" should be seen as a free product (in a sense a by-product) of the enormous explicit struggle for poetry Keats carried on in mid-1819 with *The Fall of Hyperion*. This is the poem that most fully renders the complex of Keats's will to art. It adds a social function to the personal function of art we see in, say, the "Ode to Psyche" and *Sleep and Poetry*; adds a deep realism to mythology, and magnanimous compassion to the fanciful sympathy we see in the "Ode to Psyche," while vastly enlarging the poetic personality of "To Autumn"; adds to the state of art we see in the "Ode on a Grecian Urn" a sense of vital process and intimate engagement in the things of time, as immortality itself in one form falls prey to time; adds, in the face of the separation of personal and artistic will that we have seen, a sense that artistic will can and should be a consummation of the personal will; and adds to the conflict of poetry and death variously seen in "To Autumn" and the "Ode to a Nightingale" the poet's confrontation of and triumph over his own death. Concretely, too, *The Fall of Hyperion* recapitulates Keats's thoughts on poetry from the transcendent counsellor to the transcendent draught, from the rich revelatory comprehensiveness of an autumnal moment to the sacred place and the gradus of inspiration. But it embraces these in one coherent action and one coherent experience, so coming to constitute what he had never before encompassed, a ceremony and a drama of poetization.

It is crucial to see that this ceremony and drama proceed in terms of the will. As the narrative begins, the speaker finds or fancies himself in a paradisaical place, evidently just abandoned by an angel or Mother Eve. The remnant of a feast that exceeds three mortal cornucopias causes him to experience an "appetite/More yearning than on earth I ever felt," and falling to he eats "deliciously" and as he soon grows thirsty drinks from "a cool vessel of transparent juice."[31] This is but the preamble to the action, which turns into a veritable Chinese box of visions, and so it may not be necessary to make much of the emphasis on appetite and self-indulgence. But as the action proper commences, it becomes clear that the speaker has a strong sense of his identity and will to express himself. Surprised by the narcotic potency of the drink, he imagines it as working against his will to live:

> No Asian poppy nor elixir fine
> Of the soon-fading, jealous Caliphat,
> No poison gender'd in close monkish cell,
> . . . .
> Could so have rapt unwilling life away.
> . . . .
> . . . I struggled hard against
> The domineering potion. . . .
>
> [47–54]

This initial episode, graphically developing the personality resistance to intoxication already seen in the "Ode to a Nightingale,"[32] proves a model for the progressive action of the poem. The challenge with which Moneta confronts the would-be poet—climb or perish—also involves a change from delight to imminent death; the "sacrificial fire" makes him forget "everything but bliss," but it is out of its "soft smoke" that Moneta's voice comes. The poet's first response implies a condition of will, as he "felt the tyranny/Of that fierce threat and the hard task proposed." His next response, when "a palsied chill" already is affecting him, affirms his will in language that recalls his reaction to the transparent juice:

> I strove hard to escape
> The numbness, strove to gain the lowest step.

His striving expresses his nature quintessentially. He *will* not be overcome, *will* not die without a total effort to live. As Keats said, "I must choose between despair & Energy—I choose the latter."[33] In the poem essential energy is expressed in the act of striving. Accordingly, when the protagonist's "iced foot touched/The lowest stair" and with new manifestation of life he "mounted up" the stair of poetry, we have a clear understanding of Moneta's statement, "that *thou hadst power* to do so/Is thy own safety" (142–43; italics added). The "conjuration" (291) that brings him to her side is, I think, an extension of the established efficacy of his will, and the abrupt expansion of his powers and vision manifestations of its implicit power. He does not explicitly will the first consequence of his eating, but everything thereafter depends to some extent on his will and purpose:

> . . . once more I rais'd
> My eyes *to fathom* the space every way. . . .
> [81–82]

> *I ached to see* what things the hollow brain
> Behind enwombed. . . .
> . . . .
> . . . "Shade of Memory!"
> Cried I, with act adorant at her feet,
> . . . .
> *Let me behold.* . . .
> [275–89]

> The lofty theme
> Of those few words hung vast before my mind
> With half-unravell'd web. I sat myself

Upon an eagle's watch, *that I might see. . . .*
[306-09] [italics added throughout]

Indeed it is evident that Moneta in some vital and perhaps causal way responds to the poet's will. The first concession she makes to him is couched in a line that beautifully begins with hers and ends with his will, as though the two (muse and poet) framed not just the verse but the world; "The sacrifice is done," she says, "but not the less /*Will* I be kind to thee for thy good *will*" (241-42; italics added).[34]

The consummation of the poet's will to poetry, as defined in the poem, occurs in his almost Christ-like assumption of the immortal pains of Saturn, Thea, and Moneta:

Without stay or prop,
But my own weak mortality, I bore
The load of this eternal quietude,
The unchanging gloom and the three fixed shapes
Ponderous upon my senses, a whole moon. . . .
[388-92]

But here again a consequence beyond his anticipation comes upon him:

Oftentimes I pray'd
Intense, that death would take me from the vale
And all its burthens—Grasping with despair
Of change, hour after hour I curs'd myself. . . .
[396-99]

This brings us as far as we can well be from the "Ode to Psyche": the focus is on the subject of poetry rather than the craft of the poet, on philosophy and humanized suffering instead of aesthetics and imaginative retreat. But it seems unlikely that this moment of despair could have been as happily or progressively resolved as the original unwelcome intoxication. The poet here is withstanding not an outside force but, paradoxically, himself. His cursing himself is ontological, not practical. The curse refers to his *being* such a man as to necessitate this situation, and is aimed at his nature and his will. The joy of creation which could offset its painful content would require a commitment to Apollo in the poem, or to the forward evolution and succession of the gods. But the definition of poetry and the thrust of the poem's action bear backward into nostalgia. The inescapable future is partly sacrificed to the ineluctable past.

This opposition between past and future is the most evident form of a deep-seated fault-line of focus and sympathy in *The Fall of Hyperion*. From its inception, of course, it was Hyperion's and not Apollo's poem, elegy and not triumph—so much so that in the earlier version, *Hyperion: A Fragment*, Apollo on the brink of succession is mysteriously troubled and seems like someone from the previous dispensation trying to puzzle his way into the new. In *The Fall* his role, if it has not been transferred to Hyperion, becomes obscure and almost incidental, and it is clear that the god of poetry matters far less in this process of poetization than the figure he inevitably supplants.

Two conceptions of poetry are contending, rather unequally, here. The one represented by Apollo is in the same *position* as the one rejected by Moneta, as having little or nothing to say about or to our suffering condition. This conception is summed up in the last two lines of the "Ode on a Grecian Urn": "Beauty is Truth, Truth Beauty—that is all[35] /Ye know on earth, and all ye need to know." The other conception of poetry is in part presented by Moneta, in part by the larger action in which she is dramatically engaged. It is evolutionary and self-revealing, and includes (1) the poet's taste for paradisaical food and his capacity for preternatural suffering; (2) his humility and his wit and his jealous guardianship of his own identity and being; (3) the irony that the more he gets what he wants the more difficult and burdensome his state; (4) the concomitant irony that he is commited to an insatiable desire for something that in the reminiscential structure of the poem can never be final, so that he must proceed in order to prove himself, but must be himself in order to proceed;

and, in culmination, (5) the reconciliation of aspiration and limitation in the moment of heroic compassion and sacrifice of the healing poet.

If the "Ode to Psyche" celebrates a neglected goddess for her power of beauty and love, *The Fall of Hyperion* celebrates a supplanted god and goddess for their power of suffering and symbolic mortality. The poem all but dismisses Apollo and his rights of succession, an external gift of time, in favor of the rights of passion and comprehension, an intrinsic expression of character and life. Thus the stages of the poet's growth, in the sequence of encounters with Moneta, and Saturn, and Hyperion, are the vital counterpart to the formal succession from god to god. But stages contain growth while succession offers mere substitution, and the poem is committed to what growth implies: depth, enlargement, surprise, participation. Even the loss and death that growth may entail take on a positive quality where "Sorrow [proves] more beautiful than Beauty's self." This quotation, from *Hyperion: A Fragment*, fairly summarizes Keats's bias in the Hyperion poems. He is redefining traditional artistic and cultural values, though exploiting a traditional story as a framework. On the face of it, this is no better than an unpromising venture.

In his second attempt at resolving the relationship between old and new, Keats minimizes the weight and thrust of the traditional story by making the action center around the poet figure and bringing the background figures, the ousted gods, to the foreground. But refocusing will not do what recasting must do; Apollo remains in the story as one whose time has come, and so reminds us that Keats has reconceived poetry without reconstituting its patron divinity. Perhaps after all it is not Milton or Dante who blocks Keats's path to fulfillment in this poem, but the paradoxical spirit of his own enterprise, to keep beauty, and hence Apollo, while redefining it and discovering it in the lineaments of grief: in Moneta (loyalty and compassion and wisdom), in the poet figure (integrity and courage and apprehensiveness), and in Saturn-Hyperion (passion and desolation).

In effect, where "To Autumn" proceeds from mythology to realism, Keats in *The Fall of Hyperion* approaches realism through mythology. The poem remains unresolved, but still is crucial to our understanding of what art means and does for Keats, and indeed to our understanding of his place in the romantic scheme. Keats lay great store by the possibility of producing a long poem. "Did our great poets," he trenchantly asked, "ever write short pieces?"[36] The point is, of course, that it is rarely for their short pieces that we call great poets so. And the three elements of the long poem for Keats—invention, fancy, imagination—make it apparent that he has nothing like eighteenth-century imitation in mind. He is pursuing his own greatness and he leaves little doubt, giving up *Hyperion: A Fragment* for *The Fall of Hyperion*, that it is personal as well as practical greatness, unorthodox but central, guaranteed but full of crises. His cryptic summary of the realization of art comes easily to mind: "that which is creative must create itself."

What, then, is the nature of the poet, and the poem, created in *The Fall of Hyperion*? It goes without saying that neither a monster creation nor a more than Renaissance overreaching has any part in Keats's conception of creativity. Self-creation entails an active and imaginative engagement upon the process of bringing one's possibilities into being and into play. This is why in *The Fall of Hyperion*, though Apollo is the one who officially benefits from the passage of time, the poet is the one who enters and commands it, not only recovering from the experience of its burdens but doing so as a form of resurrection. Rather than Apollo, then (according to the traditional structures of myth), the new poet emerges in place of the fallen god, with the effect of a transforming commerce between god and man: man becomes god, though fallen, and god becomes man, but exalted. And this becomes the definition of the poet, the reconciler and embodiment of two realms, enduring ultimate suffering and knowing its ultimate beauty.

The nature of the poem such a poet writes will partake of

the ambivalence (eager growth and discovered danger) and eventualism (abrupt and yet intelligible development) of his very situation. But the poem also takes its stand in relation to the history of literature and myth, with an implicitly evolutionary posture. *The Fall of Hyperion* may be termed a dream vision as epic, but in view of Keats's concern with the long poem the emphasis should probably fall on its epic character. It will not qualify as a martial-social epic, like the *Iliad*; it is no story of prowess, of man among men in society. Nor will it pass muster as a moral epic, like *Paradise Lost*; it does not foster or enunciate the terms of virtue, as a tale of man among ordained laws in the universe. Rather it presents itself as a transformative epic, a story of self-discovery and emerging courage and compassion, presenting man among his capacities and aspirations in a universe of mortality.

The *Iliad* and *Paradise Lost* rest on the possibility of man's being somehow larger than life. *The Fall of Hyperion* deals with man as somehow larger than death. And yet no absolute separation takes effect between the two approaches. One versatile category includes all these epics, and it is easy enough to see that, if Satan were its hero, *Paradise Lost* would be an epic of self-discovery, that if Hector were the hero of the *Iliad* it would be an epic of virtue, and that if Apollo were its hero *The Fall of Hyperion* would be an epic of prowess.

The oddity is of course that while it revises the protocol of the epic, *The Fall*, merely as epic, traditionally completes Keats's engagement upon the task of becoming poet.[37] He has proceeded through pastoral and satire, epistle and ode, pre-tending to the fullest conviction of himself as poet (shown in "What the Thrush Said") and to the freest expression of himself as poet (achieved in the "Ode to Psyche," perhaps, and "To Autumn"), revolving and resolving, this way and that, tracking himself near the junction of the weary world and a licentious fancy, fearing death (and faking it) until he could recognize it as a versatile and indeed prolific idea more than a rigid and terminal experience, storing power and taxing possibility, willing and second-guessing himself to the point where he could run the risk of self-abnegation in "To Autumn" and conduct the adventure of self-authorization in the culminating long poem of a truncated career, *The Fall of Hyperion*.[38]

EXCURSUS: THE WILL TO ART IN ROMANTICISM

The will to art in romanticism has little to do with a Paterian timelessness, antithetical to the flux of life, instantly autonomous, self-constituting and self-reflective. That sort of art does appear in a quiescent form in the "Ode on a Grecian Urn" and in a projective form in "Kubla Khan." But in neither case is the will viably involved. The animation it seems to preserve at the outset is soon lost to the urn, and its incapacity to preserve the full life of the "little town" leaves it at best a lopsided power. The speaker's curious eagerness to penetrate and participate in its world cools to the point where he can call it, withdrawing into paradox, a "Cold Pastoral." Only "marble men" have any existence there, and only a cryptic, marmoreal message comes from that world: "Beauty is Truth, Truth Beauty—that is all/Ye know on earth, and all ye need to know." Whatever will to art, as timelessness and autonomy, we may see in the beginning of the poem is clearly recanted by the end, either because such art proves mortally inaccessible or because it proves mortally inadequate.

By the same token the will to art in "Kubla Khan," the emulous will to re-present the awesome *effects* of absolute power in the monarch and in nature, dwindles into speculation, and paralyzed speculation at that. The basic problem is much the same as with the "Ode on a Grecian Urn": the majestic kinesis of the subject is rendered as the majestic stasis of an object, and the ellipsis and pathos of that change informs the "responsible" will it is in vain. The poet cannot "build that dome," damsel or no damsel. Mysterious though it remains, it is real; his "dome" would be as mysterious, but magical rather than real.

What makes the romantic will to art so different from the Paterian mode depends heavily on the discomfiture of the magical, with all that it suggests of escape and fascination; *Lamia* and "La Belle Dame sans Merci" are cautionary tales on the subject of the magical for English romanticism. This is not to say that the romantics deny the magical but that, from the point of that cardinal contract between Wordsworth and Coleridge, they insisted on relating it to, or finding it in, the practical. So much so, in fact, that their basic program might be seen as a redefinition of the practical, making it more inclusive, and more versatile. Thus in particular relation to art we need to recognize that for the romantics something "aesthetic" affects more than the features or principles of beauty. It goes directly and materially to life, as the antonym of "anesthetic."

Not even the early, escapist Keats fails to betray this thrust, because he retains the sense, so marked in *Paradise Lost*, that a happy place must belong to and express a happy condition of being. The would-be poet of *Sleep and Poetry*, as already shown, is more challenged than coddled by his aesthetic opportunities, and also maintains, in his own challenge to the school of Boileau, a standard for poetry that is both rigorous and humane. The consummation of art for him comes not with arbitrary or primitive freedom (as in, say, the "Ode to Psyche") but with acceptance and therewith a redeeming realization of a difficult condition of mortal suffering, including its difficult beauty (*The Fall of Hyperion*). In sum, there is a movement away from the self-insistence of the aesthetic (the immediate autonomy summarized by Pater in his remark that all art aspires to the condition of music), and a compensatory movement toward a cultivated freedom, the freedom of devotion to the labor of bringing the possible about. But the possible is here also the necessary—the poet in *The Fall of Hyperion* does not enjoy an arbitrary and cloistered (not to say fugitive) freedom, as in the "Ode to Psyche"; instead, he grows away from this freedom by virtue of the very feast which seems meant to induce it, and painstakingly realizes a second necessary freedom, adequate to the known world and the knowable capacities of man. This freedom, as we have seen, is made up of the acts of coming to terms with the force and the laws and the values of experience; the wisdom that comes from suffering and courage; compassion; knowledge of eternal principles working in time; and a grave and generous commitment to time and acceptance of mortality.

The line of Keats's career, we may say, develops from an overweening sense of the powers of poetry to a tempered, indeed chastened, sense of the status of the poet. This is a judgment that can be made quite apart from the quality of the poems in question; the poet increasingly diverts the focus of attention away from poetry, and the poems thereby bebecome more human, more charged with the idioms and economics of experience, than expressive of a need for uninhibited agency.

But it is clear that the appeal of art, the will to art in the romantic scheme, practically originates in the feeling for uninhibited agency. At the same time a rhythm of surprise also typically marks the romantic organization of experience, and as there is no agency without object, or *relation*, the status of this appeal is subject to considerable alteration. One pattern of alteration has emerged in the poetry of Keats, in a movement from indulgence to suffering, egocentricity to humanism, frailty and fancy to magnanimity. This pattern does not strictly repeat itself in the other romantic poets, but its point of origin, a desire for license, and its effective end, restraint and acceptance, can be descried in Wordsworth, say, or Byron, or Blake, to band together an unlikely trio.

It could be argued that such restraint comes with the territory of art, but we must use caution here. Both Wordsworth and Byron, for example, recognize the opportunities for license that poetry affords, and renounce them explicitly. And Keats, to use just one more example, insists on ennobling the conception of poetry by stripping it of the trappings of fancy and clothing it with a stern dignity and all but stoical temper. In a sense the poet of *The Fall of Hyperion* rises against the gods, showing them in disarray and enfeeblement; but what he loses in awe he makes up in compassion, recognizing the divinity of pain and suffering, so that what we see at last is man rising, through pain and compassion, *toward* the gods, toward the poignant grandeur of humanity. Far from inducing restraint by impositions of technique and form, art becomes a vehicle for expressing a penchant for restraint, or a movement toward restraint in a choice at once natural and calculated. The artist, like art itself, finds a proper boundary. As Keats so resonantly says of the sonnet, Wordsworth's "sufficient room": "She will be *bound* with garlands of her own" (italics added).

It is important, then, to recognize as one of the dimensions of the romantic will to art an experiential sense that mere freedom will not do. More than this, mere freedom reacts upon itself, and threatens *constraints*, not restraints, for its advocates; hence the circle woven round the would-be poet in "Kubla Khan," representing a state cogently described by Schiller:

On the wings of fancy, man leaves the narrow confines of the present in which mere animality stays bound, in order to strive towards an unlimited future. But while the infinite opens up before his reeling *imagination*, his heart has not ceased to live in the particular or wait upon the moment. In the very midst of his animality the drive towards the Absolute catches him unawares—and since in this state of apathy all his endeavour is directed merely towards the material and the temporal, and limited exclusively to himself as individual, he will merely be induced by that demand to give his own individuality unlimited extension rather than to abstract from it altogether: will be led to strive, not after form, but after an unfailing supply of matter; not after changelessness, but after perpetually enduring change; and after the absolute assurance of his temporal existence. That very drive which, applied to his thinking and activity, was

meant to lead him to truth and morality, brought now to
bear upon his passivity and feeling, produces nothing but
unlimited longing and instinctual need. The first fruits
which he reaps in the realm of spirit are, therefore, Care
and Fear.[39]

But the genius of the age, rejecting as it had at the outset the
artificial regulations of neoclassical organization, managed to
evolve a form of experience combining adventure and obedience—this is what *The Fall of Hyperion* and *The Prelude* are all
about—in a nonprescriptive and ever-unfolding order. The
will to art, though art holds up prospects of a licentious, self-
subsistent system, proves in reality an episode in a self-
correcting engagement with and upon something besides
itself, and not a positive and fixed commitment. Nor should
this surprise us; for while fantasy and escapism enter readily
into the romantic structure, the sense of the aesthetic as remote and absolute is indulged as a late Victorian phenomenon. The romantics know it as temptation, but invariably show it as dangerous (Shelley, *Alastor*) or immature
and idle (Wordsworth, *The Prelude*). The meaning of "aesthetic" to the romantics themselves, as Schiller overwhelmingly attests, carries directly to life, known more fully, lived
more deeply, valued more highly, and held more nobly:

> A thing can relate directly to our sensual condition. . . .
> Or it can relate to our intellect. . . . Or it can relate to our
> will . . . as an object of choice for a rational being. . . . Or
> finally, it can relate to the totality of our various func-
> tions without being a definite object for any single one of
> them: that is its aesthetic character. . . . And education to
> taste and beauty [the aesthetic character] . . . has as its
> aim the development of the whole complex of our sensual
> and spiritual power in the greatest possible harmony.

Or again Schiller writes:

> The power which is restored to [man] in the aesthetic
> mode [is] the highest of all bounties . . . the gift of hu-

manity itself. True, he possesses this humanity *in potentia* before every determinate condition into which he can conceivably enter. But he loses it in practice, with every determinate condition into which he does enter. And if he is to pass into a condition of an opposite nature, this humanity must be restored to him each time anew through the life of the aesthetic.

Something that is cryptic in Keats's formulation of "Negative Capability" is lucidly articulated by Schiller, who finally names the aesthetic mode "a state of Supreme Reality."[40]

In this respect art (or the aesthetic) takes on a histrionic character, embodying and exemplifying a way of living and of seeing life. If this character often has a healing influence— soothing the cares of man—it is perhaps to remind us that where Apollo takes over from Hyperion, Aesculapius would naturally take over from him. But this is to get involved with the end or function of art, instead of pursuing the will to art as such. And some dissonance exists between the two points, as inception and end do not follow one from the other with classical regularity, but in a rough process of emergency and adaptation.

LOGIC, VISION, AND ACTUALITY: THE STATE OF ART IN BLAKE

The treatment of the poet and of poetry in the work of William Blake graphically renders the range and dynamism of response which his age produces. Indeed, with Blake keeping certain character names from poem to poem while at the same time modifying the character functions associated with them, special complexities arise in his case. The question of the will to art in Blake centers around the triple figure, Orc-Blake-Los, and each member of this troika alters in himself and in his relation to the others. On the face of things, Orc would represent primary individuality and creative vitality, Blake a fundamental receptivity and devotion to creative form in all quarters of the universe, and Los, in his turn, the agent and articulation of individuality-cum-creative form. But at least two weaknesses develop at once in such a neat schema. The Orc character is intrinsically erratic and unreliable, the way all pure energy must be; he can be as magnificent and as vulnerable as the sun (vide "A Song of Liberty") in *The Marriage of Heaven and Hell*; he can be irresistible, as in the "Preludium" to *America: A Prophecy*, or eloquent in philosophy, as in the "I-am-Orc" speech in the same poem; but he remains enclosable with clouds (end of *America*) and liable to confinement and female wiles of music (*Europe: A Prophecy*), his repeated identification with the sun (conclusion of *Europe*) coming to suggest an alternating cycle of splendor and disappearance. A basic instability and uncertainty in the makeup of Orc is confirmed when Urizen overcomes him and when finally he becomes the object of sentimental comforts in a state of confinement (*The Four Zoas*, "Night the Seventh"). He does of course recover as energy and fire in "Night the Ninth," but even here he needs to be distinguished from the "living flames winged with intellect/And Reason" that mark a major gesture toward redemption, starting "the trembling millions into flames of mental fire/Bathing their Limbs in the bright visions of Eternity" ("Night the Ninth," page 119: lines 19–23); Orc's flames have been subsumed under a greater flame, "the fires of Eternity" (118:10), and it is these that afford visions of Eternity. Orc, we are informed, "quite consumd himself in Mental flames" (126:1). He could not be himself and be, in Blake's sense, "Mental"; with his insistent and possessive ways, he is flame that seizes (*rapes* is another word, as the shadowy daughter of Urthona knows) and stings, not flame that shapes and illumines.

The Los character, though his furnace is the inexhaustible fount of imaginative freedom, remains for his part curiously dependent and subject to the vicissitudes of place and person. In a sense he uses Orc, or primordial fire, in his creative furnace, and so raises Orc to a higher and stabler order by his confinement and controls. But it is this very progression that makes for an uncertainty in Los's role. For just as the Spectre of Urthona "provides [Los] with a conscious will which makes his vision consistent and purposeful,"[41] so Orc provides him with the material cause of his vision. The presence of Orc's fire, intemperate and amorphous, informs him of something correspondent in himself that needs tempering and shape. But it is Orc's fire that enables his labor to escape solipsism, and achieve objective quality and authority. The Spectre of Urthona brings out in him the principles of his behavior, if only by negation. Orc serves as the instrumentality by which those principles can be realized. As a result of Orc's fire, Los has thoughts that do not inhere in that fire. The fire is "thick-flaming" and "thought-creating" (*The Song of Los*), but not thoughtful itself.

As one endowed with a gift for shaping and refining, and supplied with fire and matter, Los would seem to be well on the way to consummating his designs. But the nature of his designs leaves much more to be supplied. The Orcian fire is a symbol of the human soul, or perhaps rather a symbol of a condition of the human soul. But no condition of the soul can be worked on from outside, as Los works on the fire, and so the symbol remains at best problematical and elided, and Los's activity likewise. He is very much the character of will in the poems where we meet him, and his activity centers around art. But his will to art—and this is a note that reverberates through the structure of romantic thought—trespasses upon the domain of practical experience and real-life philosophy. His will to erect the perfect edifice, in Golgonooza, is a metonymy for his will to "create" a perfect way of life; and herein lies a problem for Los in relation to the other figures who must also enter into his perfect world. While it is possible for him to browbeat the Spectre of Urthona,[42] in deference to his ideal, he cannot browbeat Albion or Enitharmon and so cannot make even a symbolic show of amelioration where they are concerned. For that he must wait on them. They must recognize him for what he is, shaper of truth, superintendent of the edifice of redemption, and must accept themselves and the universe in his terms. His will, inevitable in one sense, seems incidental in another; its activity does not directly extend into creation of the world he espouses, as in the case of Keats's "Ode to Psyche"; rather, it resembles the world of Keats's *The Fall of Hyperion*, where a Christ-like assumption of devaluation and grief suggests at once the heroism of human love and the heroism of aesthetic engagement. *Jerusalem*, of course, reaches a resolution *The Fall of Hyperion* does not, but this is because Albion changes as Saturn does not, and Los does not make Albion change, but rather proves that, and *how*, he can. Albion's change corresponds to Los's will, rather than resulting from it.

We are confronted, then, with a situation akin to what we have seen in *The Prelude*: a pattern of action to which a form of will seems, paradoxically, both essential and ineffectual. The case with *Jerusalem* is all the more striking in that Los makes such a clamor about his will. But we need to recall that a strictly and simply purposive will is a Urizenic phenomenon, in Blake's terms, or a repudiated neoclassical structure in terms of the larger romantic complex. The will of Los is at a primary level an irreducible value of being, an affirmation against annihilation. But it is also a will to suffer for and toward a higher, more comprehensive order of being. This objective involves the poem in a sort of reactionary prophecy. The state to be achieved has existed in memory-as-myth, toward which one struggles back, and yet it cannot begin to exist unless the vision of Los, denounced and repudiated as a meretricious illusion, is shared and brought about transcendentally by Albion and the rest, as a sort of "Miracle & a New Birth" (*Milton*).

It should not surprise us that so often in Blake the realization of prophecy hovers just beyond the next horizon; the complexities of that realization tend to leave one element or another out of line or out of phase, and so the poems end with a promise that is also a postponement. This is perhaps to be expected when ebullient Orc provides the impetus toward millennium, as in *America: A Prophecy*. Mere energy will not give needed stability and shape to a new order, though it can heave the old one out of the way. What is "furious," as Blake notes in *The Four Zoas*, must also be "controllable" ("Night the Seventh," 86:6). But it may seem odd that Los, with Orc's energy at his disposal and with his own non-Urizenic devotion to order,[43] also fails to bring about a truer world. Rather, he too brings us to the horizon of hope, and stops there, in poems as divergent as *Europe: A Prophecy*, ending with a battle joined; *The (First) Book of Urizen*, which ends with an escape from Egypt but without prospect of a promised land; and even *Milton*, which as it closes brings us to the end of admonition and preparation, suggesting images of redemption but affording no actual evidence of Los or man in the putative new world:

Los listens to the Cry of the Poor Man: his Cloud
Over London in volume terrific, low bended in anger.

Rintrah & Palamabron view the Human Harvest beneath
Their Wine-Presses & Barns stand open; the Ovens are
    prepar'd
The Waggons ready: terrific Lions & Tygers sport & play
All Animals upon the Earth, are prepard in all their strength

To go forth to the Great Harvest & Vintage of the Nations[.]
        ["Book the Second," plate 42:34–39, plate 43]

This is evocative writing, and on an ethical and imaginative level likely to seem convincing in itself. Certain things, we are led to conclude, won't happen any more, because Los won't have them, and other things are about to take place, because all the conditions are present and they follow properly and promptly. But in fact the anger of Los is not so obviously and irresistibly curative as to warrant the first conclusion, and it is not necessary to be a Humean to note that the readiness of the Wine-Presses, the Ovens, the Waggons, and the Animals does not guarantee the Harvest. The credibility of the images for one "in the mortal state," as the poet effectively is, subsists in the realm of hope, and thus undermines the overt claim of imminent occurrence in the order of realization.

Something is wanting to Los who, representing the will to freedom and form, proves hardly less limited in his effect on the actual world than Orc, who enacts only the will to freedom as unrestraint. This difficulty is the more marked in that Los is not inclined to settle for the form of art as such, but designs a form of the world. It is well to recall that he relates to the intended ideal world largely by suffering—his anger in *Milton* is a mode of suffering—or perhaps rather by patience, in the mode of a man whose activity, however intense, is really meant to insure that things have a chance to turn out right.

But how can things turn out right? Let us recall that (1) Los's will to art has a basically engaged and, for all its chiliastic temper, a basically practical dimension, and (2) this puts him in a bind since he is only a part of the system he needs to create and cannot, either qua artist or qua character in the action, proceed directly to fulfillment of his design. He would have more scope, a better chance to play his hand, if Blake had adopted a dramatic mode and had written in the vein of *Prometheus Unbound* or visionary heroic drama; but for better or worse Blake opted for a kind of lyrical-didactic epic which, though it is full of dramatic confrontations and even, as he says himself, visionary forms dramatic, cannot like a drama produce resolution within itself. If Los, especially in *Jerusalem*, seems like the director of a drama, he is directing a bunch of Pirandellian actors who will make up their own play and leave him continually in the lurch. The Christ figure is the deus ex machina of this impasse in the poetry, but is in a sense as remote from its dimension as art as Los is from its claims as redemption. His presence is the consummation of Los's capacity for patience, and reflects the limitations of that capacity, serving as an offer, not an act, a reservoir rather than a healing draught. The impasse *of the poetry* can no more be solved from one side than from the other, from that of redeemer who knows no art or that of the artist who commands no redemption.

The power and function of art in Blake does not, however, reside only in the dual character of Orc and Los. There is a third figure, combining the energy of Orc and the purpose of Los, while commanding the amplitudes of the other persons. This figure shares but is not governed by either Orc's precipitancy or Los's hesitancy. He joins with them to complete the ideal of the poet for Blake. The figure is of course Blake himself. On one level he is a mere amanuensis, as anyone who aspires to prophecy must be. But we must not overlook the fact that he is the amanuensis for his own dispensation of prophecy. At the deepest level he is less the prophet-as-amanuensis than the amanuensis-as-creator-and-master. Say what he will about following dictation, Blake is the editorial poet par excellence, prompt to intrude into the poetry, and seemingly determined to have it go one way. Unquestionably he shows a singularly candid and sensitive mind, and hides nothing of the oppositions his vision encounters, but his involvement in realizing that vision remains paramount. His mythology indeed gives a very powerful impression of an objective and long-standing order. If he is not, like Los vis-à-vis the Spectre of Urthona, simply insistent on his "dictates," perhaps we should see Blake as one obsessed with and exploiting that *dictated* order.

Blake in effect disguises the will of the poet as the will of the poem or its characters, but we must ultimately scrutinize him for answers to the behavioral peculiarities of the poems. It would seem odd that the sources of his work, after *The Marriage of Heaven and Hell*, keep giving him a truncated action if we did not realize that they give him what he wants and needs (thus always the accommodating muse). It would seem odd that his apparent surrogates, Orc and Los, remain thwarted, save that they intimate his awareness of the limits of energy and of purpose, respectively;[44] energy dissipates itself and purpose, when not crushingly compulsive, must exercise itself in patience.

As limited instruments of his will to art, Orc and Los oblige Blake to refine and enlarge that will. The easy victories and facile wisdoms of *The Marriage of Heaven and Hell* or even *The French Revolution*[45] will not finally sustain experience or, for that matter, the edifice of Blake's vision. Blake must seem, of all the great English romantics, the most masculine and arrogant in position, but his capacity for exuberance carries with it a reflex capacity for doubt, which his larger works seek to overcome and, at last, eliminate. By itself prophecy cannot eliminate doubt; faith is required for that. And we must remember that the Blake who espoused the idea of contraries feared negations, and came close to substituting "Mental war" as a practical mode of redemptiveness for the static perfection of apocalypse. It seems likely that Blake, struggling between the sharp finality of his burin and the accommodating elasticity of his verse, kept the action of his poem from going too far in the direction of abstraction and amorphous apocalypse by a kind of brinkmanship. Though he needs Orc and Los for his art, he is not satisfied with them. Though he sees his instrumental prophetic stance as a privilege, it functions also as a threat to his own being. For though his prophecy may be his greatest act, it is not as much as himself, not his *fullest* act if it makes him but its instrument. This impasse is only solved when Blake comes to add to the history of prophetic writing the personal factor whereby the prophet must attain belief, before the new truth can attain reality.

Jerusalem is the analysis and record of his attaining belief as a poet. The distance Blake traverses in it may be judged by the fact that at the start he plays the role of simple agent or amanuensis: "When this Verse was first dictated to me . . ." (1, 3). If his arbitrary choice of the "Cadence" qualifies his position, the emphasis remains on dictations, on his function as recipient and purveyor, rather than originator:

> This theme calls me in sleep night after night, & ev'ry morn
> Awakes me at sun-rise, then I see the Saviour over me
> Spreading his beams of love, & dictating the words of this
>   mild song.
>
>   [1, 4:3–5]

This might seem a simple invocation of the Muse, but Blake is virtually denying any access of power, which the Muse as a rule affords. The prose preface leaves no doubt concerning the nature of the case. Not just Blake but presumably any man would be subject to dictation: "We who dwell on Earth can do nothing of ourselves, every thing is conducted by Spirits" (1, 3).

But the sharp distinction between effective spirit and automatic man begins to break down at once. Indeed a degree of identification ensues, as the exhortation "Awake! awake O Sleeper of the land of shadows," actually addressed to Albion, seems to apply to the poet; the sequence of statements, in a way that is characteristic of Blake's prophecies, functions plausibly as a continuation, where in fact a concealed transition has occurred. By the time the impression of continuation is rectified, it has become part of the reader's response and thus, as a matter of reverberation, the source of suggestive resonances and reflections in the reader's mind.[46] The effect here is to create a sense of possible kinship between spirit and man, or even a degree of mutual involvement concerning which the poem furnishes various further clues along the way.

The first clue is not long in coming. The seemingly passive poet emerges as a man with a mission and an ideal he is strenuously pursuing. It is not his possession but his devotion that impresses his friends, and not his activity but his duty and purpose that occupy him:

> Trembling I sit day and night, my friends are astonish'd at
> me.
> Yet they forgive my wanderings, I rest not from my great
> task!
> *To open* the Eternal Worlds, *to open* the immortal Eyes
> Of Man inwards into the Worlds of Thought . . .
> . . . the Human Imagination
> O Saviour *pour upon me* thy Spirit of meekness & love:
> *Annihilate* the Selfhood in me, *be thou all my life*!
> [1, 5:16–22; italics added]

The infinitives of purpose and the subjunctives of supplica-

tion here (marked by italics) involve the poet at primary levels
of expression. Function ("to open") and essence ("be . . . all
my life") meet in one cast, whose object is the coming into
realized being of the poem and the poet alike. It will be apparent that Blake is conducting in the arena of his own mind
no less a dramatic experiment than Keats in the confrontation between the poet and Moneta in *The Fall of Hyperion*.
But Blake is more lucid about the situation than Keats, and
so struggles from the outset toward, not against, self-annihilation; he knows that to lose his life is to gain it.

In effect, the poetic will functions in terms of paradox.
Blake wills, with all his being, an abdication of will. The more
perfectly he is subjected to the superior influence of the
"Saviour,"[47] the more perfectly he overcomes the inhabitant
obstacles to his fullest humanity, the more perfectly he is
free.

A mastery of self-abnegation remains, however, an immate-
rial feat. The poet's purpose must be grasped in connection
with the "Spirit of Meekness & love" that he would receive as
from a vessel (that is the sense of *pour*). These virtues set an
ideal for character and for poetry, and it is essential to see
that they are not shibboleths but require constant defense
and sacrifice: "willing sacrifice of Self, [not] sacrifice of
(miscall'd) Enemies" (1, 28:20). They represent the way out
of "Selfhood," with its antagonism and confinement of view.
The quality of Selfhood in Albion betrays itself in the abun-
dant and assertive use of the pronoun *I* in his manifesto (as
compared with Los's profession of faith, just quoted):

I have erred! I am ashamed! and will never return more:
I have taught my children sacrifices of cruelty: what shall I
    answer?
I will hide it from Eternals! I will give myself for my
    Children!
Which way soever I turn, I behold Humanity and Pity!
He recoil'd. . . .

                                            [1, 23:16–20]

An unalterable past, an unbearable present, and an unwork-
able future: such are the terms derived from a rigid concern
with the private actions and sentiments of the single self, di-
vorced from the very values which seem to motivate its despair. That is, the logic of regretting error requires return and
rectification, not perpetual absence. In the same way, cruelty
to children is not amended but increased by a recoil from
humanity and pity. Albion is paradoxically hemmed in
("Which way soever I turn") by "Humanity and Pity," by the
very force which should enlarge him and furnish him an alternative structure of principles against his "I"-solation.

  The poet's devotion to meekness and love makes explicit
the values that animate Los in the poem as he labors to stave
off final disaster for Albion:

> For had the Body of Albion fall'n down, and from its
>   dreadful ruins
> Let loose the enormous Spectre on the darkness of the deep,
> At enmity with the Merciful & fill'd with devouring fire,
> A nether-world must have receivd the foul enormous spirit,
> Under pretense of Moral Virtue, fill'd with Revenge and
>   Law,
> There to eternity chain'd down, and issuing in red flames
> And curses, with his mighty arms brandish'd against the
>   heavens,
> Breathing cruelty, blood & vengeance, gnashing his teeth
>   with pain,
> Torn with black storms, & ceaseless torrents of his own con-
>   suming fire:
> Within his breast his mighty Sons chaind down & fill'd with
>   cursings:
> And his dark Eon, that once fair crystal form divinely clear:
> Within his ribs producing serpents whose souls are flames of
>   fire.
>
>   [2, 36:31–42]

And the poet, who has quickly proceeded from recorder to
champion of spiritual values, comes to seem their source and

philosophical possessor, while the controlling "Spirits" turn into something like their agents. Certainly one gets the sense of a new status for the poet a third of the way through the poem, and most emphatically in plate 34. He is a seer now, and the spiritual creatures act within his domain: "I see them [the Divine Family following Albion] in the Vision of God upon my pleasant valleys." More than this, he seems to introduce independent expatiations on the action proper within the poem. It is in line with the espousal of meekness and love that he defines how the "loves and tears" of others are indispensable to man's existence (2, 34:10-12). And it adds a heroic dimension to that position when, once more speaking as seer, he defines the amplitudes and manifestations of man:

> I see thee awful Parent Land in light, behold I see![48]
> Verulam! Canterbury! venerable parent of men,
> Generous immortal Guardian golden clad! for Cities
> Are Men, fathers of multitudes, and Rivers & Mountains
> Are also Men; every thing is Human, mighty! sublime!
> In every bosom a Universe expands, as wings
> Let down at will around, and call'd the Universal Tent.
> [2, 34:44-50]

The logical *for* of line 46 itself expands and comes to take a significant position through the poem. It is a gesture whereby the poet enters into the meaning of his experience, on one level, but on another it must seem the instrument whereby he initiates us into that meaning.[49] His status expands at will.

Two further points should effectively round out our understanding of the pattern of the poet's development from passive amanuensis to independent creativity. In plate 74 he commands all time as seer, and communicates all meanings as poet. Not only has his ambition escalated from the beginning of the poem, but now his ambition is virtually self-realizing, as we see in the abrupt shift from the subjunctive to the indicative mood:

> Teach me O Holy Spirit the Testimony of Jesus! let me
> Comprehend wonderous things out of the Divine Law[.]

I behold Babylon in the opening Streets of London, I
   behold
Jerusalem in ruins wandering about from house to house
This I behold the shudderings of death attend my steps
I walk up and down in Six Thousand Years: their Events
   are present before me
To tell how Los in grief & anger . . .
Drove the Sons & Daughters of Albion from their ancient
   mountains[.]

[3, 74:14-21]

Far from giving himself over, then, as in the original phase of
the poem, he is taking over control of unlikely realms. There
is paradox in comprehending wonders, if they are not to
cease to be so, but the poet sets himself just that task,
making himself positively exceptional. His capacity to grasp
what most men might boggle at appears again in the preface
to chapter 4, where he distinguishes between what "we are
told" and what "I know"; the poem thus becomes, in retrospect, a presentation of *his* singular knowledge as a rectification of ours.

His ascendancy in the poem is complete when, instead of
his praying to receive the power of the spiritual order, representatives of that order acknowledge a sort of dependency on
him: "The Poets Song [Enitharmon observes] draws to its
period & Enitharmon is no more." They are part of his world,
and implicitly adjust themselves to him. In this light the narrative index, "Time was Finished!" (4, 94:18), reflects not
just the poet's vision but his decision for the subjects of his
work. This completes the poet's progression from anxious
self-abnegating prayer, at the outset of *Jerusalem*, to an
apocalyptic activity and competence.

In a sense the poet's development parallels that of the action; that is to say, his initial plea for inspiration represents
an intuition of possibilities beyond the known, and the unfolding of the action as given coincides with the unfolding of
his capabilities as discovered. But it must be stressed that the
poet's prowess, his authority, still occurs within the prin-

ciples, though not in the form, of his initial engagement with the spiritual world. Even the final moment of triumph in the poem is a moment of sacrifice (4, 96:35), reminding us of the suffering that goes with "meekness and love." Los becomes identified with Christ (96:22) just as the poet has become identified with Christ, and the wholeness of the poet— tacitly including Orc's energy and Los's shaping force, but transcending their subjection and frustration—is manifest in terms of the redemption of suffering through love. The experience of shouldering the crosses of the world, which befalls Keats and which has no definite resolution in *The Fall of Hyperion*, is subject matter and lodestar for the *Jerusalem* poet.

Recognition of suffering—and of the only way to meet a world defined by suffering—stands as the central gesture of *Jerusalem*. The poem has been called apocalyptic, but this can be misleading, for apocalypse is oblique or mediated in it; the source and instrument of apocalypse prove to be a very humble embracing and assimilation of self-sacrifice, as when "Albion spoke & threw himself into the Furnaces of affliction" (4, 96:35). Indeed, apocalypse has no status of its own, since there is always suffering to be allayed. This makes *Jerusalem* an invitation to the self-sacrifice of meekness and love, as a perpetual transformation of a perpetually needy world, rather than a purveyor of any final apocalypse. Even the artist figure, Los, despite his apparent freedom to devise apocalyptic structures like Golgonooza, bears witness to the poem's basic reliance on sacrifice and transformation. It is not his strenuous and frenzied building but his sympathy and faith and devotion that should be credited with saving Albion.

To transform suffering by acceptance, to see the beauty inherent in suffering and sacrifice, even to become a surrogate Christ or scapegoat in society: these are the functions that link Blake and Keats,[50] and the functions that seem to bring us closest to their conception of the poet and of art. It will seem paradoxical to say so, given a long-standing opinion of the romantic poet as arrogant or ethereal or, in short, *romantic*. But, as I have brought out with respect to Keats and

Wordsworth, the whole romantic enterprise may well be regarded as an intricate and unceasing dialogue between idiocracy and community, between definitive personal impulse and the discipline of experience. In this light, the poet's choice is not between ecstasy and reality, as Keats early on seems to say, but between a grace-giving acceptance of suffering on the one hand and death on the other, as *Alastor* graphically shows.

If it does not originate as such, the will to art in romanticism quickly evolves into a confrontation of the problem of suffering in light of certain presumptions of life's positive meaning and value, thus leaving the poetry in the argumentative position of trying to reconcile a radical opposition between experience and principle. Keats and Blake afford two striking modes of response to the dilemma of suffering. A third response emerges in Wordsworth's work, where the will to art and the fact of suffering meet in a way that raises the prospect, alien to Keats and Blake, not of converting but of renouncing art itself.

WORDSWORTH AND THE STOICAL RESOLUTION OF ART

The function of healing ("To sooth the cares, and lift the thoughts of man") adds a whole new dimension to the value of poetry in the romantic period. The old Horatian aims of instruction and delight[51] address themselves as it were to particular occasions and immediate effects; but the business of healing is perennial, addressing itself directly to the very state of man as finite and suffering (the state that delight may distract from, or instruction imaginably temper here and there). It is hard to say whether the dimension of healing gives evidence of a radical departure as regards the object of poetry or merely articulates what had been latent all along. In a sense the mythology of poetry suggests that healing is the proper genealogical successor to instruction and delight. Aesculapius, god of the healing art, is son to the god of poetry, Apollo.

The poet as healer may be seen to enjoy a new social eminence, at least potentially. But this amounts to a burdensome privilege, making him vulnerable to the exposure of his very eminence. In his case the physician must heal himself simultaneously with the patient, or not at all. He knows humanity's disease as an extension of his own suffering; Schopenhauer cannily remarks that "according to the true nature of things, everyone has all the sufferings of the world as his own."[52] The poet's dual status as singular healer and common sufferer seems to give rise to a dual method of response, or, so to speak, of treatment. One method is based on the principle of ectype, with the protagonist in a Christ-like manner (1) going through the suffering of mankind, as Keats and Shelley show in *The Fall of Hyperion* and *Prometheus Unbound*, respectively, and (2) shining the healing light of compassion and courage upon the state of suffering. Its psychology seems to assume that the identification of all mankind (and of godhead) in suffering will dissipate and transform the individual case. The second method follows the principle of idealization and works by presenting the model of an achieved command over the onslaughts of suffering, the sort of command we may recognize in Wordsworth's discharged soldier or old Leech-gatherer. It invites the mind toward the security of transcendence, where an empirically unexpected freedom from suffering is taken as something all people, one by one, may attain.

Not that the model Wordsworthian figures with their balanced, impregnable mood control the amplitudes of the poems they occur in. The energy and volatility of Wordsworth's personal reaction surround characters like the Leech-gatherer or the Wanderer or the Old Cumberland Beggar, or even the old man traveling in "Animal Tranquillity and Decay" (a poem full of hushed pity and amazement, and so charged with a sort of reverse animation). The essence of the poems lies in their vibrant confrontations, even a manufactured one between Wordsworth and the audience in "The Old Cumberland Beggar." Undeniably such confrontations subsist in a dramatic atmosphere quite at odds with the quiescence of these characters by themselves. The drama and energy of the poems in question arise from an intrinsic failure of quiescence at their focal point. The poetry is not in, or even about, the Leech-gatherer; it subsists in the confrontation of his passage beyond poetry into pure wordless symbol and the poet-speaker's slide beneath poetry into pure uncontrolled phenomenality.

Wordsworth's poetry often seems to strive toward quiescence or what Perkins calls "permanence" as a state more effective and more philosophical, for all its inertia and silence, than any amount of labor or enunciation. Perhaps this attitude springs from a conception of grace as utterly given, as self-evidently out of human reach or purpose; certainly the accidental appearance and fortuitous beneficence of Wordsworth's quiet derelicts is of a piece with the eventualist myth of a poem like *The Prelude*. But their very embodiment of happiness as happenstance helps to suggest that quiescence ought not to be taken as a direct or dogmatic ideal for Wordsworth. It is a reference point that manages to be both basic and *occasional* in the career of the Wordsworthian actor. It is as much a surprise as an ideal, a humiliation as well as a comfort, to the central figure in the poetry. It is not out of place to observe that "resolution" means both objective-to-be-attained and position-attained. And both meanings apply to Wordsworth through his encounter with the Leech-gatherer; he is at once absolved of the chaos of spirit he begins by exhibiting and incapable of maintaining that state without exploiting his memory and emulation of the Leech-gatherer.

Resolution and "Memorials of a Tour on the Continent, 1820"

The failure of resolution comes out powerfully in the *Memorials of a Tour on the Continent, 1820*. The main series of thirty-seven poems cultivates stillness and stability, freedom from confusion without and from "terror or despondency" (XX, 20) within, and even seeks to stop up "the secret springs/Of that licentious craving in the mind/To act the

God among external things,/To bind, on apt suggestion, or unbind." (XXXII, 64-67). A stoical harmony is achieved where "consciousnesses"

> . . . only serve a feeling to invite
> That lifts the spirit to a calmer height,
> And makes this rural stillness more profound.
> [XXXVI, 12-14]

The earlier confusions of the poem (the word *consciousnesses* hints at a confusing and oppressive plenty) are not eliminated; Wordsworth has not withdrawn from reality, but reenters it tempered, composed. This is a natural, temporal event with a divine, eternal analog:

> "Ocean's o'erpowering murmurs have set free
> Thy sense from pressure of life's common din;
> As the dread Voice that speaks from out the sea
> Of God's eternal Word, the Voice of Time
> Doth deaden, shocks of tumult, shrieks of crime,
> The shouts of folly, and the groans of sin."
> [XXXVII, 9-14]

But the final poem in the series, "Desultory Stanzas upon Receiving the Preceding Sheets from the Press," lives up neither to its title nor to the spirit of stoical calm and conviction of the foregoing pieces. Instead a recrudescence of feeling and of self-indulgent creativity occurs. The "Desultory Stanzas" become a recapitulation rather than a conclusion; a casual temptation is enough to call forth energies that are hidden rather than controlled or converted:

> . . . unbidden feelings start
> Forth from their coverts; slighted objects rise;
> My spirit is the scene of such wild art
> As on Parnassus rules, when lightning flies,
> Visibly leading on the thunder's harmonies.
>
> All that I saw returns upon my view,
> All that I heard comes back upon my ear,

> All that I felt this moment doth renew;
> And where the foot with no unmanly fear
> Recoiled—and wings alone could travel—there
> I move at ease. . . .
>
> [XXXVIII, 5-15]

Like Yeats in "Sailing to Byzantium," Wordsworth here re-
covers what has seemed to be repudiated. He is no longer
threatened, but "at ease." He combines responsiveness and
control now, where before he had been subject to the "pressure" of his very "consciousnesses." In short, these *Memorials*
regenerate tumult and spontaneity, though ostensibly devoted to surcease of pain and safety from that preternatural
wildness of experience which the opening poem, "Fish-
Women—On Landing at Calais," so shiveringly portrays:

> . . . if the Nereid Sisters and their Queen
> Above whose heads the tide so long hath rolled,
> The Dames resemble whom we here behold,
> How fearful were it down through opening waves
> To sink, and meet them in their fretted caves,
> Withered, grotesque, immeasurably old,
> And shrill and fierce in accent!

Such fear cannot be sustained, but stoical calm cannot maintain itself either. And the poetry might seem to embody the
struggle between these two impossibilities.

In the final analysis, more is at issue than the fact that
Wordsworth does not maintain stoical resolution. At bottom
he is not satisfied with it, and may be said to treat it as instrument more than ideal. His theory of poetry is exploitative
of peace, which both saves him from the torment of immediate experience and furnishes him a means of shaping and
enjoying a recovered experience. If the "overflow of powerful feelings" that defines poetry for Wordsworth is "spontaneous," it is also systematically displaced. Poetry "takes its
origin from emotion recollected in tranquillity: the emotion
is contemplated till, by a species of reaction, the tranquillity

gradually disappears, and an emotion, kindred to that which was before the subject of contemplation, is gradually produced, and does itself actually exist in the mind" (Preface to *Lyrical Ballads*). It is clear that Wordsworth is both soliciting and undermining "tranquillity," just as he is both renouncing and cultivating emotion. One might at first suppose that his tranquillity here has no connection with stoicism, but it is useful to see the structural kinship between his behavior as regards creative tranquillity and personal composure. In neither case is he truly or definitively committed to "calm of mind, all passion spent." He pursues quiescence less for itself than for the assurance it gives him in the face of a recreated and incorporated tumult. In a sense he pursues the discovered *power of quiescence*.

This phenomenon is presented in more patently stoical terms in "Tintern Abbey," where a triple movement from confusion to tranquillity to ecstasy-in-tranquillity occurs. The "din/Of towns and cities," "hours of weariness," "the heavy and the weary weight/Of all this unintelligible world," "the fretful stir/Unprofitable, and the fever of the world": these dispossessing trials beset Wordsworth "in darkness and amid the many shapes/Of joyless daylight." He is desperate for relief, and finds it as "tranquil restoration" in the recollection of the Wye and the scene above Tintern Abbey. He has sought no more, but more is found in an imperceptible and yet inevitable process of development. Tranquillity "gently lead[s] . . . on" to ecstasy, and that ecstasy coexists with essential insight:

> That serene and blessed mood,
> In which the affections gently lead us on,—
> Until the breath of this corporeal frame
> And even the motion of our human blood
> Almost suspended, we are laid asleep
> In body, and become a living soul:
> While with an eye made quiet by the power
> Of harmony, and the deep power of joy,
> We see into the life of things.

In the last lines "power" yields "quiet," but in the passage as a whole "quiet" yields "power." This is a crucial recognition for Wordsworth and the resolution of stoicism, and it is useful to remember that stoicism itself was processive and *empowering* in the world; Marcus Aurelius's *Meditations* constitutes a course of instruction *for himself*, not a set of rules and determination for others.[53] As W.H.D. Rouse observes, Marcus Aurelius "is no head of a school to lay down a body of doctrine for students; he does not even contemplate that others should read what he writes. . . . The grim resignation which made life possible to the Stoic sage becomes in him almost a mood of aspiration."[54]

Wordsworth's response to suffering—a complex escape through an idealization of quiescence—needs to be pursued along two main lines of interest: (1) the fact that this idealization ultimately unites Wordsworth and Byron, though they start from the opposite poles of gratuitous melancholy and Promethean defiance,[55] respectively; and (2) the fact that this idealization is the more self-contradictory as it is the more efficacious, suppressing what it should foster, the reality of poetry and personality alike. For poetry, in the interest of quiescence, must take on a sober garb and beat with a sober pulse, even to the point of giving up the potential magical power that could amplify the dimensions of healing. In *Childe Harold*, canto 4 (stanzas 5–8), Byron abjures poetry as magic and with it the healing agency of escape from harsh reality; and *The Prelude* is sprinkled with Wordsworth's resistance to the magical lure of poetry and its supposed cure for his own and the world's ills. At the same time the poet's sensation of himself as poet, the sense of aesthetic acuteness or at least of human amplitude, is correspondingly played down—the element of personality is another temptation of self-indulgence. The aspiration to write drama and philosophy, in Keats and Shelley, respectively, points up the movement away from personality, as does the dramatizing tendency in Wordsworth (which Coleridge so deplored) and Byron's incorporation of a reflective historical manner into his later writing. Indeed, the elements of drama, philosophy, and history help to suggest, in the development toward quiescence, a resort to generality as a means of stabilizing and giving adequacy to the self.

If we remember that romanticism, for all its revolutionary and self-expressive fervor, remained at bottom a movement toward a redeemed catholicity, the place quiescence holds in its mental economy will come as no surprise. It arises as a need in the very openness and sensitivity of spirit that romanticism espouses, and if it finds expression in *simple figures*, it also manifests itself in complex situations, its simplicity forming a powerful resolution of the complex. In fact, the contexts in which quiescence occurs make it seem more than a product of a spiritual rhythm. It is a spiritual choice, and a philosophical statement arrived at through the drama and the energy of flesh. The peculiar nature of this philosophy I would classify as stoical, and it is to the singular and deep presence of the stoical temper in romanticism that the following pages are given.

The Articulation of Silence: From "Calm Is All Nature" to "The Excursion"

Though stoicism is late to appear in articulate form in the work of any English romantic, an oblique and primitive form of it can be discerned in the thick of much of their more impassioned and as it were turbid writing. One of Wordsworth's first poems, the sonnet "Written in Very Early Youth," can be used in illustration.

> Calm is all nature as a resting wheel.
> The kine are couched upon the dewy grass;
> The horse alone, seen dimly as I pass,
> Is cropping audibly his later meal:
> Dark is the ground; a slumber seems to steal
> O'er vale and mountain, and the starless sky.
> Now, in this blank of things, a harmony,
> Home-felt, and home-created, comes to heal
> That grief for which the senses still supply

Fresh food; for only then, when memory
Is hushed, am I at rest. My Friends! restrain
Those busy cares that would allay my pain;
Oh! leave me to myself, nor let me feel
The officious touch that makes me droop again.

This is essentially a poem about incessant grief in experience
and in memory, but it is very subtly constructed so as to hold
up "calm" or the antithesis of grief as the measure of things.
In effect, calm disguises grief in the form of the poem as well
as in the speaker's soul. More than this, too, calm proves to
be a purely mechanical (the wheel) or physical (the kine) condition, without the usual connotations of mental and spiritual
composure; it represents a "blank of things" and so an effective surcease of life with its "grief" and "pain." In effect, we
encounter a mechanical quiet even in the spirit. The "blank,"
which is not "calm" in any customary sense, is explicitly
associated with "a harmony,/Home-felt, and home-created."
Thus it seems to arise not only from nature, as something outward, but also from the inner state, home. There is no dimension of the world that does not partake of the nonvital,
insensate[56] quality of the "blank."

In effect both "calm" and "harmony" become mutually
reinforcing quasi-stoical states, an emotional (or unemotional)
analog to the philosophy of stoicism. The poem does not give
a concrete version of what makes life as such intolerable. It
does, however, contain two images that may suggest a necessity for stoicism in the given universe of uncertainty and
comfortlessness. The "resting wheel" of the first line may be
a cart wheel, but it strongly invokes thoughts of the wheel of
fortune, its momentary cessation affording a grateful relief
that would be quite consistent with a "blank of things." And
there is a suggestion, in the "starless sky," that misery predominates in this random and unilluminated world. What this
early (but surprisingly resonant) poem sets forth is a condition of causeless melancholy in the nature of human being,
and an impulse (not surprising in so young a writer) to escape,

if only into a blank of things. At the same time the quasi-stoical idioms of "calm" and "harmony" reach out toward another, more positive answer.

It is an answer to which Wordsworth does not come quickly, or smoothly. But we may see him as it were gravitating, in his poetry, toward characters or situations that either (1) demand a stoical answer, as in "Ruth" and "The Thorn," or (2) embody and promote that answer, as in "Peele Castle" or "Resolution and Independence." A search for resolution of spirit really underlies the dramatizing tendency for which Coleridge found fault with Wordsworth; the "drama" amounts to no more than a playing out of the obsessions and necessities of the ego, with a second character providing reflective philosophical dimensions, and has little of the formal or impersonal features of drama proper. The wilful and hence woeful ego approaches what Wordsworth in a cancelled stanza of the "Ode to Duty" termed "a second Will more wise." "Resolution and Independence" furnishes a fine example of Wordsworth's use of the reflective character to engage the problem of causeless or primary melancholy.

The movement of "Resolution and Independence" follows the course of the speaker's spirit, from hypersensitivity as poet to stoical acceptance as man. The poem encompasses a third phase, preliminary to the unsettling ominous storm that, lasting "all night", seems to have suggested to the speaker the end of a world—destruction by water informs the phrase, "the rain . . . fell in *floods*"; and the "roaring *in* the wind" (stanza 1; italics added), conveys a sense of nature uttering sounds of threatening or dismay. The initial, sensitively poetical phase is without specific character and effect. It has a blanket, superficial, almost lulled quality, like the calm before a storm: "My whole life I have lived in pleasant thought,/As if life's business were a summer mood." After the wakeful storm that world is indeed ended, where before it was no more than overclouded by recognition of "the ways of men, so vain and melancholy" (stanza 3). A basic threat to the self has supervened, and that self utterly redefines the terms of existence, making "dim sadness" (stanza 4) the pervasive condition and treating the "pleasant season" (stanza 3) as the kind of ostensible relief that gives new sting to pain like the drop of black paint that makes white paint brighter; "gladness" is the beginning of "despondency and madness" (stanza 7). The new world after the floods punishes the speaker with erratic emotions that image an unstable dispensation. And his being a poet only makes his sense of affliction the keener (here, explicitly, that danger of the poetical state which is propaedeutic to stoicism).

The image of the poet, apart from its prevailing pathos, is not an especially engaging one. In a sense he proves unable to see what is under his nose ("I saw a Man before me unawares"), and then, whether from bafflement or excess of wit, seems bent on making what he sees into what, as Byron might say, he wants to see ("huge stone," "a thing endued with sense," "a sea-beast").[57] Even the rhythm and rhetoric of the stanzas (9-11) become poetical and Spenserian. And yet the humanity of the old man breaks through the phalanx of the poet's imaginings. The poet does not give over his poetizing, nor his sense of the omnipotence of melancholy, but he applies them in a way that admits the Leech-gatherer's human status: "As if some dire constraint of pain, or rage/Of sickness felt by him . . . " (stanza 10).

The action of the poem essentially takes places in the "poet's" mind, and its tension derives from the difference between (1) an arbitrary imposition of his imagination on what he meets and (2) a lucid recognition in him of the intrinsic state and force of what meets him; or, to put it otherwise, between a momentary and an abiding state of things. He himself is at the mercy of the momentary ("I heard the woods and distant waters roar;/*Or heard them not*"—italics added) and can come to no more stable a footing than the weather. He has a penchant for generalization, but his generalization canonizes the momentary and inhibits its range by taking away his faith in its brighter aspects: "Even as these blissful creatures do I fare;/. . . But there may come another day to me—/Solitude, pain of heart, distress, and poverty." If he has a capacity for breaking the cycle of experienced or expected solitude, etc., it proves self-contradictory. He identifies with Chatterton, and beyond him all poets, only to reinforce the helplessness of his personal states: "We Poets in our youth begin in gladness;/But thereof come in the end despondency and madness." The last line is metrically troubled, its *thereof* standing out ominously as it advances the helplessness of tragic sequence (post hoc) into the logical ineluctability of tragedy (propter hoc).[58]

It is this principle of momentariness that the "poet" brings to the scene where the Leech-gatherer is met. In spite of the latter's complete motionlessness, the poet puts him through a protean course of similes which further involve ideas of brief and strange movement (the unaccountable stone, the sea-beast). His philosophy (momentariness) and his function (poetry) thus combine to dehumanize the old man and make him into a creature of his arrogant universe; even the rehumanizing simile of the old man's pain ("As if some dire constraint . . .," stanza 10) only confirms the poet's values—the world is full of pain, and pain cannot be borne.[59] But again the speaker has blindly approached more and deeper truth than he apprehends. The situation "upon the margin of that moorish flood" carries us back into thoughts of universal disaster (the flood) but also of profound beginning (the margin). And it is the beginning that predominates. With his "unsettling" the Leech-gatherer introduces new movement and new valences into the poem. The overt sociology and pragmatism of the speaker's interest are only a mask for the deeper question, namely, how the Leech-gatherer is himself. It is obvious after all how he lives and what he does; what is not obvious is how he *keeps* himself up, without repining or blasphemy. In short, in a solipsistic vein, how can he be different from the poet himself?

The "dream" of unrealization into which the poet falls (stanza 16) constitutes, psychologically, a breakdown of rigidity and resistance to whatever may be alien to himself.

Thus his sense of the Leech-gatherer as one "sent," with "apt admonishment." But unreality ("in a dream") and remoteness ("from some far region") undermine this good effect. The poet cannot grasp the message, and the old man, no longer insensate "stone," takes on for him the vague and passing properties of a "stream." This is sheer projection. Instability marks the poet's mind; his former thoughts recur and bring him back to philosophical fretfulness and defiant incomprehension of the old man (stanza 17). He is struggling with incomprehension here, expressing old prejudices but also exposing himself to possible new revelation, if the old man will only explain. What the poet, the creature of the moment, experiences is the fact of *repetition as revelation*. The Leech-gatherer repeats his words, as he has repeated the very acts of his life, as essential and obvious truth, which thus stands revealed. By contrast with the poet's gratuitous imagery and even his didactic dream, the revelation takes the form of reality itself, with all the austere naturalism of a chastised "imagination":

> In my mind's eye I seemed to see him pace
> About the weary moors continually,
> Wandering about alone and silently.

The poet sees the Leech-gatherer *as himself*, solitary, and to that extent deprived; but also eternal, and to that extent transcendent. Acceptance is the source of his transcendence, the stoical composure he offers the speaker as a means of becoming what is more than a pathetic poet, a competent man.

In effect "Resolution and Independence" dramatizes the metaphysical power of stoicism, in the Leech-gatherer, and the spiritual need for it, in the poet. In a sense, then, the poet has been tacitly receptive to the Leech-gatherer all along. In another sense the two figures remain at odds; the poet does not envisage himself becoming "a veritable Leech-gatherer," but will only invoke the old man's state and his powers on suitable occasions, which he obviously expects to recur indefinitely. Indeed, qua poet, he may not aspire to become like the Leech-gatherer, whose powers are the *powers of silence*. In relation to the Leech-gatherer the poet may express a certain idealism and convey a certain consummate human state; in himself, he cannot even effectively represent his state, because it is consummate, removed from process, from attention, from response, in a way that oddly induces the poet's first false assessment of the Leech-gatherer as unalive or inhuman.

The energy, in fact the possibility, of the poem stems from the natural friction generated between the poetic and the stoical state, for implicitly stoicism runs counter to poetry. Wordsworth's better poetry of stoicism ("Peele Castle," "Ode to Duty," "Character of the Happy Warrior," "Laodamia," "Nuns fret not," *The White Doe of Rylstone, Memorials of a Tour on the Continent, 1820*) thrives on a state of struggle or aspiration, and may be said to come into being in the gap between imperfect humanity and perfect stoicism. The radical weakness of *The Excursion* as a poem derives precisely from its assertion and assumption of, as opposed to an inspiration toward, stoicism. We are too much outside the Wanderer, in mutual detachment, as we learn that "he strove/To mitigate the fever of his heart" (1, 299–300). In like manner the "just equipoise" of his mind (1, 355) conjures up the image of a scale without a grasp of character. The radical dialogue between poet and Leech-gatherer is missing in the relation of poet to Wanderer. Description supersedes drama; the poem does not move and educate us, it presumes on our capitulation or credulity.

The early portrait of the Wanderer offers a compendium of stoical traits:

> Serene [his mind] was, unclouded by the cares
> Of ordinary life; unvexed, unwarped
> By partial bondage. In his steady course,
> No piteous revolutions had he felt,
> No wild varieties of joy and grief.
> . . . .

> . . . in himself
> Happy, and quiet in his cheerfulness,
> He had no painful pressure from without
> That made him turn aside from wretchedness
> With coward fears. He could *afford* to suffer
> With those whom he saw suffer.
>
> [1, 356–71]

But perhaps this is a specious bubble rather than the substantial sphere of stoicism. The enlarging and ennobling compassion that marks Keats's stoicism in *The Fall of Hyperion* might seem to be paralleled here. The lines in fact yield almost an ironic resonance. Wordsworth underlines the word *afford*, which, because it picks up the commercial life the Wanderer has led, makes his apparent compassion little different from his early retirement ("provision for his wants/Had been obtained"—he could afford it). This comes dangerously close to the angelic stoicism we see in *Paradise Lost*, where the fate of the fallen angels, though clearly known, fails and must fail to disturb the fate of the loyal ones. Such imperturbability makes sense, especially in the ontology of angels, but it proves problematical in humanity.

The fact is of course that the Wanderer—*The Excursion* itself—is fully aware of "the strong creative power/Of human passion" (1, 480–81), which "the Poets" show, and also of the shattering power of passion, which Margaret and the Solitary exemplify. But this knowledge yields, instead of a vital tension and grounds for growth, the inconsistency of the Wanderer's weeping (1, 598) or the inert opposition of the Solitary's way and the stoical ideal (3, 263 f.). The poetry, given over too simply to the blank philosophy or isolated states of the Wanderer, loses amplitude, variety, relish, and, in a word, plausible humanity. The "wanderer" of "Resolution and Independence" has become the Wanderer, impressive but somehow inanimate, drifted off into abstraction if not informal allegory.

It is important to observe that, whether for reasons of

self-protection or of a nobler self-abnegation, Wordsworth evinced a definite disposition toward stoicism, or what Abrams has called a "passivist psychology." This disposition served his poetry in the first decade of the nineteenth century, but by the time of *The Excursion* (1814) had begun to undermine it. Within a few years the conflict between stoicism and poetry becomes all but explicit in the *Memorials of a Tour on the Continent, 1820*, where the mastery of feeling (which proves both positive as rapture and negative as mortal vulnerability) leads toward an ultimate threat of silence. We should consider that stoicism, rather than apocalypse, was the enemy of Wordsworth's muse, and we should observe that the efficacy of that muse depended not on a forward movement into apocalypse but, as shown in discussion of the *Memorials*, on the backward movement into memory, the reservoir of feeling and strenuous, revelatory engagement.

CONCLUSION

Ultimately, stoicism posed a threat to romantic poetry, to the romantic spirit itself. That spirit, I have tried to demonstrate, demanded stoicism, but only as a metaphysical version of the Gödelian theorem that every system contains the grounds of its own refutation. Perhaps it would be proper to regard romanticism as a movement from Prometheanism to stoicism, a movement exemplified in such single documents as Byron's *Childe Harold*, canto 3, and, no less tellingly, Shelley's *Prometheus Unbound*. The initial superhuman defiance of Shelley's Prometheus proves an obstacle to development in the drama; Demogorgon's final address formally renounces defiance and enjoins the active characters to an austere ideal of endurance that is more availably and more fruitfully superhuman in relation to the real audience, mankind itself:

> Gentleness, Virtue, Wisdom, and Endurance,
> These are the seals of that most firm assurance
> Which bars the pit over Destruction's strength;
> . . . .

These are the spells by which to reassume
An empire o'er the disentangled doom.
To suffer woes which Hope thinks infinite;
To forgive wrongs darker than death or night:
To defy Power, which seems omnipotent;
To love, and bear; to hope till Hope creates
From its own wreck the thing it contemplates;
Neither to change, nor falter, nor repent;
This, like thy glory, Titan! is to be
Great, good and joyous, beautiful and free;
This is alone Life, Joy, Empire, and Victory!

Where Prometheanism and stoicism effectively frame *Prometheus Unbound*, an evolutionary movement from one to the other can be discerned in *Childe Harold*, canto 3. From the outset Childe Harold—"he of the breast which fain no more would feel"—is set against a background of stoicism; he embodies, or *thinks* he embodies, what we may recognize as the popular conception of the stoic: imperviousness to feeling, independence and firmness of soul, an almost clinical pursuit of the meaning of what is permanent, and concern with the basic, if not the recondite, ways of God and nature in material terms:

Secure in guarded coldness, he had mix'd
Again in fancied safety with his kind,
And deem'd his spirit now so firmly fix'd
And sheathed with an invulnerable mind,
That, if no joy, no sorrow lurk'd behind;
And he, as one, might 'midst the many stand
Unheeded, searching through the crowd to find
Fit speculation, such as in strange land
He found in wonder-works of God and Nature's hand.

[stanza 12]

Even the pantheism of the early stanzas (6, 13) would be compatible with stoical principles, which Byron was sufficiently acquainted with.

But stoicism, as the poem says, is something of a "sheath";

the true mettle of Childe Harold's spirit at this juncture proves vividly misanthropic and Promethean:

> untaught to submit
> His thoughts to others, though his soul was quell'd
> In youth by his own thoughts; still uncompell'd,
> He would not yield dominion of his mind
> To spirits against whom his own rebell'd;
> Proud though in desolation; which could find
> A life within itself, to breathe without mankind.
>
> [stanza 12]

Childe Harold, indeed, emerges as a complete Promethean syndrome; like a tyrant he exiles himself (16) and he is his own eagle and punisher: "the heat/Of his impeded soul would through his bosom eat." The movement of this third canto of the poem is toward escape from an erosive Prometheanism, into sublimity if possible, or stoicism if possible, or through the opportunism of travel into history as novelty-and-meditation.

The development of the canto suggests that sublimity is impossible, and offers a view of history itself as a domain where stoicism is indispensable to the observer and its absence a tragedy for the actor-sufferer. A stoical obligation as it were emerges from the elegiac stanzas on the Battle of Waterloo (27–34), and becomes focused in the trenchant reading of Bonaparte's station and character. He embodies, he enacts the consequences of a failed stoicism. His mind can be with "firmness fixt" (36), but it is so by temporary obsession and proves intrinsically inconstant and indiscriminate (36); he inspires the observation that "quiet to quick bosoms is a hell" (42) and the sad litany of those who suffer the "fatal" fever of unquiet, the "madmen who have made men mad":

> Conquerors and Kings,
> Founders of sects and systems, to whom add
> Sophists, Bards, Statesmen, all unquiet things. . . .
>
> [stanza 42]

The irony of it all is that Napoleon ends up, like Childe Harold, *looking like* a stoic, whether as a result of "wisdom, coldness, or deep pride." He meets his enemies and detractors "with a sedate and all enduring eye" (39). The emotional imperialism of Childe Harold and the political imperialism of Napoleon alike recoil upon themselves and lead to or necessitate stoicism. In effect Childe Harold is proceeding through a world of loss (of beauty and chivalry as well as love and humane order) and destruction, and so reconfirming and refining the message his own jaded nerves had sent him concerning the need of an "invulnerable mind." The continual impulse to mingle with sky or peak or ocean or star in the poem may be ultimately a metaphor of stoicism rather than a philosophy of mystical naturalism; it is a displacement into geography of the need to find a position in spirit that remains secure against circumstance and human finitude.

The "phrensied" Rousseau, whose "life was one long war with self-sought foes" and "whose desire/Was to be glorious" (76), is the philosophical analog of Napoleon, and the storm-tossed Rhone the natural one. Byron explicitly sets up a triple analogy of nature, love, and war (94), and it is not difficult to see that Voltaire and Gibbon (105–08), though given little space in themselves, expand backward through the material as further versions of the torment and conflict and overwhelming ambition that inform human life. In a sense the entire canto shuttles between two improbable aspirations—one to idealism, one to power, the former beyond our nature, the latter, as even Napoleon found, beyond our control.

It is important in this light to recognize that Rousseau and Voltaire, though they have achieved a permanent fame and so a transcendence of slippery time, are not celebrated but by and large lamented in the poem. A third option slowly but irresistibly arises in the course of Childe Harold's pilgrimage; a recognition that there is always "room/And food for meditation" (98), a tempered spirit of forgivingness and acceptance not only of pain and imperfection but of death itself (108) occur as the positive valences of the repudiation of

Napoleon et al. If the canto begins with a false presumption of stoicism, it earns its way at last to a lucid aspiration to stoicism:

> to steel
> The heart against itself; and to conceal,
> With a proud caution, love, or hate, or aught,—
> Passion or feeling, purpose, grief, or zeal,—
> Which is the tyrant spirit of our thought,
> Is a stern task of soul;—no matter—it is taught.
>
> [stanza 111]

Perhaps this represents a bent toward the psychology rather than the full philosophy (logic, ethics, physics) of stoicism. No claim is being made for Byron as a neo-Stoic. But it is unmistakable that for practical and spiritual purposes even he, the improper, tumultuous lord, cultivated stoicism in and for his writing.

Within the poles of Prometheanism and stoicism, the romantic mind engages itself with the problematics of an assertion of being, centered in the self but radiating, with a tentative imperialism and at the same time a bold obedience, out into the world. This problematics of being not only invites but demands a response of the metaphysical will; the practical will, addressed to specific ends, proves eminently unreliable—philosophy from Boehme to Schiller and Schopenhauer repudiates the particular will, but poetry subsists not on formal axioms but on forming life. The romantic poet-personality meets the world, either as society or as a vision, in unpredictable encounter and on paradoxical grounds. Wordsworth embodies his dilemma at the outset of *The Prelude*: he knows he cannot miss his way, but cannot tell where to turn. Yet the metaphysical will must have its occasions, as Schopenhauer insisted,[60] and is involved in processes of action as well as revelation. If it insists too much on any of its moments it becomes Promethean, with the kind of obsession we find in Gothic drama and in Byron's tales.[61] If it too much surrenders itself, it resolves into stoicism or Wordsworth's "second" Will more wise."

This again Schopenhauer points out, and indeed proffers as an ideal. Placing virtue well above mere happiness or "satisfied willing." he commends a "complete renunciation in which all willing comes to an end," and regards this as a perfect achievement of "freedom" that is "removed from the effect of *motives* . . . whose objects are only phenomena." Such "complete will-lessness" provides an apt description for the state of Wordsworth's aged solitaries, and it is striking that they should possess a kind of didactic silence, since Schopenhauer associates will-lessness with a "knowledge of the whole, of the inner nature of the thing-in-itself."[62] It is as though Wordsworth poetically intuited what Schopenhauer painstakingly enunciated in his philosophy, when he recognized the folly of any isolated will, and advocated the purification of the will by dissolution.

Such wisdom, though, promotes not only inaction but silence; for all they signify, how little such figures as Demogorgon and the Leech-gatherer have to say. In this context poetry—speech itself—in romanticism must be seen as an expression of a basic strife and discontent (of which apocalyptic aspiration is only the obverse). The basic object of the poetry is to reconcile a primary metaphysical conviction of meaning and of value with experience of change, loss, denial, and ultimately death.[63] In response to this experience the romantic will conceded enough to espouse stoicism, which functions as an anti-form of life or approximation of death. But an antinomical will to death largely exceeds romantic amplitudes, belonging to Victorian and post-Victorian modes of mind. Perhaps Beddoes' *Death's Jest Book* and Shelley's *Adonais*[64] constitute straws in the wind, but these fall far short of the sense of death as heroism that we find in, say, Arnold's *Empedocles on Etna* and Browning's "Childe Roland to the Dark Tower Came." And Lawrence's later poetry—especially such pieces as "Bavarian Gentians," "Death is Not Evil, Evil Is Mechanical," "The Ship of Death," and "The

End, The Beginning"—raises the will to death to a pseudo-Platonic height, as does Virginia Woolf's *To the Lighthouse*. Though suggesting the paramountcy of the will in so many ways, romanticism strikingly avoids the two extremes of the will—its impulse to mere arbitrary definition, or solipsism, and its smothering in the possessiveness of death. Accordingly, we may regard the period as a negotiation between the necessary self and an inevitable world, with the will at once underlying and burdened by every action, and the state of being both assumed and problematically pursued.

NOTES

CHAPTER 1

1 "The 'Uncanny'," in *Studies in Parapsychology*, p. 20.
2 See Geoffrey H. Hartman, "Romanticism and Anti–Self-Consciousness," in *Beyond Formalism*, pp. 298-310.
3 See in particular "La Princesse Lointaine; or The Nature of Romanticism," in *The Decline and Fall of the Romantic Ideal*. John Jones gives a more favorable reception to the presence of feeling in romanticism in *John Keats's Dream of Truth*, esp. pp. 189-213, 287-95; so does Herbert Read in *The True Voice of Feeling*.
4 The argument from the authority of feeling really comes into its own in the Victorian era. Tennyson's declaration, "I have felt," as also his confession, "I do not understand, I love," clearly derived primary and unanalyzable conviction from feeling as a known form of reality, equivalent to a formula or a tree.
5 *The Phenomenology of Perception*, trans. Colin Smith, p. xvii. See also "Phenomenology and the Sciences of Man," in *The Primacy of Perception*, ed. James M. Edie, p. 50.
6 The pertinent bibliography includes: Harold Bloom, "The Interiorization of Quest-Romance," in *Romanticism and Consciousness*, ed. Harold Bloom, pp. 3-24. *The Visionary Company*, rev. ed., pp. 1-3, and *The Ringers in the Tower*; Geoffrey H. Hartman, "Romanticism and Anti–Self-Consciousness," pp. 298-310, *Wordsworth's Poetry: 1787-1814*, pp. 33-69, 73-75, and *The Unmediated Vision*, pp. 156-73; Paul de Man, "The Rhetoric of Temporality," in *Interpretation: Theory and Practice*, ed. Charles S. Singleton, pp. 173-209, and *Blindness and Insight*; Morse Peckham, "Toward a Theory of Romanticism: 11. Reconsideration," in *The Triumph of Romanticism*, pp. 27-35; Northrop Frye, *A Study of English Romanticism*, pp. 3-51, esp. 37-38, 46-48, and "The Drunken Boat," in *Romanticism Reconsidered*, ed. Northrop Frye, pp. 1-25, esp. 10-11, and *Fearful Symmetry*; Meyer H. Abrams, *The Mirror and the Lamp*, pp. 1-69, and *Natural Supernaturalism*, pp. 19-140, esp. 88-94; Earl R. Wasserman, "The English Roman-

tics: The Grounds of Knowledge," in *Romanticism: Points of View*, ed. Robert F. Gleckner and Gerald E. Enscoe, 2d ed., pp. 331-46; Owen Barfield, *Romanticism Comes of Age*, new and augmented ed., and *What Coleridge Thought*.

7   "Wordsworth's Wavering Balance: The Thematic Rhythm of *The Prelude*," *The Wordsworth Circle* 4 (1973): 228.

8   A variety of books and articles amply and sensitively set forth the interplay of poetry and politics (and show this interplay to be not only persistent but variable, according to the development of political circumstances and artistic interests): David V. Erdman, *Blake: Prophet Against Empire*, rev. ed.; Carl Woodring, *Politics in English Romantic Poetry* and *Politics in the Poetry of Coleridge*; Meyer H. Abrams, "English Romanticism: The Spirit of the Age," in *Romanticism: Points of View*, pp. 314-30; J. R. Ebbatson, "Coleridge's Mariner and the Rights of Man," *Studies in Romanticism* 11, no. 3 (Summer, 1972): 171-206; William Empson, "The Ancient Mariner," *Critical Quarterly* 6 (1964): 298-319; Basil Willey, *The Eighteenth Century Background*; Jacques Barzun, *Classic, Romantic and Modern* 2d rev. ed.; Allan Rodway *The Romantic Conflict*; F. M. Todd, *Politics and the Poet*.

9   Abrams gives a concise and lucid summary of this evolution in "English Romanticism: The Spirit of the Age." The phenomenon is international in romanticism; Shelley is a prime English example, Schiller a prime German example. Though not without modification in recent years, the traditional view of Schiller remains tenable —that he was "in his youth a revolutionary enthusiast . . . ; in later years a withdrawn philosopher" (intro. to *On the Aesthetic Education of Man*, ed. and trans. Elizabeth M. Wilkinson and L. A. Willoughby, p. 15).

10 *Reveries*, Second Promenade.

11 Mircea Eliade declares that "modern man considers himself to be constituted by History" (*Myth and Reality*, trans. Willard R. Trask, p. 12). Whether by way of reaction against this conclusion, or as a separate element in a complex vision, a radical push toward self-determination seems no less apparent.

12 Quoted by George Armstrong Kelly in his introduction to Johann Gottlieb Fichte, *Addresses to the German Nation*, pp. ix, xi, xxvi.

13 *Biographia Literaria*, 1:65-66. Coleridge's pronouncements on the will are legion, his position on it complex if not tangled. He regarded the will as the cardinal question for philosophy, and gave considerable attention to the German philosophers, from Boehme to Fichte, Kant, and Schelling, who enunciated major positions on the question. In general, he moves between the extremes of mechanical necessitarianism as a young man and providential, Leibnizian

necessitarianism as an older man. The greatest interest and the greatest energy in his utterances comes where he foregoes the simplicity of the extremes and tries not just to define but, more important, to cope with our experience of ourselves as finitely free. The discussion of Coleridge hereafter pivots around this position, but it may be of use here to outline schematically a wide range of Coleridgean positions on the will as an index of his incessant wrestling with the issue:

1. "I am a compleat Necessitarian," an "Advocate of the Automatism of Man" (though this glides into a form of Christian Unitarianism).
2. "Will is opposed to Nature, as *Spirit*, and raised above Nature, as *self-determining* Spirit."
3. Will is "strictly synonymous with the individualizing Principle, the 'I' of every rational Being."
4. The "secondary" imagination, "coexisting with the conscious will," upon the duplication of creation of the world for the self, purposively "struggles to idealize and unify" its terms.
5. "A finite will *constitutes* a true Beginning . . . but the *finite* Will *gives* a beginning only by coincidence with that *absolute* Will, which is at the same time *Infinite* Power."
6. "Will any reflecting man admit that his own Will is the only and sufficient determinant of all he is, and all he does? Is nothing to be attributed to the harmony of the system to which he belongs, and to the pre-established Fitness of [all that acts] *on* the will, though doubtless, *with* it likewise?"
7. "In its utmost abstraction and consequent state of reprobation, the will becomes Satanic pride and rebellious self-idolatry in the relations of the spirit to itself, and remorseless despotism relatively to others."

This is a schematic rather than a chronological ordering of viewpoints. The extreme positions both resemble and repudiate each other, the internal positions refine and rebalance one another. Schematization is not meant to deny chronology and development, but to suggest, in keeping with Thomas McFarland's warning against canonizing these concerns (*Coleridge and the Pantheist Tradition*, p. 161), that modulation and analytical pattern provide important data concerning the substance of Coleridge's thought. Owen Barfield in *What Coleridge Thought* also indicated the limitations of the chronological approach (p. 5).

14 *Goethe's Literary Essays*, ed. J. E. Spingarn, p. 181.
15 *On the Aesthetic Education of Man*, nineteenth letter, p. 135. This

idea is repeated in the twentieth letter (p. 139), and represents a fundamental position in his thought.

16 Emerson's fairly typical romantic phrase, used in the introduction to his first book, *Nature*. It would be pointless to say that Coleridge had anticipated him with the distinction between nature and self or intelligence, or to say that Schelling had anticipated Coleridge and been himself anticipated by Leibniz. The dichotomy is a constant issue for philosophy. We may find it echoed and modernized by Henri Bergson, who in *Matter and Memory* speaks of nature and self or consciousness as making up the universe. As McFarland writes in *Coleridge and the Pantheist Tradition*, "All systematic philosophy must account for the status and interrelations of . . . the ego or subject, the external or object, and [making a combined third term] the questions arising" from their peculiar relationship (p. 55).

17 *Biographia Literaria* 2:12. This idea of wholeness has an interesting precedent in classical thought. In his recent study, *Stoic Philosophy*, J. M. Rist has pointed out that *hegemonikon* corresponds to the full or true self of the individual human being. Rist, one commentator states, "sees the early Stoics as moving towards the conceptions of a unitary self and of human activity as psychosomatic activity, away from models of conflicting faculties or parts of the soul that we find in Plato and elsewhere" (*TLS*, 1 Aug. 1971, p. 45).

18 E. D. Hirsch, Jr., has fruitfully discussed the place of enthusiasm in the romantic complex; see *Wordsworth and Schelling*, pp. 15–25.

19 This bias has beset much of the Coleridge criticism devoted to the statement on imagination, and even enters into J. R. de J. Jackson's discussion of it, *Method and Imagination in Coleridge's Criticism*, though his thesis centers around questions of theology in Coleridge's thought.

20 *On the Origin of Languages: Jean-Jacques Rousseau, Essay on the Origin of Languages; Johann Gottfried Herder, Essay on the Origin of Language*, trans. John H. Moran and Alexander Gode, pp. 109–10.

21 A powerful modern statement of this position is given in H. Wildon Carr's *A Theory of Monads*. See, for example, pp. 10, 17, 30.

22 As a matter of interest, both Schelling and Schopenhauer reject this possibility outright. Schopenhauer makes short work of it as *liberum arbitrium indifferentiae* (*Essay on the Freedom of the Will*, pp. 8–18), and Schelling finds it idle to speculate on "a completely undetermined power to will either one of two contradictory opposites without determining reasons, simply because it is desired" (*Of Human Freedom*, p. 59). And it is of interest to note that Thomas Hobbes allowed man free will, but not freedom in relation to will, insofar as free will is ordained for him. In *The Question Concerning Liberty, Necessity and Chance*, he writes, "No man can

determine his own will, for the will is appetite; nor can a man more determine his will than any other appetite, that is, more than he can determine when he shall be hungry and when not. When a man is hungry, it is in his choice to eat or not eat; this is the liberty of the man; but to be hungry or not hungry, which is that which I hold to proceed from necessity, is not in his choice"; and again, "true liberty . . . doth not consist in determining itself, but in doing what the will is determined unto" (*The English Works*, ed. Sir William Molesworth (London, 1841) 5:34, 35).

23   A. O. Lovejoy, "Coleridge and Kant's Two Worlds," *ELH* 7 (1940): 348, 350.

24   Further comment on this point is available in Marshall Suther's *The Dark Night of Samuel Taylor Coleridge*, pp. 13–25.

25   Schelling, *Of Human Freedom*, p. 29.

26   As do Walter Jackson Bate in his *Coleridge*, pp. 161–62, and James Volant Baker before him in *The Sacred River*, pp. 114–25. See also Thomas Middleton Raysor's introduction to Coleridge's *Shakespearean Criticism*, 1:xxviiin, and George Watson, *Coleridge the Poet*, pp. 125–26. Though ostensibly rectifying a limitation in Bate's reading of the primary imagination, J. R. de J. Jackson may in fact have been responding to Watson's suggestion that Coleridge on the imagination was a dead issue with special value for archeologists of philosophy and criticism. But it seems to me that he does not so much refurbish as reconstitute the issue. His is a learned and provocative response, but it does an evident injustice to the context and to the text of Coleridge's statement. By making a *parti pris* of the theological possibilities of the context, Jackson undervalues what he glancingly acknowledges: Coleridge's preoccupation with the *human*, even the egotistical, orientation of the *Biographia* at this crucial point; and he further undervalues the *autobiographical* development of the statement on imagination as well as the fact that the theology of the end of the *Biographia* is a relinquishment of the vital challenge of imagination, and not so much a destination as a dam for the eruptive forces of Coleridge's experience and conception of himself in the world. In dealing with the text Jackson continually contrives a series of analogs and associations that are somehow treated as identifications. This is highly problematical with a writer whose philosophy, as Jackson notes, is "slipping and by no means static" (*Method and Imagination*, p. 171). To avoid these peaks is perhaps to be somewhat pedestrian, but it looks as though the statement on imagination may be encountered, text and context, in its own explicit terms, as a significant philosophical autobiographical statement. My discussion has sought to encounter it so.

27   "The English Romantics: The Grounds of Knowledge," pp. 331–46.

28   *Of Human Freedom*, p. 63.
29   *The Primacy of Perception*, p. 25.
30   Quoted in Abrams, *Natural Supernaturalism*, p. 362.
31   "Theory of Metaphor in Rousseau's *Second Discourse*," in *Romanticism: Vistas, Instances, Continuities*, ed. David Thorburn and Geoffrey Hartman.
32   In his *Essay on the Freedom of the Will*, Schopenhauer distinguishes between two stages of the "cognitive faculty" and "self-consciousness" on similar grounds: "At first our cognitive faculty grasps this world perceptively, but that which is thus obtained is forthwith worked over, as it were in a ruminating fashion, into concepts." But Schopenhauer here separates "the self-consciousness" from the "endless combinations of concepts" which "thinking" generates; perhaps he does the same in *The World as Will and Representation*: "Everyone knows without further help what the world is, for he himself is the subject of knowing of which the world is representation. . . . But this is a knowledge of perception, is in the concrete. The task of philosophy is to reproduce this in the abstract, to raise to a permanent rational knowledge successive, variable perceptions" (p. 82). Coleridge, however, sees the one—conception—in the other —perceptions—indissolubly. For Coleridge "thinking" is more intrinsically a matter of selfhood than for Schopenhauer; and by the same token, willing is more intrinsically a matter of selfhood for Coleridge than for Schopenhauer, in that Schopenhauer's will is incorrigibly empirical, other-oriented: "Our willing always has external things for its object. It is directed toward them, it revolves around them, and is at least motivated by them" (*Freedom of Will*, p. 12). Coleridge, I think, adds something vital in recognizing the practicality, indeed the *personality*, of knowledge per se.
33   This is the effective bearing of Coleridge's comment that "know thyself" must be taken "at once practically and speculatively" (*Biographia Literaria*, 1:173). One notes with interest its recurring as the home idea of Bergson's *Matter and Memory*.
34   I am using *experience*, following Hegel, to mean "the inseparable and continuous interrelation of subject and object," with the presumption "of conscious awareness of an object" on the part of the subject (J. B. Baillie, introduction to *The Phenomenology of Mind*, p. 53).
35   *Aids to Reflection*, Aphorism 10, 178*n*.
36   The word *echo*, which Coleridge uses in this connection, is on the face of things problematical. Probably it takes the place of a more straightforward term, *image*, and is adopted to get rid of a conflict of meanings; but *echo* seems to have the meaning of the Hobbesian *image*, the retention in the mind or, alternatively, the recollection

of discrete perception (the matter, in this context, of the primary imagination). The secondary imagination, then, in relation to the primary, is materially subordinated as an echo, but is distinctive in mode and result.

37 It is interesting that Goethe uses the term *decomposition* to indicate a process very similar to the work of the secondary imagination (see Löwth, *From Hegel to Nietzsche*, p. 12). One is struck, too, with Bergson's expression of the same idea in relation to the mastery of bodily gestures: "The true effect of repetition is to decompose, and then to recompose, and thus appeal to the intelligence of the body" (*Matter and Memory*, p. 137). Clearly we are dealing in all these cases with a theory of learning (an epistemology) founded on a theory of the quality of the learner and of his life (an ontology). This double valence is present at every stage of imagination; for Coleridge, perception is as much a personal *act* as conception, and attention to the will in imagination does something by merely bringing this out.

38 If it remains difficult to divorce the idea of hierarchy from the case, we should note that Coleridge goes to some lengths to warn us against this incidental effect of his vocabulary. *Primary* and *secondary*, he insists, do *not* differ in kind, only in degree and mode; also, he keeps things in perspective by making the secondary imagination, which on one level is the apparent source of meaning and value, an "echo." In this respect the definition of the imagination includes an explicit effort to correct a habitual bias toward hierarchical analysis of the human mind and state, just as the imagination itself supersedes the discrete "faculties."

39 Schelling, *Of Human Freedom*, p. 36.

40 As Coleridge points out in chapter 12 of *Biographia Literaria*, "Where the spirit of man is not filled with the consciousness of freedom (were it only from its restlessness, as of one still struggling in bondage) all spiritual intercourse is interrupted, not only with others, but even with himself" (1:168). Kierkegaard repeats this idea in a humble and concrete context, but with no loss of cogency:

> What gives this struggle [for daily bread] such a high educative value is the fact that the prize of victory is so small, in fact nonexistent: the struggle goes on only so that man may continue the struggle. The greater and more extrinsic the reward of the struggle becomes, the more surely he may rely on all the ambiguous passions that have their abode in man: ambition, vanity, pride. [But] these passions leave [a man] in the lurch. . . . If he has no other source of strength, he is lost. . . . This is why the struggle for bread educates and ennobles man: it gives him

no possibility of being deceived about himself. If he can see nothing higher in this struggle, then it is really a wretched, miserable situation. . . . But for this very reason this struggle forces man to see something else in it. If a man does not want to be discarded in this struggle, he must see in it a struggle for honor, a struggle, which brings greater honor the lesser the reward is. Thus although one indeed struggle for sustenance, in reality he is struggling for himself [quoted by Löwth, *From Hegel to Nietzsche*, p. 284].

41 Not to be active and creative and self-expressive, in the mode of the secondary imagination, has a near analog in the romantic period in Blake's state of Experience. Blake depicts Experience not as the absence of *experiences*, but as the lack of resiliency, resolution, coherence, and viability of personal response to experiences, and in this sense as the loss of Innocence. Blake's Innocence and Experience, then, would be nearly equivalent to Coleridge's Joy and Disintegration or loss of Imagination. It is important to recognize that Imagination for Coleridge is always and intrinsically ontological. It may involve an aesthetic action, as critics like Brett, Watson, Appleyard, R. H. Fogle, and Bate have observed, but should not be confined to or identified with the aesthetic.

42 Regarding the general question of influences on Coleridge's thinking, see, for example, René Wellek, *Immanuel Kant in England, 1793–1838*, pp. 63–135, and Norman Fruman, *Coleridge, the Damaged Archangel*. With particular reference to influences on Coleridge's formulation of the idea of imagination, it is crucial to consider Thomas McFarland's "The Origin and Significance of Coleridge's Theory of Secondary Imagination," in *New Perspectives on Coleridge and Wordsworth*, ed. Geoffrey Hartman, pp. 195–246. For some well-tempered comments on the relation Coleridge bears to his "antecedents" in philosophy, criticism, and poetry, Jackson's *Method and Imagination* may be readily recommended.

43 My article, "*Quisque Sui Faber*: Coleridge in the *Biographia Literaria*," *Philological Quarterly* 50 (April, 1971): 208–229, may appropriately be cited here; we may also note that in the very first paragraph of chapter 12 of the *Biographia* Coleridge postulates an individual being that strives to apprehend or *find* itself "in [the] infinity of the world" (1:196).

44 J. A. Appleyard, "Coleridge and Criticism: 1. Critical Theory," in *Writers and their Background: S. T. Coleridge*, ed. R. L. Brett, pp. 137–38.

45 We may note here Fichte's almost mathematical formulation that

perfect freedom equals perfect obedience, and Schelling's statement that absolute freedom and absolute necessity are identical.

46 *Letters*, 1:279, and *Notebooks* 1:1515, respectively.

47 Schopenhauer provides a neat summary of Kant's distinction between the "empirical" and the "intelligible" or implicit will in *Freedom of Will*, pp. 83, 96.

48 Isabella Fenwick records the fact that the line in question was supplied by Wordsworth (*Poetical Works* 1:360–61), but this, I think, is adventitious; the spirit of the poem elicited and dictated Wordsworth's contribution, and he acknowledged that he did not and could not radically share in the undertaking: "As we endeavoured to proceed conjointly . . . our respective manners proved so widely different that it would have been presumptuous in me to do anything but separate from an undertaking upon which I could only have been a clog" (ibid.).

49 There is a sense that the ship's "drop" out of the ordinary world is a drop into directionless space without "shapes of men [or] beasts." Certainly the kirk, the hill, and the lighthouse top cease to be points of reference, even to the memory. The continual echo of a Christian vocabulary in the early parts of the poem seems residual only, the survival of an idle formula. The fact that the men drop "merrily" betokens naiveté, if not improvidence. Something about the way the mariners drop out and the way the Ancient Mariner pops up into the world again is reminiscent of the *Inferno*. The absence of a guide and of ultimate orientation in the modern poem sets it worlds apart from the medieval one, though. Coleridge's Mariner may be said to achieve a vision of salvation, but he cannot find the way.

50 It is tempting to think that *one* mariner, the ancient one, is being identified, so that the shooting becomes a specific betrayal of trust. But this is implausible, and unnecessary; the betrayal resides in the situation, not in a specific relationship.

51 *Origin of Language*, p. 109.

52 Hartman, "Romanticism and Anti–Self–Consciousness," pp. 293–94.

53 Leslie Brisman, in "Coleridge and the Ancestral Voices," also acknowledges the Mariner's "act of will." He interprets it as breaking the spell "that bound nature and supernature in mysterious communion," and makes it equivalent to an interruption "from Porlock." This is part of a provocative reading of the poem as an investigation of the "origin of evil" and a way of redeeming nature into imagination (*The Georgia Review* 19 [Summer, 1975]: 469–98).

54 William Wordsworth, *Poetical Works*, 1:360–61.

55 The idea of adventure and the Ancient Mariner has been broached in different ways by E. M. W. Tillyard in *Five Poems: 1470-1870*, by W. H. Auden in *The Enchafed Flood*, and by R. A. Foakes in *The Romantic Assertion*, but the adventure of becoming an individual, with all its blindness and its purpose, has not hitherto been brought out. While something akin to it, existentialism, has come up, the tendency has been to set up an opposition between consciousness and nature and postulate the "alienated man" (see Frye, *A Study of English Romanticism*, p. 18), whereas it seems to me that individuality and indifference (or indifferentiation) are the issue. Existential alienation seems likelier in "Dejection: An Ode" and, subject to redemption, "This Lime-Tree Bower My Prison." Concerning the latter, see especially R. A. Durr's "'This Lime-Tree Bower My Prison' and a Recurrent Action in Coleridge" *ELH* 26, no. 4 (December, 1959): 514-30.

56 *Coleridge*, p. 96.

57 The same ineradicability is manifest in *Childe Harold*, canto 3, where Byron admonishes the Rhine of the limits of its power to cleanse man and the marks of his action: "But o'er the blacken'd memory's blighting dream/Thy waves would vainly roll, all sweeping as they seem" (stanza 51, lines 8-9).

58 Schopenhauer, *Freedom of Will*, p. 17.

59 This reading of *The Ancient Mariner*, naturalistic-metaphysical in character, departs from the ethical and/or religious orientation that criticism (in part influenced by Coleridge's afterthought gloss) has favored. Such an orientation can be pursued in a variety of strong and stimulating studies: *The Rime of the Ancient Mariner, with an Essay*, ed. Robert Penn Warren; S. F. Gingerich, *Essays in the Romantic Poets*; H. W. Piper, *The Active Universe*; W. J. Bate, *Coleridge*; Humphry House, *Coleridge*; George Herbert Clarke, "Certain Symbols in *The Rime of the Ancient Mariner*," *Queens Quarterly* 40 (February, 1933): 27-45 ; John A. Stuart, "The Augustinian 'Cause of Action' in Coleridge's *Rime of the Ancient Mariner*," *Harvard Theological Review* 60, no. 2 (April, 1967): 177-211; N. P. Stallknecht, *Strange Seas of Thought*; Coleman O. Parsons, "The Mariner and the Albatross," *Virginia Quarterly Review* 26, no. 1 (January, 1950): 102-23; James D. Boulger, intro. to *Twentieth Century Interpretations of "The Rime of the Ancient Mariner"*; John B. Beer, *Coleridge the Visionary*; E. E. Bostetter, *The Romantic Ventriloquists*. Attention should also be directed to Mary Jane Lupton, "*The Rime of the Ancient Mariner*: The Agony of Thirst," *American Imago* 27 (Summer, 1970): 140-59, which argues a tortured psychology as the groundwork of the poem, suggesting, for example, that it embodies a death wish, immature fears

of genital sexuality, and rejection as well as rebellion against established authority. My sense of the poem as an adventure in individuality is more positive, and identifies the speaker's difficulty with that adventure, not with personal pathology.

60 *The Symbolism of Evil*, trans. Emerson Buchanan, p. 299.

61 Hartman, *Wordsworth's Poetry*, pp. 11–12, 13.

62 This is the self-presentation of the poem. In biography, the experience is a remembered one, going back two years (*Poetical Works*, 3:444–45) and coming over Wordsworth as abruptly and compellingly, almost, as memory over the Mariner.

63 The tyranny of the eye, which Wordsworth and Coleridge recognized, and Joyce's "ineluctable modality of the visible" do not take away from this position. In any situation where attention and interest are being called upon, the eye is free and not unlikely to turn away. For, as Goethe says, "What we apprehend with the eye (the most facile of our organs of receptivity) seems alien and unimpressive considered in and for itself" ("Shakespeare ad Infinitum," *Goethe's Literary Essays*, p. 177).

64 *Wordsworth's Poetry*, p. 17.

65 Hartman sums up the issue as one of "the appropriateness or decorum of the poets's feelings ... to be resolved ... by individual critical decision, or by these decisions as they indicate a consensus" (*Wordsworth's Poetry*, p. 3). With a consensus wanting, he moves to establish the elements of self-consciousness and "spiritual" egotism in the poem, showing it as a case of "self-acquired revelation," with overtones of the universality of death (pp. 4–5, 14–16). The speaker presumes, though, that the audience will respond; he *makes* the audience respond before any of these elements comes into direct play. This can but suggest the presence of a cryptic community of response, or something infallibly efficacious in the object to which the response is made. The origin or character of this community of response is what needs further attention, especially since it is *not* based on a consensus, on a reliable orthodoxy, but rather on spontaneous evocation.

66 *Wordsworth and the Poetry of Encounter*, p. 3.

67 John Dewey, *Art as Experience*, p. 24.

68 The sound and, presumably, the rhythm of the song would naturally help the reaper to go on longer and less wearied with her work. Wordsworth explicitly invokes this functional aspect of song in his poem "On the Power of Sound":

> Unscorned [be] the peasant's whistling breath, that lightens
> His duteous toil of furrowing the green earth.
> For the tired slave, Song lifts the languid oar,

> And bids it aptly fall, with chime
> That beautifies the fairest shore,
> And mitigates the harshest clime.
> . . . .
> Nor friendless he, the prisoner of the mine,
> Who from the well-spring of his own clear breast
> Can draw, and sing his griefs to rest.

69 In his suggestive study, *The Ways of the Will*, Leslie H. Farber remarks that "even if it were to disappear altogether from the scholarly disciplines, the subject of will would nevertheless survive as an essential and literal part of our language, that is, in the simple and volitive future tense of verb forms" (p. 4). His further remarks on this subject will repay the reader's attention.

70 This is a tacit feature of the singing of the Highland Lass, which becomes in this respect a cryptic forerunner of Stevens "Ideas of Order at Key West." Art and will in the romantic scheme get ample attention hereafter; for now, the salience of the relation may be suggested in the case of poems like "Kubla Khan," *The Fall of Hyperion*, *The Marriage of Heaven and Hell*, "Alastor," and *Childe Harold*, cantos 3 and 4.

71 *Freedom of Will*, p. 11.

CHAPTER 2

1 A question of a vital dualism has been raised before in connection with romanticism by Abrams in *The Mirror and the Lamp* and by Wasserman in "The English Romantics: The Grounds of Knowledge." Abrams speaks of subject-object dualism, Wasserman of man-nature dualism. A learned and elegant statement of the background and terms of this dualism is furnished by McFarland, *Coleridge and the Pantheist Tradition*, p. 53. In speaking of the self and the system I am not vainly seeking to parade a merely terminological originality, but pointing to an important element in the "other" that somehow both "object" and "nature" tend to gloss over, namely, a distinct and perhaps definitive organization in every sense precedent to man, and strictly tending to co-opt him. This would be equivalent, perhaps, to an inexorable pantheism.

2 For the relation of Coleridge to Leibniz, see McFarland, *Coleridge and the Pantheist Tradition*, p. 135.

3 This use of "given," suggesting *datum* rather than *donum*, differs markedly from what obtains in "Dejection: An Ode," discussed in the preceding chapter. Schopenhauer is incensed at Kant's adoption of this term ("Criticism of the Kantian Philosophy," *World as Will*

and Representation, 1:440, but his insistence on the unthinkability of "an *absolute object*" (p. 442), which chimes with his maintaining the indispensability of a subject if an object is to be known as such, does not dispense with the point that the object, though "as such [it] exists always only for and in *perception*" (p. 442), still and all exists to be perceived. Perception may occur as the product of pathology, fantasy, "imagination" (p. 442), but it is common—and Schopenhauer readily grants this—for it to "be brought about through the senses" (p. 443), as objectively capable of duplication and validation. The issue between Schopenhauer and Kant admits of two perspectives. One of these is God's, and makes perception primary and causal; Berkeley perhaps offers the definitive statement where he maintains that God sustains the world in perceiving it. The other is more peculiarly human, and on this level the issue seems to become less philosophical than semantic. Thus, though Schopenhauer holds that "suns and planets with no eye to see them and no understanding to know them can be spoken of in words" (p. 30), it seems clear that to think of "an absolute object" is ipso facto to convert it into a *"perceived object"* (p. 442), even if it is only imaginatively perceived. Berkeley rather merrily makes this point in the *First Dialogue between Hylas and Philonous*. Language in actuality does not allow us to deal with an absolute object, but logic does not allow us to yield the existent object entirely to the domain of perception. Schopenhauer himself, to "express the compatibility of empirical reality with transcendental ideality," quotes Sir William Jones: "'The fundamental tenet of the Vedanta school consisted not in denying the existence of matter . . . (to deny which would be lunacy), but in correcting the popular notion of it, and in contending that it has no essence independent of mental perception'" (*World as Will and Representation*, p. 4). Schopenhauer by and large seeks to maintain an antinomical position, at one point saying that the "action" of matter "on the immediate object (which is itself matter) conditions the perception in which alone it exists" (pp. 8-9), then again asserting that "the world . . . requires the knowing subject as the supporter of its existence" (p. 30). At bottom, though, his position is not unlike that of Levi-Strauss, who writes that "the Universe signified long before man began to know what it signified." An earlier philosopher also gives precedence to the world over the ego; writing in *The Phenomenology of Mind*, Hegel observes that the "object . . . is the real truth, is the essential reality; it *is*, quite indifferent to whether it is known or not; it remains and stands even though it is not known while the knowledge does not exist if the object is not there" (p. 151). And Schelling writes, in a letter to Hegel in 1795, "Consciousness without object is impossible." Perhaps the thought should run "Cognosco, ergo sum."

4   Introduction to Fichte, *Addresses to the German Nation*, p. xvii.

5   "The Drunken Boat," p. 308.

6   As we may note in a letter of Coleridge to Sotheby, 10 September 1802: "A poet's *Heart & Intellect* should be *combined, intimately* combined & *unified*, with the great appearances in Nature" (*Letters*, 2:864). The use of "should" obligates the poet, but promises him nothing, and empowers him in no way.

7   "The Romantic Mind Is Its Own Place," *Comparative Literature* 15 (Summer, 1963): 250–68, quotes pp. 251–52. On the question of heroes and the will, the reader may profitably consult Eugene M. Waith's *The Herculean Hero*.

8   Thorslev, "The Romantic Mind," p. 267.

9   The play is based on the *Vitae Sanctorum* of the sixteenth-century monk, Surius, and is set in early Christian Armenia.

10 For a full and cogent discussion of this change, see Stuart M. Tave, *The Amiable Humorist.*

11 An incident in this pattern of self-opposition has been noted by Jean H. Hagstrum, who observes that "the quarrel between pictorialist and antipictorialist [in the Augustan age] was not owing to important change in taste and thought. Burke, in vigorously attacking pictorialist doctrine, used precisely the same empirical psychology that Addison had used in supporting it. Neoclassicist lifted his sword against neoclassicist" (*The Sister Arts*, p. 151).

12 Substantial and enlightening treatments of the general literary-cultural movement from the eighteenth to the nineteenth century will be found in: Walter Jackson Bate, *From Classic to Romantic*; Abrams, *The Mirror and the Lamp*; Willey, *The Eighteenth Century Background*; and Frederick W. Hilles and Harold Bloom, eds., *From Sensibility to Romanticism.*

13 G. Wilson Knight in *The Starlit Dome* takes Kubla Khan for God (p. 93); McFarland in "The Origin and Significance of Coleridge's Theory of the Secondary Imgination" calls him "'a notable *prosopopeias*' that represents God himself" (p. 203); House in his *Coleridge* makes Kubla Khan an Emersonian figure or Representative Man (like Jesus); Carl Woodring, in "Coleridge and the Khan," *Essays in Criticism* 9, (1959): 361–68, treats him firmly as an Eastern potentate or "Nimrod" trying to encompass the sacred within his sphere of power.

14 In a late, poignant letter to Gillman, Coleridge all but seems to enunciate the indwelling failure of ultimate creative or subjective aspiration:

> In Youth and early Manhood the Mind and Nature are, as it were, two rival Artists, both potent Magicians, and engaged,

like the King's Daughter and the rebel Genie in the Arabian Nights' Enters., in sharp conflict of Conjuration—each having for it's object to turn the other into Canvas to paint on, Clay to mould, or Cabinet to contain. For a while the Mind seems to have the better in the contest, and makes of Nature what it likes. . . . But alas! alas! that Nature is a wary wily long-breathed old Witch, tough-lived as a Turtle and divisible as the Polyp, repullulative in a thousand Snips and Cuttings, integra et in toto! She is sure to get the better of Lady Mind in the long run. [*Letters*, 5: 496–97]

15 The contraries of the poem are discussed by Knight, *The Starlit Dome*, p. 90; Irene H. Chayes, "'Kubla Khan' and the Creative Process," *Studies in Romanticism* 6 (1966): 11: Woodring, "Coleridge and the Khan," 364; and R. H. Fogle, "The Romantic Unity of 'Kubla Khan,'" *College English* 13 (1951): 13–18. Knight and Fogle and Chayes see reconciliation of the contraries; Woodring suggests that the poet encompasses the contraries. The contraries, though, seem to me to present an impasse situation for, if not in, the speaker's mind.

16 *The Symbolism of Evil*, p. 299.

17 Abrams, *Natural Supernaturalism*, p. 234.

18 Quoted in ibid., p. 349.

19 Carlyle, in such essays as "Labour" and "Of Heroes and Hero-Worship" takes what is really the traditional escape from this position by making one man autonomous and other men identify themselves with him, thereby as it were enjoying *his* autonomy. But even for the leader this is gregariousness, not individualism.

20 One may note that Coleridge, introducing the notion of stoical opposition or indifference to experience, makes room for the inference that this egotism suppresses the self. In full, Coleridge's charge is that Fichte's theory "degenerated into a crude *egoismus*, a boastful and hyperstoic hostility to *Nature*, as lifeless, godless, and altogether unholy" (*Biographia Literaria*, 1:101–02).

21 From *On the Ego as the Principle of Philosophy*, quoted by Abrams, *Natural Supernaturalism*, p. 355.

22 Hegel, *Phenomenology of Mind*, p. 130.

23 The absorption of "finite self-consciousness" into "absolute self-consciousness," of the single being into a total scheme, is apparent in the conclusion to Hegel's *Lectures on the History of Philosophy* (see Abrams, *Natural Supernaturalism*, p. 354).

24 *World as Will and Representation*, 1:58.

25 *Wordsworth's Poetry*, p. 75.

26 This question of freedom in romantic contexts is cogently discussed by Abrams, *Natural Supernaturalism*, pp. 367.

27 This opposition of luxury and vigor, and its suggestion of an in-

structive asceticism, appears in Wordsworth's earliest pictures of himself. In his "School-Time" reminiscences (2, 78–81) he writes:

> Our daily meals were frugal, Sabine fare!
> More than we wished we knew the blessing then
> Of vigorous hunger—hence corporeal strength
> Unsapped by delicate viands. . . .

28 *Theory of Monads*, pp. 152 (extract), 123.
29 Ibid., p. 153.
30 "Fortunata," p. 42.
31 In *Sincerity and Authenticity* Lionel Trilling brings out a central "ontological concern" and a "preoccupation with the sentiment of being" in Wordsworth's poetry (p. 92). This reaffirms his position taken in "Wordsworth and the Rabbis" (see *The Opposing Self*, pp. 118–50).
32 The "self-sufficing power of Solitude," if anything too irresistible in nature (2, 77), proves at this stage inadequate to the challenge of society.
33 The unearthliness of Wordsworth's aged figures and their remoteness from ordinary humanity is discussed by David Ferry, *The Limits of Mortality*, pp. 59–60, 62, 95, 141–42; Trilling also considers these figures, stressing, however, their capacity to reveal and reaffirm the "intensity of human existence" ("Wordsworth and the Rabbis," p. 138).
34 "Wordsworth's Wavering Balance," p. 228.
35 The "spots of time" frequently serve as the focus for investigating the material or structural principles of *The Prelude*. In *On Wordsworth's "Prelude"* Herbert Lindenberger analyzes a development from naturalistic to extraordinary modes in the "spots," while Hartman emphasizes the interplay in them of action and memory, nature and mind, in *Wordsworth's Poetry*; Jonathan Bishop, in "Wordsworth and the 'Spots of Time',," is at pains to isolate the imagistic and conceptual motifs that connect the political and personal "spots" (*ELH* 26 [1959]: 45–65). Developing a critical issue raised in Lindenberger's study, Jonathan R. Grandine takes another, rhetorical tack in *The Problem of Shape in 'The Prelude'*. Foakes concentrates on the "journey as an image of development" in *The Romantic Assertion*. E. A. Horsman provides a judicious and discerning study, "The Design of Wordsworth's *Prelude*," in *Wordsworth's Mind and Art*, ed. A. W. Thomson, pp. 95–109; he recognizes in book 1 of the poem a pattern of "repetition with progressively increasing awareness," without establishing this as a principle for the entire work, and goes through book by book with an astute treatment of the poem's imagistic, actional, and conceptual points of coherence. A singular, indeed oblique, but evocative ap-

proach to the structure of *The Prelude* is furnished by Jonathan Wordsworth in *Usurpation and Reality: Wordsworth's Great Six Weeks*.

36 It seems that, as he gets older, moments of crucial import for Wordsworth occur with someone else around, on his heels as it were. It is remarkable that in his earlier years these moments either find him alone or, as in the ice-skating episode, allow for a subordination of his companions that borders on their elimination. Bishop makes an "emergence of a solitary figure from a crowd" characteristic of the "many" episodes that might be housed in that category ("Wordsworth and the 'Spots of Time'," pp. 45–46, 47); but relation of a solitary to a crowd seems a more apt description for the instances he gives. It may be observed that an emphasis on himself, not as end but as source of concern, remains invariable in Wordsworth's position.

37 See, e.g., Hartman, *Wordsworth's Poetry*, pp. 16–17, 43–48, 240–41; but we should note that John Jones speaks of the episode as dwelling "upon potentiality rather than present possession" (*The Egotistical Sublime*, p. 49).

38 Altieri, in "Wordsworth's Wavering Balance," also argues against transcendence, insofar as that entails disjunction. He sees an "epiphany" though, and evidence that "apocalyptic desire can be satisfied within time" (pp. 231–32). His treatment of the episode seems to me unduly positive, and misleading in its assumptions of a climax and resolution in the episode.

39 Leslie Brisman, *Milton's Poetry of Choice and Its Romantic Heirs*, p. 287.

40 Woodring in *Politics in English Romantic Poetry* undertakes a detailed, acute, and judicious study of the political dimensions of *The Prelude*, and of the place of the poet qua poet in the ferment of a revolutionary situation.

41 Not to harp on a point that may be sufficiently clear, this seems a salient statement of the lesser position of consciousness as such, in relation to action and conduct, and of knowledge in relation to becoming and will.

42 Spenser, with his peerless brilliance as a psychological realist, sets a precedent for Wordsworth's use of the double-bottom of despair. As the Redcrosse Knight expects to be purged of himself and the Dungeon of Orgoglio by a conquest of Despayre, but finds his plight ultimately revealed instead, so Wordsworth in the French Revolution-Godwin sequence.

43 This phrase clearly puts a special stress on the will ("wanted" as expressing lack and desire) in a statement overtly focusing on reason. The following ejaculation speaks for itself.

44 Wordsworth seems to use this word to refer to the lucid and com-

municable activity of the spirit, and in opposition to conventional "reason" (see *The Prelude*, 12, 44 f.). It will prove useful to consult Francis Christensen, "Intellectual Love: The Second Theme of *The Prelude*," *PMLA* 80 (1965): 69–75. Also, we should note Wordsworth's use of the phrase "imaginative power" (12, 203) in circumstances which make "imaginative" for him an indisputable synonym of "intellectual."

45 See, for example, Hartman, *Wordsworth's Poetry*, p. 211, and Bishop, "Wordsworth and the 'Spots of Time,'" pp. 45–46; Horsman, "The Design of Wordsworth's *Prelude*," p. 106, and Bostetter, *Romantic Ventriloquists*, pp. 42–48, on the "subjection of nature to the mind"; and Lindenberger's remark that the "three final books celebrate [Wordsworth's] triumphant restoration to the inner world" (*On Wordsworth's "Prelude*," p. 170).

46 In this connection the reader may well wish to consult my essay "On the Mode of Argument in Wordsworth's Poetry," in *Romantic and Victorian*, ed. Paul W. Elledge and Richard L. Hoffman, pp. 95–109; also of interest will be Richard J. Onorato's observation that Wordsworth's personal doubts lead to a troubled undernote in his assertions (*The Character of the Poet*, pp. 10, 11, 33).

47 Harold Bloom has observed that the action of *Jerusalem* occurs "primarily . . . within Blake's own psyche" (*The Poetry and Prose of William Blake*, ed. David V. Erdman, with commentary by Harold Bloom, p. 862), or within the psyche of Blake-Los. But perhaps the action and issue of the poem have to do with the extent and authenticity of the correspondence between Los-Blake's conceptions and the operations of the world. Neither Albion's guilt nor Jerusalem's feminine patience are properly attributable to Los, though they are obviously attributes of the situation Los lives in.

48 As a matter of design, it must be noted that Blake sets up the poem more in Spenser's vein, with poet and protagonist separate, than in the innovative Wordsworthian vein, where poet and protagonist are virtually joined as one. Thus Wordsworth, though as the person composing the poem he has command of all the material of *The Prelude*, lets it seem that the protagonist is proceeding ad lib, moment by moment. Blake, through Los, predicates a world that Albion proceeds toward ad lib, moment by moment.

49 The principle of shape in *Jerusalem* has received continual attention; though critics disagree in emphasis and in conception, they have tended to deal with the poem in large formal segments and rhythms and parallelisms, rather than in terms of its inner dynamism of experience and purpose and conviction. The following may be singled out for their contribution to the understanding of structure in *Jerusalem*: Frye, *Fearful Symmetry*, p. 356; Bloom,

Blake's Apocalypse, p. 404; Karl Kiralis, "The Theme and Structure of *Jerusalem*," in *The Divine Vision*, ed. Vivian de Sola Pinto, pp. 141–62; E. J. Rose, "The Structure of Blake's *Jerusalem*," *Bucknell Review* 11 (1963): 35–54; Henry Lesnick, "Narrative Structure and the Antithetical Vision of *Jerusalem*," in *Blake's Visionary Forms Dramatic*, ed. David V. Erdman and John E. Grant, pp. 391–412; Stuart Curran, "The Structures of *Jerusalem*," in *Blake's Sublime Allegory*, ed. Stuart Curran and Joseph Anthony Wittreich, Jr., pp. 329–46.

50 Bloom, commentary in *Poetry and Prose of Blake*, p. 843.

51 The text later suggests a *trompe-l'oeil* identification between Albion's Spectre and Vala. If this "identification" is followed up, then the explanation of "the appearance in the frowning Chaos" has to do with the repression of "Albion's Emanation . . . in Jealousy." This is, we may say, the original cause, while the turning from the Divine Vision is the immediate cause of the appearances.

52 Perhaps it is the most poignant mark of the bewilderment which results from the failure to make Albion come home that the Cities (1) give themselves over to Los now that he has lost his own self-mastery (2, 39:21–31), and (2) begin to preach "mercy" as the only cure when they have just abandoned it for "violence" (2, 40–41).

53 Frye, evidently influenced by the "dazzling pyrotechnics" accompanying the reversal in *The Four Zoas*, does not recognize one here, and concludes that Blake may have been at pains to suppress "crisis" in *Jerusalem* (*Fearful Symmetry*, pp. 357, 358).

54 Plate 56 of *Jerusalem* has long taxed commentary; for other interpretations the reader should consult Bloom, commentary in *Poetry and Prose of Blake*, pp. 855–56, and S. Foster Damon, *William Blake*, p. 456.

55 Max Plowman calls this "a particularly obvious example of Blake's habit of inserting an extra plate whenever he wished to expand a theme" (in Blake, *Poems and Prophecies*, p. 232*n*).

56 Heliocentric and geocentric theories of the universe and a flat earth vs. global theory of our planet pale to insignificance here beside the *quality* of the earth.

57 This emerges continually in Bloom's commentary on Blake's poetry, and enters significantly into Fred Kaplan's *Miracles of Rare Device*, pp. 15, 21, 26–27.

58 To the extent that it always, whether oriented to the world as mimesis or to the self, encountering the world, as expressive, whether it takes the form of a *nouvelle vague* litany or of a surrealist outburst, amounts to presentation rather than origination. (Perhaps this makes criticism tertiary; so be it.)

59 This comment is patently based on Abrams's brilliant analysis of the movement from mimetic to expressive modes in the rise of romanticism in *The Mirror and the Lamp*. I suggest only a degree of eddying and ambivalence in that movement. Perhaps some of that ambivalence persists into our century, though it must be observed that a perfect resolution, maintaining both mimetic and expressive modes in impeccable harmony, appears in James Joyce's *Ulysses*. The triumph of the expressive mode may be seen in modern African poetry of negritude and in recent Latin American fiction (Marquez, Donoso).

CHAPTER 3

1 *World as Will and Representation*, 1:223 (all quotes).
2 *Letters*, 1:238.
3 The sense of a superior world in covert comes up again in connection with the violet in Keats's "To George Felton Mathew," as the fit setting for the Muse not only has obvious treasures but also proves a place "where to pry, aloof,/Atween the pillars of a sylvan roof/Would be to find where violet beds were nestling."
4 "Keats's Epic Design in *Hyperion*," *Studies in Romanticism* 14 (1975): 183.
5 I would contrast this manipulative aesthetics with the contemplative aesthetics of preceding eras. The Elizabethan play, for example, may work on us by means of an epilogue (already something extrinsic), but it hereby seeks our tolerance, not our submission or conversion. And the playwright formally resists the tendency of the audience to treat his play directly as phenomenon in life, a response which breeds a confusion, in Maritain's terms, of *agibilia* and *factibilia*. The classic statement of this view occurs of course in Beaumont's *The Knight of the Burning Pestle*. It may be remarked here that a medium between manipulative and contemplative aesthetics occurs in the case of satire, where the renovation of standards demands manipulation, while at the same time the presumption of standards permits contemplation through the act of art.
6 By way of quick comparison, Byron continually chafed at his vocation, and would have been a doer and liberator, Shelley a philosopher and liberator, Coleridge a philosopher and seer, and Wordsworth, whose vocation in a sense befell him, a teacher and seer. Within my limited knowledge of the European writers of the age, only Hölderlin seems to have had a will to poetry like Keats's, and that in a problematical if not pathological vein.
7 Thomas A. Vogler in his provocative study, *Preludes to Vision*, has

observed that in Keats's career the crucial question was one "of will, of achieving confidence in poetic vision . . . and in the finished poem as an embodiment of truth" (p. 116).

8 The reader may with profit consult Harold Bloom, *The Anxiety of Influence*, for a stimulating hypothesis concerning the interplay between composition and preemption in writing new poetry.

9 The *rolling* of the *vast* idea inevitably suggests the overwhelmings of the earlier passage, and enables us to see more precisely the freedom, from overwhelming, that Keats recognizes in *Sleep and Poetry*.

10 Referring, of course, to sleep.

11 The charioteer, Reason, who is prominent in the Platonic conception of the soul, would make an improbable identification here. If he is involved, he has been infused (or confused) with eagerness and uncertainty in relation to an elusive exaltation. He is Wordsworth's more than Plato's Reason, imaginative more than judgmental.

12 *Letters*, 1:374.

13 See Clarence D. Thorpe, *The Mind of John Keats*, pp. 65–70.

14 *Letters*, 1:238–39.

15 Ibid., 1:193–94.

16 It is clear enough from "A Prophecy: to His Brother George in America" that Keats regarded poetry as innate in the poet, no matter how much difficulty or labor might be entailed in manifesting this:

> Little child
> O' th' western wild,
> Bard art thou completely!
> Sweetly with dumb endeavor,
> A Poet now or never,
> Little child
> O' th' western wild,
> A Poet now or never!

17 I have been quoting from the letter of 19 February 1818 to John Hamilton Reynolds, in which "What the Thrush Said" first occurs as a poetic statement of Keats's thoughts on "the flower [and] the Bee," exemplars of opposite conditions of life (*Letters*, 1:232–33). On 19 March 1819 Keats clearly states his divided views on indolence, which he thought might take "an easy" or "an uneasy" form, with "a great difference between" them (*Letters*, 2:77; see also p. 78).

18 Ibid., 2:105–06.

19 Both "The Eve of St. Agnes" and *Lamia* contain special versions of

the poetical or fabricated enclave, a charmed "world-within-the-world" that elicited Keats's powers in striking ways; the command of language and *of the audience* in these two poems is virtuosity at a conspicuous height. At the same time this charmed world is full of internal tension, as again both poems show. Madeline and Porphyro cannot stay in it, but leave its antithesis, the castle, for a highly problematical home across the moors. Lamia, who may be seen as the arbitrary creator, the poet-within-the-poem, suffers the consequences of her own magic—Lycius will have it seen, will force it on the world without, and thus gives that world usurpative access to the charmed world. Keats puts himself in the position of indulging and yet also of chiding the arbitrary appeal of charm.

20 The particular reference to a nightingale in the poem, and in Charles Armitage Brown's account of its origin (see Hyder E. Rollins, ed., *The Keats Circle*, 2:65) has troubled Keats's most devout scholars and editors, prompting the practical question, How can the particular bird, which obviously must be subject to death, be any more immortal than the particular man addressing it? Nor does the maneuver of isolating one of its attributes, such as its voice, really make the proposition more sensible. Attributes persevere in the species, and man is as much a species as the nightingale. It would seem likeliest that Keats is responding to the nightingale's music in particular, and also to its generic status as a bird. The song starts him thinking, but his thought is the age-old association of the bird with the soul, with untrammeled freedom of being, and immortality. The phrase "immortal *Bird*" then addresses the nightingale generically, indeed mythically, and couches a peculiar redundancy: "immortal symbol of the immortal soul."

21 It will be of interest to compare Blake's reformulation of the meaning of "death" in *Jerusalem*, p. 132 above and after.

22 Another indication that no natural "draught" can do for the effect he seeks. If Bacchus is taken not as god of the vine but as god who inspires to music and poetry, an interesting extension of the poet's self-will emerges, since the poet flying on the "wings of Poesy" without recourse to Bacchus and his pards would seem to become his own Muse. It is well also to remember the lines "To—[Fanny Brawne]" written late in 1819, where Keats not only insists on his "old liberty" or subjective will, but also specifically repudiates wine as a source of elevation: "Shall I gulp wine? No, that is vulgarism" (line'24); an ampler and more carefully analyzed idea of wine occurs in Keats's *Letters*, 2:56, 64.

23 Possibly the preoccupation with knowledge which, in light of the present reading, thwarts the will to poetry while ostensibly promoting it.

24 We may note too the reinforcement of this startling reversal in the use of the verb *fade*. At first the poet seeks to fade, into the forest with the bird; the fading is from one point to another point that presumably should grow more graphic as more nearly approached (the fact that the forest remains dim, in the fifth stanza, may be only a reflection of the poet's ecstasy, or of his mortal limitation). But the "plaintive anthem" of the bird "fades" progressively into the state where it is "buried deep." One is forced to wonder if the bird is singing its own requiem.

25 The threat of bounty is an undercurrent in stanza 5 of the "Ode to a Nightingale," and also helps to explain the deathly association of the first stanza of that poem. Andrew Marvell of course offers the consummate statement of the threat of bounty, in the fifth stanza of "The Garden":

> What wondrous life is this I lead!
> Ripe apples *drop about my head*;
> The luscious clusters of the vine
> *Upon my mouth do crush* their wine:
> The nectarine, and curious peach,
> Into my hands themselves do reach;
> *Stumbling* on melons, as I pass,
> *Insnared with flowers, I fall* on grass. [italics added]

26 James Lott, in "Keats's 'To Autumn:' The Poetic Consciousness and The Awareness of Process," *Studies in Romanticism* 9 (1970): 71-81, deals tellingly with this subject.

27 We may recall that lyric poetry, the predominant mode of the romantics, tends to be self-referential, as though the feeling for the poem identified itself with the impulse to write, and feelings about writing took precedence over writing about something. Of course a self-referential quality can be recognized in the Renaissance as well. But the romantic lyric distinguishes itself in exploring, rather than asserting, its immunity to circumstance, as we see in the relation it bears to time. The Renaissance lyric looks at itself perfunctorily and postulates that its existence as durable *book* confers immortality; the romantic lyric suggests that immortality resides in its creation—the substance, not the existence, of the lyric—or in some way *in itself*. Wordsworth explicitly laments the *frailty* of books in *The Prelude*, book 5. A new enduringness-in-process enters into the self-image of the romantic lyric. Decay and dilapidation provide a good image of the possibilities of this eternal moment in Wordsworth's woods (*Prelude*, book 6) or Byron's place where Ruin greenly dwells (*Childe Harold*, canto 3, stanza 46).

28 On 21 September 1819—two days after composing "To Autumn"—

Keats wrote to John Hamilton Reynolds: "How beautiful the season is now—How fine the air. A temperate sharpness about it. Really, without joking, chaste weather—Dian skies—I never lik'd stubble fields so much as now. Aye better than the chilly green of the spring. Somehow a stubble plain looks warm—in the same way that some pictures look warm—this struck me so much in my sunday's walk that I composed upon it" (*Letters*, 2:167).

29 Without forcing, much may be made of the hilly bourn, the hedge, the garden-croft. The poem does not come down (death) without going up (life), and it is significant that, within its natural rhythm and amplitude, it ends on an up stroke. We may note in passing, too, that the bourn and the croft, despite the contrast between hill and garden, pick up the enclosure image of autumn "sitting careless on a granary floor," while adding the humanistic values of protection and husbandry to the naturalistic, almost indifferent bounty of the season.

30 We need but observe the gnats "sinking" in the third stage to temper any zeal for perfect correspondence between active and passive in grammar and in fact.

31 It is customary to observe that the scene takes place in a postlapsarian world, with all that implies of lost power and grace. But surely the return to the place of the garden tends to counteract any negative implications of the scene. Later in the poem the poet, who here eats after angels, climbs the gradus of the temple "as once fair angels on a ladder flew / From the green turf to heaven," a description which suggests an expanding parallelism of imitation instead of any humiliating contrast. We may note, in more immediate and practical terms, that the poet hardly flinches from the offered food; clearly he calls it the "refuse of a meal" in a neutral and not emotional way. Rather than feeling himself or it disgraced, he approaches it eagerly as a surpassing bounty. His mind is on recovered munificence, with Eve's garden and Proserpine's fields equally surpassing anything he has known, and thus giving rise to a more than earthly appetite. While the thought of partaking of someone's leftovers sticks in the craw, the poet is not eating after just anybody; as our dogs after us, so perhaps we after our mythical heroes.

32 Attention may be called to my essay, "De Quincey, Coleridge, and the Formal Uses of Intoxication," *Yale French Studies* 50 (1974): 26–40.

33 *Letters*, 2:113.

34 The relationship between Moneta and the poet is full of problems, which are judiciously set forth by Vogler (*Preludes to Vision*, p. 127). One factor, though, calls for special attention, and that is Moneta's dual function as lofty preceptor and pained actor in the

scene. This duality has its counterpart in the poet's alternating reverence and ironic familiarity. Its critical implications are far from negligible, especially in relation to Moneta's analysis of the types of poetry and dismissal of the poet (though his superior quality has already been proven on the stairs) as one "of the dreamer tribe." Her remarks must carry weight, but cannot be definitive. They are as much dramatic as philosophical, and one of their effects as drama is to show her grief and vindictiveness and need. In a sense she knows less than the poem, in which three pieces of data work counter to her postulates: (1) to dream is a universal phenomenon; (2) the poet is *literally* a dreamer; (3) the crucial question is whether the dream that includes Moneta is a fanatic's (restricted to sect) or a poet's (apt for all mankind). As regards Moneta herself a further qualification presents itself, in that her treatment of the poet is affected by her inability to respond to him aesthetically. Caught up in a realistic situation, she wants a psychopolitical solution, not an aesthetic balm. Her impatience reflects her frustration more than the poet's quality. His dream is her reality, and her question therein boils down to what good he can do her and hers. But his position, both repudiating "proud bad" versifiers and honoring poets as physicians to all men, paves the way for further development of their relationship. In a way he is not only proving himself worthy of her instruction but instructing her in the worth of his art.

35 Part of the limitation of this vision is already apparent in the ominous ring of this line, where the simple turning of the verse gives a chilling finality to the phrase "that is all."

36 *Letters*, 1:170.

37 Keats's development toward competence in epic is neatly summarized by Vogler, *Preludes to Vision*, p. 15.

38 The study of Keats's development as a poet has over the years attracted an impressive roster of scholars, and one can only hope in joining the field that it is possible to walk in others' footsteps without galling their kibes. To ask a new question is to solicit a new answer; emphasis on the state and degree of will evinced in the poems, first and foremost, makes for something of a new departure, and raises new issues for Keats's poetry. This reading clearly has been facilitated and enriched by various critics and commentators. Walter Jackson Bate has published two books that enter centrally into our consideration of Keats: *Negative Capability* and *John Keats*. J. M. Murry's *Keats and Shakespeare* and his "Keats's Thought: A Discovery of Truth" (in *The Major English Romantic Poets*, ed. Clarence D. Thorpe et al., pp. 252–58) have great value for students of the poet's mind and mastery of his art. Douglas

Bush has enlarged understanding of the freight and movement of
Keats's art with his *Mythology and the Romantic Tradition in En-
glish Poetry*, pp. 81–128, and *John Keats*. A number of works are
devoted specifically to Keats's development as a poet: Hugh
I'Anson Fausset, *Keats;* Claude Lee Finney, *The Evolution of
Keats's Poetry*; Bernard Blackstone, *The Consecrated Urn*; Morris
Dickstein, *Keats and His Poetry*; and Maurice Roy Ridley, *Keats's
Craftmanship*. Astute and weighty consideration of Keats as a com-
mitted and increasing artist can also be found in Mario D'Avanzo,
Keats's Metaphors for the Poetic Imagination; Earl R. Wasserman,
The Finer Tone; E. E. Bostetter, *The Romantic Ventriloquists*,
pp. 136–80; Lionel Trilling, introduction to the *Selected Letters of
John Keats*; Norman Talbot, *The Major Poems of John Keats*; Ian
Jack *English Literature: 1815–1832*, pp. 105–29. Stuart M. Sperry,
Jr., in his recent study, *Keats the Poet*, considers sensation and
thought, "conscious intention and unconscious creativity" as pri-
mary tensional poles in Keats's development; this work gives
Sperry a place among the foremost Keatsians.

39 *On the Aesthetic Education of Man*, fourteenth letter, p. 175.

40 Ibid., pp. 141 (first extract), 147 (second extract), 151.

41 Northrop Frye, *Anatomy of Criticism*, p. 298. It would perhaps be
more just to say that the Spectre of Urthona, by recognizing and
trying to play on Los's own weakness, drives him in reaction to
enunciate and espouse a genuine "will" and "purpose." This is
certainly the conclusion indicated in *Jerusalem*, plates 7–12.

42 And proper within the scheme of the poem, for here, after a number of failures ranging from *The Marriage of Heaven and Hell* to
The Four Zoas, Blake makes contraries truly coexist, and eschews
the trap of negation. Los does not try to cancel the Spectre out, as
Blake does the angel in *The Marriage*, but instead uses him, concep-
tually and practically, to advance his own cause: "Without Contraries is no progression."

43 As *The (First) Book of Urizen* makes clear, he is by nature "af-
frighted/At the formless unmeasurable death" (3, 7:8–9). This is
repeated in chapter 5, where "the space, undivided by existence
/Struck horror into his soul" (14:46–47).

44 No clearer sign of this weakness can be found than Orc's capitulation before Urizen in *The Four Zoas* ("Night the Seventh"). Orc
does not become Urizen, as Frye perhaps too schematically suggests (*Fearful Symmetry*, p. 210), but becomes susceptible to
Urizen's structuring of things, or aware of his own need for structure. To admit this criticism of himself is tantamount to nullifying
himself as energy, in much the same way that a moment of sympathy in *The Four Zoas* undoes Urizen as system. What Blake does,

to retain and yet to reconcile these two essential character-states in his poetry is to create in *Jerusalem* a merger between Urizen's impulse to structure and Orc's to ebullience, as we see in the character-state of Los. Thus the superficial Orc-Urizen dichotomy becomes the profound and decisive confrontation of Los (vital system) and Urizen (mechanical systematization).

45 William F. Halloran provides a good account of the basis of engagement and conviction in this poem (see "*The French Revolution*: Revelation's New Form," in *Blake's Visionary Forms Dramatic*, ed. D. V. Erdman and J. E. Grant, pp. 30–56).

46 The fact that Albion, who here turns away from the Saviour's summons is regarded as a "saviour" (1, 23:12) creates yet another evolutionary identification of apparent opposites in the poem. The danger for the poem is of course that if all things are identical, nothing will have identity, a state of confusion that presumably could give grounds for Urizen's analytical rigidities. But in fact there is identity, distinction, without categorization or incompatibility.

47 Here again the sequence, "Human Imagination/O Saviour," leaves a vital double meaning. The Human Imagination enjoys an apposition with the Worlds of Thought and with the Saviour. To recognize this is to reinforce the connection between spirit and man, which the poem is at pains to generate.

48 Clearly these last words are more than a simple redundancy. They show that the poet is not just seeing but demanding that he be recognized in and for that act.

49 The explanatory impulse is concentrated in plate 69, for example, where *hence* and *for* serve as the mode of progression from statement to statement. This mode of progression infuses into the apparent narrative contract of the poem a strong logical element (see, again, plates 72, 73).

50 Various critics have investigated the problem of suffering in Keats's poetry, with advantageous results. A. C. Bradley's *Oxford Lectures on Poetry*, D. G. James's *The Romantic Comedy*, and Albert Gérard's "Keats and the Romantic *Sehnsucht*," *University of Toronto Quarterly* 28 (1959): 160–75, may be particularly cited. Also Brian Wilkie in *Romantic Poets and Epic Tradition* speaks tellingly of Keats's epic cultivation of "sternness of matter as well as approach and viewpoint" (p. 145).

51 It may be observed that these aims persist, but substantially modified. One is not so much instructed as reeducated in the terms of romanticism. The poet is left "to create the taste by which he is to be relished." And the delight he affords is less aesthetic than human; Wordsworth takes care to keep any imputation of frivolity

from the "pleasure" of poetry, deriving this pleasure from "an acknowledgment of the beauty of the universe," to be sought by anyone who "looks at the world in the spirit of love," and who would pay "homage . . . to the native and naked dignity of man, to the grand elementary principle of pleasure, by which he knows, and feels, and lives, and moves." In a sense the twentieth century revives but also subdues the idea of instruction and delight. Wallace Stevens perhaps best exemplifies the case, with his Yeatsian poet in "that old coat, those sagging pantaloons":

> It is of him, ephebe, to make, to confect
> The final *elegance*, not to console
> Nor sanctify, but plainly to *propound*.
> [*Notes Toward a Supreme Fiction*, 1, 10;
>   italics added]

It is as though Stevens were rejecting Keats and reinstating Horace, but without the latter's sense of immediate, purposive involvement with an audience. "Delight" is distanced into elegance, and "instruction" reduced to propounding.

52 *World as Will and Representation*, 1:353.

53 The movement Wordsworth observes from blood to heart to mind may derive from self-observation or from associationist philosophy; it is striking all the same to see that it chimes with stoical epistemology and theory of being. The Stoics held that all reality is one, and that everything that exists, acts, or is acted upon is body, and they maintained that all reality is informed with an active principle or logos. A passage from the *Meditations* of Marcus Aurelius will both sum up this position and suggest the Wordsworthian ascent from material to spiritual states:

> Ever consider and think upon the world as being but one living substance, and having but one soul, and how *all things in the world, are terminated into one sensitive power*; and are done by one general motion as it were, and deliberation of that one soul; and how all things that are, concur in the cause of one another's being, and by what manner of connection and concatenation all things happen. [p. 44, Meric Casaubon translation; italics added]

54 Ibid., p. xviii.

55 A good discussion of a stoical temper of acceptance in Byron, emphasizing his comic writing, is provided by G. R. Elliott, "Byron and the Comic Spirit," *PMLA* 39 (1924): 897–909; and general commentary on stoicism in Byron's work appears in my study, *The Blind Man Traces the Circle* (see esp. pp. 181–83, 203–05).

David Perkins, *The Quest for Permanence*, offers a suggestive discussion of the "retreat into stoicism" by Wordsworth (p. 8). Cleanth Brooks analyzes what he terms Wordsworth's Olympian perspective in "Wordsworth and Human Suffering," in *From Sensibility to Romanticism*, pp. 373–88. And Jonathan Wordsworth has valuable comments on the tragic dimensions of Wordsworth's art in *The Music of Humanity*. Valuable background material and useful insights into Wordsworth's position on stoical "virtue" and conformity to nature are available in Jane Worthington, *Wordsworth's Reading of Roman Prose*. Further specialized discussion of Wordsworth and stoicism has appeared in Stallknecht, *Strange Seas of Thought*, pp. 25–26, and "Wordsworth's 'Ode to Duty,' and the Schöne Seele," *PMLA* 52 (1937): 230–37; E. A. Sonnenschein, "Stoicism in English Literature," *The Contemporary Review* 124 (1923): 355–65; Trilling, "Wordsworth and the Rabbis"; Bostetter, *The Romantic Ventriloquists*, pp. 53–81; and Melvin G. Williams, "A New Look at Wordsworth's Religion," *Cithara* 2 (1962): 20–32.

56 The poem includes the phrase, "a slumber seems to steal," which is startlingly close to "A slumber did my spirit seal"; the idea of withdrawal from the terms of life and by extension of lifeless identification with natural or nonhuman objects would be common to both pieces.

57 The conflict between a balanced view of reality and the "encroachments of fantasy" in ''Resolution and Independence" is well developed by W. W. Robson, "Wordsworth: *Resolution and Independence*," in *Interpretations*, ed. John Wain, pp. 113–28. Valuable commentary on the tensional structure and philosophy of the poem is provided by Albert Gérard, "*Resolution and Independence*: Wordsworth's Coming of Age," *English Studies in Africa* 3 (1960): 8–20, and by Anthony E. M. Conran, "The Dialectic of Experience: A Study of Wordsworth's *Resolution and Independence*," *PMLA* 75 (1960): 66–74, and A. W. Thomson, "Resolution and Independence," in *Wordsworth's Mind and Art*, pp. 181–99.

58 His rejection of the consolations offered in the Sermon on the Mount (stanza 6) deserves special notice; he is rejecting a positive theory of the momentary (or occasionalist) possibilities of life in favor of a stubborn and, again, logical negative ("how can He expect that others should/Build for him, sow for him, and at his call /Love him, who for himself will take no heed at all?"). But the "poet's" negative logic of the moment, here applied strictly to himself, is proleptically addressed to the Leech-gatherer, who refutes it by *not* kicking, by *not* expecting, by simply being as metaphysically strong as he is physically weak. On the surface it is Christian stoicism that the poem encourages. But finally the Leech-gatherer,

himself a Christian, does not inculcate Christianity so much as stoicism; the hope and positive faith of the Sermon on the Mount are
not urged by the poem's final lines, only the curative image of the
old man perfect in his endurance. A stronger claim for the Christian possibilities of the poem is made by Alan Grob in "Process and
Permanence in 'Resolution and Independence'," *ELH* 28 (1961):
89–100.

59   The contrast in sensitivity and values between the self-avowed poet
and the "old sea-captain" in "The Thorn" works heavily to the
former's discredit. The captain is at once more alert to reality and
more spontaneously sympathetic than the poet. To be sure he *mis-
takes* Martha Ray for "a jutting crag," but in the worst of weather,
and he instantly and profoundly corrects his vision: "I did not
speak—I saw her face;/Her face! it was enough for me;/I turned
about and heard her cry,/'Oh misery!'" That unbearable face of
hers ("I turned about") is stamped on his mind, and her voice of
woe rings forever in his ear. He becomes her champion, by an in-
stant access of human sympathy, which may be increased by the
shame of his first mistake and his first weakness of response. By
contrast the poet *takes* the Leech-gatherer for stone and sea-
beast. Not in the least embarrassed by almost stumbling upon the
old man who is standing "beside a pool bare to the eye of heaven,"
he persists in patronizing him, and cannot let go his own pointless
monomania: "How is it that you live, and what is it you do?"

60   *World as Will and Representation*, 1:503.

61   It has been customary to call this kind of will Byronic; this does
the versatile peer an injustice, as I have tried to demonstrate in *The
Blind Man Traces the Circle*; see esp. chapters 3 and 4.

62   *World as Will and Representation*, 1:527, 1:404, 1:379.

63   Attention may be called to Evelyn Shakir, "Books, Death, and
Immortality: A Study of Book V of *The Prelude*," *Studies in Romanticism* 8 (1968): 156–67.

64   Benjamin P. Kurtz in *The Pursuit of Death* proposes that Shelley in
his poetry tries to accommodate himself to death, but the main
thrust of his argument is toward a position where death is for
Shelley a thrice-conquered enemy and is finally avoided and transcended (see esp. pp. xiv, xvi, xx–xxi, 48–49, 177–84, 215). It is
useful also to recall Northrop Frye's comment on Beddoes and the
subject of death: "Beddoes, identifying (the) invisible and underlying reality with death, seems . . . to have hit a bullseye that many
of his contemporaries *saw but tried not to hit*" (*A Study of English
Romanticism*, p. 85; italics added).

BIBLIOGRAPHY

Abrams, Meyer H. "English Romanticism: The Spirit of the Age." In *Romanticism: Points of View*, 2d ed, edited by Robert F. Gleckner and Gerald E. Enscoe. Englewood Cliffs, N.J.: Prentice-Hall, 1970.
———. *The Mirror and the Lamp: Romantic Theory and the Critical Tradition*. New York: Oxford University Press, 1953.
———. *Natural Supernaturalism*. New York: W. W. Norton, 1971.
Addison, Joseph. *Cato, a Tragedy, in Five Acts*. With an illustration, and notes, biographical and critical, by D. G., London and New York: S. French, n.d.
———, and Steele, Richard. *Selections from the Tatler and the Spectator*. 2d ed. Introduction and notes by Robert J. Allen. New York: Holt, Rinehart and Winston, 1970.
Adler, Gerhard. *The Living Symbol: A Case Study in the Process of Individuation*. New York: Pantheon Books, 1961.
Altieri, Charles. "Wordsworth's Wavering Balance: The Thematic Rhythm of *The Prelude*." *The Wordsworth Circle* 4 (1973): 226–40.
Anscombe, G. E. M. *Intention*. Oxford:Blackwell, 1957.
Appleyard, J. A. "Coleridge and Criticism: 1. Critical Theory." In *Writers and their Background: S. T. Coleridge*, edited by R. L. Brett. Columbus: Ohio University Press, 1973.
———. *Coleridge's Philosophy of Literature: The Development of a Concept of Poetry, 1791-1819*. Cambridge: Harvard University Press, 1965.
Arieti, Silvano. *The Will To Be Human*. New York: Quadrangle Books, 1972.
Auden, Wystan Hugh. *The Enchafed Flood, or, The Romantic Iconography of the Sea*. New York: Vintage Books, 1967.
Auerbach, Eric. *Mimesis: The Representation of Reality in Western Literature*. Translated by Willard Trask. Princeton: Princeton University Press, 1953.
Aurelius Antoninus, Marcus. *Meditations Concerning Himself*. Translated with notes by Meric Casaubon. Edited with an introduction, appendix, and glossary, by W. H. D. Rouse. New York: Dutton, 1900.
Bacon, Francis, viscount St. Albans. *Essays, Advancement of Learning,*

New Atlantis, and Other Pieces. Selected and edited by Richard Foster Jones. New York: Odyssey Press, 1937.

Baker, James Volant. *The Sacred River: Coleridge's Theory of the Imagination*. Introduction by Richard Harter Fogle. Baton Rouge: Louisiana State University Press, 1957.

Barfield, Owen. *Romanticism Comes of Age*. New and augmented edition. Middletown: Wesleyan University Press, 1967.

———. *What Coleridge Thought*. Middletown: Wesleyan University Press, 1971.

Barker, Sir Ernest, ed. *Social Contract: Essays by Locke, Hume and Rousseau*. New York: Oxford University Press, 1962.

Barrell, John. *The Idea of Landscape and the Sense of Place, 1730–1840: An Approach to the Poetry of John Clare*. Cambridge: Cambridge University Press, 1972.

Barzun, Jacques. *Classic, Romantic and Modern*. 2d rev. ed. Garden City: Doubleday, 1961.

Bate, Walter Jackson. *Coleridge*. New York: Macmillan, 1968.

———. *From Classic Romantic: Premises of Taste in Eighteenth-Century England*. Cambridge: Harvard University Press, 1946.

———. *John Keats*. Cambridge: Belknap Press of Harvard University Press, 1963.

———. *Negative Capability: The Intuitive Approach in Keats*. Cambridge: Harvard University Press, 1939.

Beaumont, Francis. *The Knight of the Burning Pestle*. Edited by John Doebler. London: Edward Arnold, 1967.

Beddoes, Thomas Lovell. *The Works*. Edited with an introduction by H. W. Donner. London: H. Milford, Oxford University Press, 1937.

Beer, John B. *Coleridge the Visionary*. London: Chatto & Windus, 1959.

Bergson, Henri Louis. *Matter and Memory*. Authorized translation by Nancy Margaret Paul and W. Scott Palmer. New York: Macmillan, 1929.

———. *Time and Free Will: An Essay on the Immediate Data of Consciousness*. Translated by F. L. Pogson. 2d ed. New York: Macmillan, 1912.

Bishop, Jonathan. "Wordsworth and the 'Spots of Time'." *ELH* 26 (1959): 45–65.

Blackstone, Bernard. *The Consecrated Urn: An Interpretation of Keats in Terms of Growth and Form*. London: Longman's, Green, 1959.

Blake, William. *Poems and Prophecies*. Edited with an introduction by Max Plowman. New York: Everyman's Library, 1925.

———. *The Poetry and Prose of William Blake*. Edited by David V. Erdman. Commentary by Harold Bloom. Garden City: Doubleday, 1965.

Bloom, Harold. *The Anxiety of Influence: A Theory of Poetry*. New York, Oxford University Press, 1973.

——. *Blake's Apocalypse: A Study In Poetic Argument*. Garden City: Doubleday, 1963.

——. *The Ringers in the Tower: Studies in Romantic Tradition*. Chicago: University Of Chicago Press, 1971.

——, ed. *Romanticism and Consciousness: Essays in Criticism*. New York: W. W. Norton, 1970.

——. *The Visionary Company: a Reading of English Romantic Poetry*. Rev. and enl. ed. Ithaca: Cornell University Press, 1971.

Boehme, Jakob. *The High and Deep Searching Out of the Threefold Life through the Three Principles*. English ed. by J. Sparrow. Reissued by C. J. B. Introduction by the Rev. G. W. Allen. London: J. M. Watkins, 1909.

——. *Mysterium Magnum; Or, An Exposition of the First Book of Moses, Called Genesis*. Translated by J. Sparrow. Edited by C. J. B. London: J. M. Watkins, 1924.

——. *Six Theosophic Points, and Other Writings*. Introduction by Nicholos Berdyaev. Translated by John Rolleston Earle. Ann Arbor: University of Michigan Press, 1958.

——. *The Way to Christ, Described in the Following Treatises: Of True Repentance; Of True Resignation; Of Regeneration; Of the Super-sensual Life*. London: J. M. Watkins, 1911.

Boileau, Nicolas, *Oeuvres complètes*. Vol. 2. *Epitres. Art Poetique. Lutrin*. Edited by Charles-H. Boudhors. Paris: Société des Belles lettres, 1934.

Bostetter, E. E. *The Romantic Ventriloquists: Wordsworth, Coleridge, Keats, Shelley, Byron*. Seattle: University of Washington Press, 1963.

——. "The Nightmare World of *The Ancient Mariner*." *Studies in Romanticism* 1 (1962): 241–54.

Boulger, James D., ed. *Twentieth Century Interpretations of "The Rime of the Ancient Mariner": A Collection of Critical Essays*. Englewood Cliffs, New Jersey: Prentice-Hall, 1969.

Bourke, Vernon J. *Will in Western Thought: An Historio-Critical Survey*. New York: Sheed and Ward, 1964.

Bradley, A. C. *Oxford Lectures on Poetry*. 2d ed. New York: St. Martin's Press, 1955.

Brett, R. L. *Reason and Imagination: A Study of Form and Meaning in Four Poems*. London and New York: Oxford University Press, 1960.

——, ed. *Writers and their Background. Samuel Taylor Coleridge*. Columbus: Ohio University Press, 1973.

Brisman, Leslie. "Coleridge and the Ancestral Voices." *The Georgia Review* 29 (1975): 469–98.

——. *Milton's Poetry of Choice and Its Romantic Heirs*. Ithaca: Cornell University Press, 1973.

Brooks, Cleanth. "Wordsworth and Human Suffering: Notes on Two Early Poems." In *From Sensibility to Romanticism*, edited by F. W. Hilles and Harold Bloom. New York: Oxford University Press, 1965.

Buchan, A. M. "The Sad Wisdom of the Mariner." *Studies in Philology* 61 (1964): 669–88.

Bush, Douglas. *John Keats, His Life and Writings*. New York: Macmillan, 1966.

——. *Mythology and the Romantic Tradition in English Poetry*. New York: Pageant, 1957.

Byron, George Gordon Noel, Lord. *Don Juan*. 4 vols. Edited by T. G. Steffan and W. W. Pratt. Austin: University of Texas Press, 1957.

——. *The Poetical Works*. Edited with a memoir by Ernest Hartley Coleridge. London: John Murray, 1972.

——. *The Complete Poetical Works*. Cambridge ed. Boston: Houghton Mifflin, 1933.

Carr, H. Wildon. *A Theory of Monads: Outlines of the Philosophy of the Principle of Relativity*. London: Macmillan, 1922.

Cassirer, Ernst. *The Individual and the Cosmos in Renaissance Philosophy*. New York: Barnes and Noble, 1963.

Caton, Hiram Pendleton. *The Origin of Subjectivity: An Essay on Descartes*. New Haven: Yale University Press, 1973.

Chayes, Irene H. "Dreamer, Poet and Poem in *The Fall of Hyperion*." *Philological Quarterly* 46 (1967): 499–515.

——. "'Kubla Khan' and the Creative Process." *Studies in Romanticism* 6 (1966): 1–21.

Christensen, Francis. "Intellectual Love: The Second Theme of *The Prelude*." *PMLA* 80 (1965): 69–75.

Clare, John. *The Poems*. Edited with an introduction by J. W. Tibble. London: J. M. Dent, 1935.

——. *Poems of John Clare's Madness*. Edited with an introduction by Geoffrey Grigson. London: Routledge and Kegan Paul, 1949.

Clarke, C. C. *Romantic Paradox: An Essay on the Poetry of Wordsworth*. London: Routledge and Kegan Paul, 1962.

Clarke, George Herbert. "Certain Symbols in *The Rime of the Ancient Mariner*." *Queens Quarterly* 40 (1933): 27–45.

Coleridge, Samuel Taylor. *Aids to Reflection and the Confessions of an Inquiring Spirit*. New ed., rev. London: G. Bell (Bohn's standard library), 1884.

——. *Biographia Literaria*. Edited with his Aesthetical essays by J. Shawcross. 2 vols. Oxford: Clarendon Press, 1907.

——. *Biographia Literaria, Or Biographical Sketches of My Literary Life and Opinions*. 2d ed. Edited by Henry Nelson Coleridge, completed and published by his widow. London: W. Pickering, 1847.

———. *Collected Letters*. Edited by Earl Leslie Griggs. 6 vols. Oxford: Clarendon Press, 1956–59.

———. *The Complete Poetical Works, Including Poems and Versions of Poems Now Published for the First Time*. Edited with textual and bibliographical notes by Ernest Hartley Coleridge. 2 vols. Oxford: Clarendon Press, 1957.

———. *Inquiring Spirit: A New Presentation of Coleridge From his Published and Unpublished Prose Writings*. Edited by Kathleen Coburn. London: Routledge and Kegan Paul, 1951.

———. *The Notebooks*. Edited by Kathleen Coburn. 2 vols. in 4. New York: Pantheon Books, 1957–61.

———. *The Rime of the Ancient Mariner*. With "A Poem of Pure Imagination: An Experiment in Reading," by Robert Penn Warren. New York: Reynal and Hitchcock, 1946.

———. *Shakespearean Criticism*. Edited by Thomas Middleton Raysor. 2d ed. 2 vols. New York: Dutton, 1960.

———. *The Statesman's Manual*; *Or, The Bible the Best Guide to Political Skill and Foresight: A Lay Sermon, Addressed to the Higher Classes of Society*. Burlington: C. Goodrich, 1832.

Conran, Anthony E. M. "The Dialectic of Experience: A Study of Wordsworth's *Resolution and Independence*." *PMLA* 75 (1960): 66–74.

Cook, Albert Stanburrough. *The Art of Poetry: The Poetical Treatises of Horace, Vida, and Boileau*. With the translations by Howes, Pitt and Soame. New York: G. E. Stechert, 1926.

Cooke, Michael G. *The Blind Man Traces the Circle: On the Patterns and Philosophy of Byron's Poetry*. Princeton: Princeton University Press, 1969.

———. "De Quincey, Coleridge and the Formal Uses of Intoxication." *Yale French Studies* 50 (1974): 26–40.

———. "On the Mode of Argument in Wordsworth's Poetry." In *Romantic and Victorian: Studies in Memory of William H. Marshall*, edited by Paul W. Elledge and Richard L. Hoffman, Rutherford, N.J.: Fairleigh Dickinson University Press, 1971.

———. "*Quisque Sui Faber*: Coleridge in the *Biographia Literaria*." *Philological Quarterly* 50 (1971): 208–29.

Corea, Peter Vincent. *The Will and Its Freedom in the Thought of Plato, Aristotle, Augustine, and Kant*. Ph.D. dissertation, Boston University, 1961.

Corneille, Pierre. *Le Cid, Horace, Polyeucte*. In *Nine Classic French Plays*, edited by Joseph Seronde and Henri Peyre. Boston: D.C. Heath, 1936.

Curran, Stuart and Wittreich, Joseph Anthony, eds. *Blake's Sublime Allegory: Essays on "The Four Zoas," "Milton," "Jerusalem."* Madison: University of Wisconsin Press, 1973.

Currie, Peter. *Corneille: Polyeucte.* Great Neck: Barron's Education Series, 1960.

Damon, S. Foster. *William Blake: His Philosophy and Symbols.* Gloucester, Mass.: Peter Smith, 1958.

Darbishire, Helen. *The Poet Wordsworth.* Oxford: Clarendon Press, 1950.

D'Avanzo, Mario. *Keats's Metaphors for the Poetic Imagination.* Durham: Duke University Press, 1967.

DeMan, Paul. *Blindness and Insight: Essays in the Rhetoric of Contemporary Criticism.* New York: Oxford University Press, 1971.

------. "The Rhetoric of Temporality." In *Interpretation: Theory and Practice,* edited by Charles S. Singleton. Baltimore: Johns Hopkins University Press, 1969.

------. "Theory of Metaphor in Rousseau's *Second Discourse.*" In *Romanticism: Vistas, Instances, Continuities,* edited by David Thorburn and Geoffrey Hartman. Ithaca: Cornell University Press, 1974.

DeQuincey, Thomas. *Confessions of an English Opium Eater and Other Writings.* Edited by Aileen Ward. New York: New American Library, 1966.

Descartes, René. *A Discourse on Method, and Selected Writings.* Translated by John Veitch. With an introduction by A. D. Lindsay. New York: Dutton, 1951.

------. *Philosophical Writings: A Selection.* Translated and edited by Elizabeth Anscombe and Peter Thomas Geach. With an introduction by Alexandre Koyré. London: Nelson, 1969.

Dewey, John. *Art as Experience.* New York: Capricorn Books, 1958.

Dickstein, Morris. *Keats and His Poetry: A Study in Development.* Chicago: University of Chicago Press, 1971.

Donne, John. *The Anniversaries.* Edited with introduction and commentary by Frank Manley. Baltimore: Johns Hopkins University Press, 1963.

Dryden, John. *Poetical Works.* New ed., rev. and enl. by George R. Noyes. Boston: Houghton Mifflin, 1950.

------. *Essays.* Selected and edited by W. P. Ker. 2 vols. Oxford: Clarendon Press, 1900.

------. *Selected Dramas, With "The Rehearsal," by George Villiers, duke of Buckingham.* Edited with introduction and notes by George R. Noyes. New York: Scott, Foresman, 1910.

DuBos, Charles. *Byron and the Need of Fatality.* Translated by Ethel Colburn Mayne. London: Putnam, 1932.

Durr, R. A. "'This Lime-Tree Bower My Prison' and a Recurrent Action in Coleridge." *ELH* 26 (1959): 514–30.

Ebbatson, J. R. "Coleridge's Mariner and the Rights of Man." *Studies in Romanticism* 11 (1972): 171–206.

Edelstein, Ludwig. *The Meaning of Stoicism*. Cambridge: Harvard University Press, 1966.

Eliade, Mircea. *Myth and Reality*. Translated by Willard R. Trask. New York: Harper Torchbooks, 1968.

Eliot, T. S. *The Use of Poetry and the Use of Criticism: Studies in the Relation of Criticism to Poetry in England*. London: Faber and Faber, 1955.

Elliott, G. R. "Byron and the Comic Spirit." *PMLA* 39 (1924): 897–909.

Emerson, Ralph Waldo. *Complete Essays and Other Writings*. Edited with a biographical introduction by Brooks Atkinson. New York: Modern Library, 1940.

Empson, William. "The Ancient Mariner." *Critical Quarterly* 6 (1964): 298–319.

Erdman, David V. *Blake: Prophet Against Empire*. Rev ed. Princeton: Princeton University Press. 1969.

———, and Grant, John E., eds. *Blake's Visionary Forms Dramatic*. Princeton: Princeton University Press, 1970.

Farber, Leslie H. *The Ways of the Will: Essays Towards a Psychology and Psychopathology of Will*. New York: Basic Books, 1966.

Farrelly, Daniel. *Goethe and Inner Harmony: A Study of the "Schöne Seele" in "Wilhelm Meister."* Shannon: Irish University Press, 1973.

Fausset, Hugh I'Anson. *Keats: A Study in Development*. Hamden, Conn.: Archon Books, 1966.

Ferry, David. *The Limits of Mortality: An Essay on Wordsworth's Major Poems*. Middletown: Wesleyan University Press, 1959.

Fichte, Johann Gottlieb. *Addresses to the German Nation*. Translated by George Armstrong Kelly. New York: Harper Torchbooks, 1968.

———. *The Popular Works*. Translated by William Smith. 4th ed. London: Trübner, 1889.

———. *The Vocation of Man*. Translated by William Smith. Biographical introduction by E. Ritchie. Chicago: Open Court, 1925.

Finney, Claude Lee. *The Evolution of Keats's Poetry*. New York: Russell, 1936.

Foakes, R. A. *The Romantic Assertion: A Study in the Language of Nineteenth Century Poetry*. London: Methuen, 1958.

Fogle, R. H. "The Romantic Unity of 'Kubla Khan'," *College English* 13 (1951): 13–18.

Franklin, R. L. *Freewill and Determinism: A Study of Rival Conceptions of Man*. London: Routledge and Kegan Paul, 1968.

Freud, Sigmund. *The Standard Edition of the Complete Psychological Works*. Translated under the general editorship of James Strachey in collaboration with Anna Freud, assisted by Alix Strachey and Alan Tyson. London: Hogarth Press, 1953–74.

Vol. 2. *Studies on Hysteria.*

Vol. 7. *A Case of Hysteria, Three Essays on Sexuality, and Other Works.*

Vol. 21. *The Future of an Illusion, Civilization and Its Discontents, and Other Works.*

———. *Studies in Parapsychology.* Introduction by Philip Rieff. New York: Collier Books, 1963.

Frosch, Thomas. "The Descriptive Style of John Clare." *Studies in Romanticism* 10 (1971): 137-49.

Fruman, Norman. *Coleridge, the Damaged Archangel.* New York: Braziller, 1971.

Frye, Northrop. *Anatomy of Criticism: Four Essays.* Princeton: Princeton University Press, 1957.

———. "The Drunken Boat." In *Romanticism Reconsidered*, edited by Northrop Frye. New York: Columbia University Press, 1963.

———. *Fearful Symmetry: A Study of William Blake.* Princeton: Princeton University Press, 1947.

———. *A Study of English Romanticism.* New York: Random House, 1968.

Garber, Frederick. *Wordsworth and the Poetry of Encounter.* Urbana: University of Illinois Press, 1971.

Gardner, W. H. "The Poet and the Albatross (A Study in Symbolic Suggestion)." *English Studies in Africa* 1 (1958): 102-25.

Garrod, H. W. *Keats.* 2d ed. Oxford: Clarendon Press, 1957.

Gérard, Albert S. *English Romantic Poetry: Ethos, Structure, and Symbol in Coleridge, Wordsworth, Shelley, and Keats.* Berkeley: University of California Press, 1968.

———. "Keats and the Romantic *Sehnsucht.*" *University of Toronto Quarterly* 28 (1959): 160-75.

———. "*Resolution and Independence*: Wordsworth's Coming of Age." *English Studies in Africa* 3 (1960): 8-20.

Gingerich, S. F. *Essays in the Romantic Poets.* New York: Macmillan, 1929.

Gleckner, Robert F. *Byron and the Ruins of Paradise.* Baltimore: Johns Hopkins University Press, 1967.

Godwin, William. *Enquiry Concerning Political Justice and Its Influence on Morals and Happiness.* 3rd ed., corr. and ed., with variant readings of the 1st and 2d eds., and with a critical introduction and notes by F. E. L. Priestley. Toronto: University of Toronto Press, 1946.

Goethe, Johann Wolfgang von. *Faust.* Translated by Philip Wayne. Baltimore: Penguin Books, 1949.

———. "Shakespeare ad Infinitum." In *Goethe's Literary Essays: A Selection in English.* Arranged by J. E. Spingarn, with a foreword by Viscount Haldane. New York: Harcourt, Brace & Co., 1921.

———. *Wilhelm Meister's Apprenticeship and Travels.* Translated by Thomas Carlyle. 2 vols. In *The Works of Thomas Carlyle.* London: Chapman and Hall, 1907.

Grandine, Jonathan R. *The Problem of Shape in "The Prelude": The Conflict of Private and Public Speech.* Cambridge: Harvard University Press, 1968.

Grob, Alan. "Process and Permanence in 'Resolution and Independence'." *English Literary History* 28 (1961): 89–100.

Grunsky, Hans Alfred. *Jakob Böhme als schöpfer einer germanischen philosophie des willens.* Hamburg: Hanseatische verlagsanstalt, 1940.

Hagstrum, Jean H. *The Sister Arts: The Tradition of Literary Pictorialism and English Poetry from Dryden to Gray.* Chicago: University of Chicago Press, 1958.

Halloran, William F. "*The French Revolution*: Revelation's New Form." In *Blake's Visionary Forms Dramatic*, edited by David V. Erdman and John E. Grant. Princeton: Princeton University Press, 1970.

Hartman, Geoffrey H., ed. *New Perspectives on Coleridge and Wordsworth: Selected Papers from the English Institute.* New York: Columbia University Press, 1972.

———. "Romanticism and Anti-Self-Consciousness." In *Beyond Formalism: Literary Essays 1958–1970.* New Haven: Yale University Press, 1970.

———. *The Unmediated Vision: An Interpretation of Wordsworth, Hopkins, Rilke, and Valéry.* New York: Harcourt, Brace & World, 1966.

———. *Wordsworth's Poetry: 1787–1814.* New Haven: Yale University Press, 1964.

Haven, Richard. *Patterns of Consciousness: An Essay on Coleridge.* Amherst: University of Massachusetts Press, 1969.

Heffernan, James A. W. *Wordsworth's Theory of Poetry: The Transforming Imagination.* Ithaca: Cornell University Press, 1969.

Hegel, G. W. F. *The Phenomenology of Mind.* Translated with an introduction by J. B. Baillie. Introduction by George Lichtheim. New York: Harper Torchbooks, 1967.

Herder, Johann Gottfried von. *On the Origin of Language: Jean-Jacques Rousseau, Essay on the Origin of Languages; Johann Gottfried Herder, Essay on the Origin of Language.* Translated, with afterwords, by John H. Moran and Alexander Gode. Introduction by Alexander Gode. New York: F. Ungar, 1967.

Hilles, Frederick W., and Bloom, Harold, eds. *From Sensibility to Romanticism: Essays Presented to Frederick A. Pottle.* New York: Oxford University Press, 1965.

Hirsch, E. D., Jr. *Wordsworth and Schelling: A Typological Study of Romanticism.* New Haven: Yale University Press, 1960.

Hobbes, Thomas. *The English Works.* Vol. 5. *The Questions Concerning Liberty, Necessity, and Chance, Clearly Stated and Debated between Dr. Bramhall and Thomas Hobbes.* Edited by Sir William Molesworth. London: J. Bohn, 1841.

Hood, Thomas. *Selected Poems.* Edited with an introduction and notes by John Clubbe. Cambridge: Harvard University Press, 1970.

Horney, Karen. *Neurosis and Human Growth: The Struggle Toward Self-Realization.* New York: W. W. Norton, 1950.

Horsman, E. A. "The Design of Wordsworth's *Prelude.*" In *Wordsworth's Mind and Art,* edited by A. W. Thompson. Edinburgh: Oliver and Boyd, 1969.

House, Humphry. *Coleridge.* London: R. Hart-Davis, 1953.

Jack, Ian. *English Literature: 1815–1832.* Oxford: Clarendon Press, 1963.

Jackson, J. R. de J. *Method and Imagination in Coleridge's Criticism.* London: Routledge and Kegan Paul, 1969.

James, D. G. *The Romantic Comedy.* London and New York: Oxford University Press, 1949.

Jones, Henry John Franklin. *The Egotistical Sublime: A History of Wordsworth's Imagination.* London: Chatto and Windus, 1954.

———. *John Keats's Dream of Truth.* New York: Barnes and Noble, 1969.

Jung, Carl Gustav. *Basic Writings.* Edited with an introduction by Violet Staub de Laszlo. New York: Modern Library, 1959.

———. *The Collected Works.* Translated by R. F. C. Hull. Princeton: Princeton University Press, 1960–73.
   Vol. 6. *Psychological Types.*
   Vol. 15. *The Spirit in Man, Art and Literature.*
   Vol. 17. *The Development of Personality.*

———. *The Undiscovered Self.* Translated by R. F. C. Hull: Boston: Little, Brown, 1958.

Kant, Immanuel. *Critique of Practical Reason and Other Works on the Theory of Ethics.* Translated by Thomas Kingsmill Abbott. 6th ed. London and New York: Longmans, Green, 1948.

———. *The Essential Kant.* Edited with an introduction by Arnulf Zweig. New York: New American Library, 1970.

Kaplan, Fred. *Miracles of Rare Device: The Poet's Sense of Self in Nineteenth-Century Poetry.* Detroit: Wayne State University Press, 1972.

Keats, John. *Complete Poems and Selected Letters.* Edited by Clarence DeWitt Thorpe. New York: Odyssey Press, 1935.

———. *The Letters . . . , 1814–1821.* 2 vols. Edited by Hyder Edward Rollins. Cambridge: Harvard University Press, 1958.

———. *Poems.* Edited with an introduction by John Middleton Murry. London: P. Nevill, 1948.

———. *The Poetical Works*. Edited by H. W. Garrod. Oxford: Clarendon Press, 1939.

Kelly, George Armstrong. Introduction to *Addresses to the German Nation* by Johann Gottlieb Fichte. New York: Harper Torchbooks, 1968.

Kiralis, Karl. "The Theme and Structure of *Jerusalem.*" In *The Divine Vision: Studies in the Poetry and Art of William Blake*, edited by Vivian de Sola Pinto. London: Victor Gollancx, 1957.

Knight, G. Wilson. *The Starlit Dome: Studies in the Poetry of Vision.* Introduction by W. F. Jackson Knight. New York: Barnes and Noble, 1960.

Kurtz, Benjamin P. *The Pursuit of Death: A Study of Shelley's Poetry.* New York: Oxford University Press, 1933.

Lawrence, D. H. *The Complete Poems.* Collected and edited with an introduction and notes by Vivian de Sola Pinto and F. Warren Roberts. New York: Viking Press, 1971.

Leibniz, Gottfried Wilhelm von. *The Monadology and Other Philosophical Writings.* Translated with an introduction and notes by Robert Latta. Oxford: Clarendon Press, 1898.

Lesnick, Henry. "Narrative Structure and the Antithetical Vision of *Jerusalem.*" In *Blake's Visionary Forms Dramatic*, edited by David V. Erdman and John E. Grant. Princeton: Princeton University Press, 1970.

Lindenberger, Herbert. *On Wordsworth's "Prelude."* Princeton: Princeton University Press, 1963.

Locke, John. *An Essay concerning Human Understanding.* Abridged and edited by A. S. Pringle-Pattison. Oxford: Clarendon Press, 1924.

———. *An Essay concerning Human Understanding.* Collated and annotated, with prolegomena, biographical, critical, and historical, by Alexander Campbell Fraser. New York: Dover Publications, 1959.

Lott, James. "Keats's *To Autumn*: The Poetic Consciousness and the Awareness of Process." *Studies in Romanticism* 9 (1970): 71–81.

Lovejoy, A. O. "Coleridge and Kant's Two Worlds." *English Literary History* 7 (1940): 341–62.

Löwth, Karl. *From Hegel to Nietzsche: The Revolution in Nineteenth Century Thought.* Translated by David E. Green. New York: Doubleday Anchor Books, 1967.

Lucas, F. L. *The Decline and Fall of the Romantic Ideal.* New York: Macmillan, 1936.

Lucas, J. R. *The Freedom of the Will.* Oxford: Clarendon Press, 1970.

Lupton, Mary Jane. "*The Rime of the Ancient Mariner*: The Agony of Thirst." *American Imago* 27 (1970): 240–59.

Marchand, Leslie A. *Byron's Poetry: A Critical Introduction.* London: John Murray, 1965.

Marlowe, Christopher. *Doctor Faustus*. Edited by Keith Walker. Edinburgh: Oliver and Boyd, 1973.

——. *Tamburlaine the Great: Parts I and II*. Edited by J. W. Harper. New York: Hill and Wang, 1973.

McFarland, Thomas. *Coleridge and the Pantheist Tradition*. Oxford: Clarendon Press, 1969.

——. "The Origin and Significance of Coleridge's Theory of Secondary Imagination." In *New Perspectives on Coleridge and Wordsworth*, edited by Geoffrey H. Hartman. New York: Columbia University Press, 1972.

McGann, Jerome. *Fiery Dust: Byron's Poetic Development*. Chicago: University of Chicago Press, 1968.

McGill, V. J. *Schopenhauer: Pessimist and Pagan*. New York: Brentano's, 1931.

Maritain, Jacques. *Creative Intuition in Art and Poetry*. New York: Meridian Books, 1955.

Merleau-Ponty, Maurice. *The Phenomenology of Perception*. Translated by Colin Smith. New York: Humanities Press, 1962.

——. *The Primacy of Perception*. Edited by James M. Edie. Evanston: Northwestern University Press, 1964.

Miller, Jonathan, ed. *Freud: The Man, His World, His Influence*. Boston: Little, Brown, 1972.

Milton, John. *The Poems*. Edited with introduction and notes by James Holly Hanford. 2d ed. New York: Ronald Press, 1953.

Molière, Jean Baptiste Poquelin. *The Misanthrope, and Tartuffe*. Translated into English verse by Richard Wilbur. New York: Harcourt, Brace & World, 1965.

Morgenthau, Sidney, and Walsh, James, eds. *Free Will*. Englewood Cliffs, N.J.: Prentice Hall, Spectrum Books, 1962.

Morris, Herbert, ed. *Freedom and Responsibility: Readings in Philosophy and Law*. Stanford: Stanford University Press, 1961.

Muirhead, J. H. *Coleridge as Philosopher*. London: G. Allen & Unwin, 1930.

Murry, J. M. *Keats*. 4th ed., rev. and enl. New York: Noonday Press, 1955.

——. *Keats and Shakespeare: A Study in Keats's Poetic Life from 1816 to 1820*. London: H. Milford, Oxford University Press, 1925.

——. "Keats's Thought: A Discovery of Truth." In *The Major English Romantic Poets: A Symposium in Reappraisal*, edited by Clarence D. Thorpe et al. Carbondale: Southern Illinois University Press, 1957.

Nauen, Franz Gabriel. *Revolution, Idealism and Human Freedom: Schelling, Hölderlin and Hegel and the Crisis of Early German Idealism*. The Hague: Nÿhoff, 1971.

Nietzsche, Friedrich. *The Will to Power*. Translated by Walter Kaufmann and R. J. Hollingdale. Edited by Walter Kaufmann, with fac-simile of the original manuscript. New York: Random House, 1967.

Oates, Whitney J., ed. *The Stoic and Epicurean Philosophers: The Complete Extant Writings of Epicurus, Epictetus, Lucretius, Marcus Aurelius.* New York: Random House, 1940.

Onorato, Richard J. *The Character of the Poet: Wordsworth in "The Prelude."* Princeton: Princeton University Press, 1971.

Orsini, G. N. G. *Coleridge and German Idealism: A Study in the History of Philosophy, with Unpublished Materials from Coleridge's Manuscripts.* Carbondale: Southern Illinois University Press, 1969.

Paley, Morton D. *Energy and the Imagination: A Study of the Development of Blake's Thought.* New York: Oxford University Press, 1970.

Parsons, Coleman O. "The Mariner and the Albatross." *Virginia Quarterly Review* 26 (1950): 102–23.

Pater, Walter, *The Renaissance.* Introduction by Arthur Symons. New York: Modern Library, 1919.

Peckham, Morse. *The Triumph of Romanticism.* Columbia: University of South Carolina Press, 1970.

Perkins, David. *The Quest for Permanence: The Symbolism of Wordsworth, Shelley and Keats.* Cambridge: Harvard University Press, 1959.

Piper, H. W. *The Active Universe.* New York: Oxford University Press, 1962.

Pope, Alexander. *The Poems. A One-Volume Edition of the Twickenham Text, With Selected Annotations.* Edited by John Butt. New Haven: Yale University Press, 1963.

Potts, Abbie Findlay. *Wordsworth's "Prelude": A Study of its Literary Form.* Ithaca: Cornell University Press, 1953.

Prickett, Stephen. *Coleridge and Wordsworth, The Poetry of Growth.* Cambridge: Cambridge University Press, 1970.

Rader, Melvin. *Wordsworth: A Philosophical Approach.* Oxford: Clarendon Press, 1967.

Radway, Allan. *The Romantic Conflict.* London: Chatto and Windus, 1963.

Read, Herbert. *The True Voice of Feeling: Studies in English Romantic Poetry.* London: Faber and Faber, 1935.

Renwick, W. L. *English Literature: 1789–1815.* Oxford: Clarendon Press, 1963.

Richards, I. A. *Coleridge on Imagination.* Bloomington: Indiana University Press, 1960.

Ricoeur, Paul. *Freedom and Nature: The Voluntary and the Involuntary.* Translated with an introduction by Erazim V. Kohák. Evanston: Northwestern University Press, 1966.

——. *Philosophie de la Volonté: Le Volontaire et L'Involontaire.* Paris: Editions Montaigne, 1948.

———. *The Symbolism of Evil*. Translated by Emerson Buchanan. Boston: Beacon Press, 1967.

Ridley, Maurice Roy. *Keats's Craftmanship: A Study in Poetic Development*. New York: Russell and Russell, 1962.

Rist, J. M. *Stoic Philosophy*. London: Cambridge University Press, 1969.

Robson, W. W. "Wordsworth: Resolution and Independence." In *Interpretations: Essays on Twelve English Poems*, edited by John Wain. London: Routledge and Kegan Paul, 1955.

Rollins, Hyder Edward, ed. *The Keats Circle: Letters and Papers, and More Letters and Poems of the Keats Circle*. 2d ed. Cambridge: Harvard University Press, 1965.

Rose, E. J. "The Structure of Blake's *Jerusalem*." *Bucknell Review* 11 (1963): 35–54.

Rosenfeld, Alvin H., ed. *William Blake: Essays for S. Foster Damon* Providence: Brown University Press, 1969.

Rousseau, Jean-Jacques. *On the Origin of Language: Jean-Jacques Rousseau, Essay on the Origin of Languages; Johann Gottfried Herder, Essay on the Origin of Language*. Translated, with afterwords, by John H. Moran and Alexander Gode. Introduction by Alexander Gode. New York: F. Ungar, 1967.

———. *The Confessions*. Translated with an introduction by J. M. Cohen. Baltimore: Penguin Books, 1954.

———. *The Reveries of a Solitary*. Translated with an introduction by John Gould Fletcher. London: George Routledge, 1927.

———. *The Social Contract and Discourses*. Translated with an introduction by G. D. H. Cole. New York: Dutton, 1950.

Rutherford, Andrew. *Byron: A Critical Study*. Stanford: Stanford University Press, 1962.

Schelling, Friedrich Wilhelm Joseph von. *Of Human Freedom*. Translated with a critical introduction and notes by James Gutmann. Chicago: Open Court, 1936.

Schiller, J. C. F. von. *On the Aesthetic Education of Man*. Edited and translated by Elizabeth M. Wilkinson and L. A. Willoughby. Oxford: Clarendon Press, 1967.

Schopenhauer, Arthur. *Essay on the Freedom of the Will*. Translated with an introduction by Konstantin Kolenda. New York: Liberal Arts Press, 1960.

———. *The Essays*. Translated by T. Bailey Saunders. New York: Wiley, 1942.

———. *The World as Will and Representation*. Translated by E. F. J. Payne. New York: Dover Publications, 1966.

Schorer, Mark. *William Blake: The Politics of Vision*. New York: H. Holt, 1946.

Seneca. *The Stoic Philosophy of Seneca: Essays and Letters.* Translated and with an introduction by Moses Hadas. New York: W. W. Norton, 1958.

Shakespeare, William. *The Tragedy of Troilus and Cressida.* Edited by Jackson I. Campbell. New Haven: Yale University Press, 1956.

Shakir, Evelyn. "Books, Death, and Immortality: A Study of Book V of *The Prelude.*" *Studies in Romanticism* 8 (1968): 156–67.

Shelley, Percy Bysshe. *The Complete Poetical Works.* Edited by Thomas Hutchinson. London: Oxford University Press, 1943.

———. *Defence of Poetry.* In *Peacock's "Four Ages of Poetry": Shelley's "Defence of Poetry"; Browning's "Essay on Shelley,"* edited by H. F. B. Brett-Smith. 2d ed. Oxford: Blackwell, 1923.

Shorey, Paul. *Platonism Ancient and Modern.* Berkeley: University of California Press, 1938.

Sonnenschein, E. A. "Stoicism in English Literature." *The Contemporary Review* 124 (1923): 355–65.

Sperry, Stuart M., Jr. *Keats the Poet.* Princeton: Princeton University Press, 1973.

Spinoza, Benedictus de. *"Ethics" Preceded by "On the Improvement of the Understanding."* Edited with an introduction by James Gutmann. New York: Hafner, 1949.

Stallknecht, Newton P. *Strange Seas of Thought: Studies in William Wordsworth's Philosophy of Man and Nature.* Bloomington: Indiana University Press, 1958.

———. "Wordsworth's Ode to Duty and the Schöne Seele." *PMLA* 52 (1937): 230–37.

Steele, Richard, *The Plays.* Edited by Shirley Strum Kenny. Oxford: Clarendon Press, 1971.

Stillinger, Jack. *The Texts of Keats's Poems.* Cambridge: Harvard University Press, 1974.

Stuart, John A. "The Augustinian 'Cause of Action' in Coleridge's *Rime of the Ancient Mariner.*" *Harvard Theological Review* 60 (1967): 177–211.

Suther, Marshall. *The Dark Night of Samuel Taylor Coleridge.* New York: Columbia University Press, 1960.

Swingle, L. J. "Stalking the Essential John Clare: Clare in Relation to his Romantic Contemporaries." *Studies in Romanticism* 14 (1975): 273–84.

Talbot, Norman. *The Major Poems of John Keats.* University Park: Pennsylvania State University Press, 1968.

Tave, Stuart M. *The Amiable Humorist: A Study in the Comic Theory and Criticism of the Eighteenth and Early Nineteenth Centuries.* Chicago: University of Chicago Press, 1960.

Thomas, Gordon Kent. *Wordsworth's Dirge and Promise: Napoleon, Wellington, and the Convention at Cintra.* Lincoln: University of Nebraska Press, 1971.

Thomson, A. W. "Resolution and Independence." In *Wordsworth's Mind and Art,* edited by A. W. Thomson. Edinburgh: Oliver and Boyd, 1969.

Thorslev, Peter L. *The Byronic Hero: Types and Prototypes.* Minneapolis: University of Minnesota Press, 1962.

———. "The Romantic Mind Is Its Own Place." *Comparative Literature* 15 (1963): 250-68.

Tillyard, E. M. W. *Five Poems: 1470-1870: An Elementary Essay on the Background of English Literature.* London: Chatto and Windus, 1948.

———. *The Elizabethan World Picture.* London: Chatto and Windus, 1956.

Thorpe, Clarence D. *The Mind of John Keats.* New York: Oxford University Press, 1935.

Todd, F. M. *Politics and the Poet: A Study of Wordsworth.* London: Methuen, 1957.

Trilling, Lionel. Introduction to *Selected Letters of John Keats.* New York: Doubleday Anchor Books, 1956.

———. *Sincerity and Authenticity.* Cambridge: Harvard University Press, 1972.

———. *The Opposing Self: Nine Essays in Criticism.* New York: Viking, 1955.

Vitoux, Pierre. "Keats's Epic Design in *Hyperion.*" *Studies in Romanticism* 14 (1975): 165-83.

Vogler, Thomas A. *Preludes to Vision: The Epic Venture in Blake, Wordsworth, Keats, and Hart Crane.* Berkeley: University of California Press, 1971.

Waith, Eugene M. *The Herculean Hero in Marlowe, Chapman, Shakespeare and Dryden.* New York: Columbia University Press, 1962.

Warren, Robert Penn. "A Poem of Pure Imagination: An Experiment in Reading." Commentary on *The Rime of the Ancient Mariner* by Samuel Taylor Coleridge. New York: Reynal and Hitchcock, 1946.

Wasserman, Earl R. "The English Romantics: The Grounds of Knowledge." In *Romanticism: Points of View,* edited by Robert F. Gleckner and Gerald E. Enscoe. 2d ed. Englewood Cliffs, N.J.: Prentice-Hall, 1970.

———. *The Finer Tone: Keats's Major Poems.* Baltimore: Johns Hopkins University Press, 1953.

Watson, George. *Coleridge the Poet.* London: Routledge and Kegan Paul, 1966.

Wellek, René. *Immanuel Kant in England, 1793-1838.* Princeton: Princeton University Press, 1931.

Welsford, Enid. *Salisbury Plain: A Study in the Development of Wordsworth's Mind and Art.* Oxford: Blackwell, 1966.

Wesling, Donald. *Wordsworth and the Adequacy of Landscape.* London: Routledge and Kegan Paul, 1970.

Wilkie, Brian. *Romantic Poets and Epic Tradition.* Madison-Milwaukee: University of Wisconsin Press, 1965.

Willey, Basil. *The Eighteenth Century Background: Studies on the Idea of Nature in the Thought of the Period.* London: Chatto and Windus, 1940.

Williams, Charles. *The English Poetic Mind.* Oxford: Clarendon Press, 1932.

Williams, Melvin G. "A New Look at Wordsworth's Religion." *Cithara* 2 (1962): 20-32.

Wood, Mary Hay. *Plato's Psychology in its Bearing on the Development of Will.* New York: H. Frowde, 1907.

Woodring, Carl. "Coleridge and the Khan," *Essays in Criticism* 9 (1959): 361-368.

———. *Politics in English Romantic Poetry.* Cambridge: Harvard University Press, 1970.

———. *Politics in the Poetry of Coleridge.* Madison: University of Wisconsin Press, 1961.

———. *Wordsworth.* Boston: Houghton Mifflin, 1965.

Wordsworth, Dorothy. *Journals of Dorothy Wordsworth: The Alfoxden Journal, 1798; The Grasmere Journals, 1800-1803.* Introduction by Helen Darbishire. Edited by Mary Moorman. New York: Oxford University Press, 1971.

Wordsworth, Jonathan. *The Music of Humanity: A Critical Study of Wordsworth's Ruined Cottage.* London: Nelson, 1969.

———. *Usurpation and Reality: Wordsworth's Great Six Weeks.* Oberlin: Oberlin College Press, 1974.

Wordsworth, William. *The Early Letters of William and Dorothy Wordsworth (1787-1805).* 2 vols. Arranged and edited by Ernest De Selincourt. Oxford: Clarendon Press, 1935.

———. *The Letters of William and Dorothy Wordsworth: The Later Years.* 3 vols. Arranged and edited by Ernest De Selincourt. Oxford: Clarendon Press, 1939.

———. *The Letters of William and Dorothy Wordsworth: The Middle Years.* 2 vols. Arranged and edited by Ernest De Selincourt. Oxford: Clarendon Press, 1937.

———. *Lyrical Ballads: Wordsworth and Coleridge. The Text of the 1798 Ed. with the Additional 1800 Poems and the Preface.* Edited with introduction, notes and appendixes by R. L. Brett and A. R. Jones. New York: Barnes and Noble, 1963.

———. *Poems in Two Volumes, 1807*. Edited by Helen Darbishire. 2d ed. Oxford: Clarendon Press, 1952.

———. *Poetical Works*. With introductions and notes. Edited by Thomas Hutchinson. A new ed., rev. by Ernest De Selincourt. New York: Oxford University Press, 1956.

———. *The Poetical Works*. 5 vols. Edited from the manuscripts with textual and critical notes by Ernest De Selincourt. Oxford: Clarendon Press, 1940–49.

Worthington, Jane. *Wordsworth's Reading of Roman Prose*. New Haven: Yale University Press, 1946.

Yeats, William Butler. *Essays and Introductions*. New York: Macmillan, 1961.

INDEX

Abrams, Meyer H., 34, 216, 223*n*6, 224*nn*8-9, 228*n*30, 234*nn*1, 12, 237*nn*17, 21, 26, 242*n*59
Addison, Joseph, 57, 58, 60, 74; *Cato* 63-65
Aeschylus, 39
Aesculapius, 187, 201
Aids to Reflection. See Coleridge, Samuel Taylor
Alastor. See Shelley, Percy Bysshe
Altieri, Charles, 5, 98, 239*n*38
Antaeus, 113
Anti-self-consciousness. *See* Hartman, Geoffrey H.
Apocalypse, 6, 216, 221, 239*n*38
Apollo, 179, 180, 187, 201. *See also* Bacchus; Phoebus
Appleyard, J. A., 230*nn*41, 44
Aristotle, 67
Arnold, Matthew, 221
Art, 51, 112, 142, 183, 201; in Blake, 142-44, 187-201 passim; in Keats, 150-82 passim; in romanticism, 182-87; and will, 51, 143-44, 145-50, 192-96, 234*n*70
Art Poétique, L'. See Boileau, Nicolas
Auden, W. H., 232*n*55
Auerbach, Erich, 91
Augustanism. *See* Neoclassicism
Augustine, Saint, 97
Aurelius, Marcus, 207, 250*n*53
Autobiography, 9

Bacchus, 168, 224*n*22
Bacon, Lord Francis, 60
Baker, James Volant, 227*n*26
Balboa, Vasco Núñez de, 33
Barfield, Owen, 224*n*6, 225*n*13

Barzun, Jacques, 224*n*8
Bate, W. J., 227*n*26, 232*n*59, 236*n*12, 247*n*38
Beaumont, Francis, 242*n*5
Beddoes, Thomas Lovell, 221, 252*n*64
Beer, John B., 232*n*59
Being, 4, 9, 25, 34, 35, 38, 90, 183, 196; levels in *Ancient Mariner,* 35; in romanticism, xii, xiii, 11; as sin in *Ancient Mariner,* 37; in Schelling, 19; will of, 29, 34. *See also* Identity
Bergson, Henri, 226*n*16, 228*n*33, 229*n*37
Berkeley, George, 235*n*3
Biographia Literaria. See Coleridge, Samuel Taylor
Bishop, Jonathan, 238*n*35, 239*n*36, 240*n*45
Blackstone, Bernard, 248*n*38
Blake, William, 10, 11, 36, 112, 184, 230*n*41, 248*n*43; as amanuensis, 193; and art, 142-44, 187-201 passim; *The Four Zoas,* 46-47, 173, 188, 191, 241*n*53, 248*nn*42, 44; *Jerusalem,* xii, xiv, 6, 10, 77, 119-42, 147, 149, 190, 192, 194-201, 240*nn* 47-49, 241*nn*54-55, 249*n*44; *The Marriage of Heaven and Hell,* 188, 194, 234*n*70, 248*n*42; negotiations in, 124-27, 128-30, 138-40; Orc-Blake-Los, 187-201 passim; selfhood, 119, 123, 140; states, 127, 138, 140; and system, 80, 123-24, 140-41; and time, 10, 131, 133, 142; *Visions of the Daughters of Albion,* 36, 82; and will, 120-42, 189-201 passim, see esp. 192-96
Bloom, Harold, 79, 223*n*6, 236*n*12,